Men And Organizations

MEN AND ORGANIZATIONS

THE AMERICAN ECONOMY IN THE TWENTIETH CENTURY

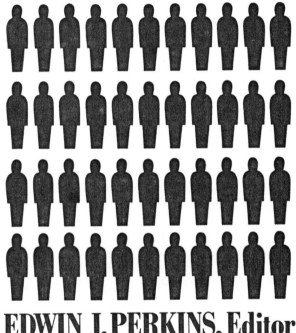

EDWIN J. PERKINS, Editor

G. P. PUTNAM'S SONS, NEW YORK

SBN: 399-11890-X hard-cover
SBN: 399-50370-6 soft-cover

Library of Congress Cataloging in Publication Data

Main entry under title:

Men and organizations.

    1.   United States—Economic conditions.
I.   Perkins, Edwin J.
HC106.M4   1977   330.9'73'09   76-48150

78-5707

PRINTED IN THE UNITED STATES OF AMERICA

Contents

PREFACE   vii

INTRODUCTION   1

The Emerging Organizational Synthesis
in American History

by Louis Galambos   3

SECTION I
THE STRUCTURE OF THE ECONOMY   16

Vertical Integration in American
Manufacturing, 1899-1948,

by Harold C. Livesay and Glenn Porter   20

The Structure of American Industry in the
Twentieth Century: A Historical Overview,

by Alfred D. Chandler, Jr.   26

The Development of Diversified and Conglomerate Firms in the United States, 1920-1970,

by Jon Didrichsen   38

SECTION II
LABOR AND AGRICULTURE   51

The Emergence of
Mass-Production Unionism,

by David Brody   58

Corporate Farming in the United States,

    by Philip M. Raup   86

SECTION III
BUSINESS, GOVERNMENT, AND THE MILITARY   97

Bernard Baruch: Symbol and Myth
in Industrial Mobilization,

    by Robert D. Cuff   104

Concept of the Organization,

    by Alfred P. Sloan   120

Herbert Hoover, the Commerce Secretariat,
and the Vision of an "Associative State,"
1921-1928,

    by Ellis W. Hawley   131

Eisenhower and the Creation of a Command
Structure, 1942-1945,

    by Alfred D. Chandler, Jr.   149

The Truman Administration and the Enlistment
of the Aviation Industry in Postwar
Defense,

    by Donald J. Mrozek   168

CONCLUSION   187

The Development of Large-Scale Economic
Organizations in Modern America,

    by Alfred D. Chandler, Jr., and Louis Galambos   188

Men And Organizations

PREFACE

Most editors of anthologies seek in some manner to achieve the dual yet elusive goals of presenting a diversity of subject matter while maintaining a framework consisting of one or two unifying themes. I have attempted to reach these goals in this volume. For diversity, I have included articles on business, labor, agriculture, government, and the military. Among the issues examined are the trend toward concentration in the industrial sector of the economy, the extent of corporate penetration in agriculture, and the emergence of the so-called military-industrial complex.

For unity, I have relied primarily on an organizational theme, a concept which is explained more fully by Louis Galambos in the first essay of this book. A related source of unity derives from the inclusion of articles by several historians who are linked in one way or another with what has emerged as the Chandlerian school of economic and business history. Alfred D. Chandler, Jr., gives his name to this school because the publication of his book *Strategy and Structure* in 1962 altered the course of institutional economic history. A number of the authors—including Glenn Porter, Harold Livesay, Jon Didrichsen, and the editor—were Chandler's students. Others were previously colleagues at M.I.T., Johns Hopkins, or Harvard. Even those authors without close professional ties have been influenced by his work and he, undoubtedly, by theirs.

One professional trait most of these authors share is a dispassionate, nonideological approach to the study of twentieth-century institutions. They are often less concerned with the ideals and goals of modern institutions than with the everyday functioning of a given organization and with how organizational values and norms have affected the outlook of leaders and permeated American society in general. Many of these historians seek intellectual inspiration not so much from Adam Smith, Karl Marx, or other economic theoreticians but from the conceptualizations of Max Weber, the German sociologist and historian. Weber identified the drive toward bureaucracy as one of the primary forces at work in the modern world, and his organizational theories have been broad enough to span a host of academic disciplines. Although critics have occasionally attacked organizational interpretations of American history because of their alleged conservative bias, the approach nonetheless has thrived in recent years and has cut a broad swath across traditional historical boundaries. Moreover, this brand of history is to my mind neither ideological nor cold and impersonal; four of the selections in this volume focus exclusively on the professional careers of individuals, men who contributed in highly individual ways to America's development in the twentieth century.

The articles in this book have been slightly edited and the notes that have been retained have been renumbered.

In the course of thinking about and finally putting together this volume, I received encouragement and solid advice from my good friend and colleague at the University of Southern California, Frank Mitchell. An old friend and former colleague, Bill Cullison, read my note on labor history and recommended a number of improvements.

INTRODUCTION

This book examines some of the main forces shaping American society in the twentieth century. The modern world has seen the emergence of powerful new institutions in many sectors of the economy and increasingly in government as well. One common characteristic of these institutions was their vast size, which required new methods of rationalization and administration. Initially, citizens were reluctant to accept the legitimacy of such concentrated power, but, as the decades passed, Americans became more acclimated to an environment dominated by some combination of big business, big government, big labor, a permanent military establishment, and agri-business.

A major theme of this volume is that an organizational revolution followed this expansion in the sheer size of modern institutions. The formal structures of these units changed, and the attitudes and values of the individual participants and ultimately the American people shifted too. Before the turn of the century, only the business sector had been strongly influenced by organizational concepts, and much of that influence was confined to a single industry—the nation's railroads. Beginning in the 1850s, the large railroad networks, with thousands of employees spread over hundreds of miles of track, started the process of developing more complex and responsive administrative structures. The result in transportation and other industries was a new form of highly centralized, powerful, and relatively efficient business firm. Even more sophisticated forms of business organization emerged in the 1920s, when a new type of bureaucracy was adopted almost simultaneously by executives at the Du Pont and General Motors corporations.

Although businessmen led the way in the United States, other institutions in American society eventually borrowed many of the same organizational concepts first introduced by the business community. In the case of the military, the strain of fighting two world wars was a catalyst leading to the implementation of a new command structure which improved internal operations and overall planning. Meanwhile, public officials gradually came to the realization that American society was increasingly, and probably irreversibly, shaped by organizational forces and that the first requirement of government was to come to terms with this radically changed world. Indeed the leaders of the twentieth-century institutions were less likely than their predecessors to refer solely to an individualistic, competitive frame of reference in problem solving; they were more inclined to consider models that stressed cooperation and a unity of purpose.

Viewed from an organizational perspective, business, government, and the military faced a surprising number of common administrative difficulties in this century, problems that were usually associated with the growing size and complexity of institutions. Moreover, these sectors passed through similar stages of organizational development, for common problems elicited similar solutions.

THE EMERGING ORGANIZATIONAL SYNTHESIS IN MODERN AMERICAN HISTORY

By Louis Galambos

With the demise of progressive history, scholars interested in modern America are left without an effective historical synthesis.[1] For many, a new conceptual framework may seem unnecessary. Some will be content to level another revisionist broadside at the crumbling structure of liberal ideas.[2] Others will find the lack of a synthesis appealing on the grounds that our sophisticated age can no longer use ideas which might blind us to some of the complexities of man's past behavior.[3] To many, the New Left will provide the best alternative, either because of or in spite of its heavy ideological orientation.[4] Meanwhile, quantification beckons, although most historians must already know that statistical analyses are only tools for testing hypotheses; the ideas themselves must come from the historian's view of society and social change.

Those who reject all of these options may be attracted by the synthesis which is emerging from the organizational school of history.[5] While their work varies in subject matter and emphasis, historians contributing to the development of this new synthesis share certain premises. One is the assumption that some of the most (if not the single most) important changes which have taken place in modern America have centered about a shift from small-scale, informal, locally or regionally oriented groups to large-scale, national, formal organizations. The new organizations are characterized by a bureaucratic structure of authority. This shift in organization cuts across the traditional boundaries of political, economic, and social history. Businesses, reform groups, professional and labor organizations—all developed along somewhat similar lines. These organizations could and did conflict, but they nevertheless shared certain modes of orientation, certain values, and certain institutionally defined roles.

As John Higham suggests, organizational history of this stripe can be distinguished from the earlier variety of institutional history. The nineteenth-century institutionalists described and analyzed the evolution of particular political or economic organizations; they interpreted their subject's development in a way which compartmentalized their findings along traditional lines. They studied a political party, for instance, in order to reach conclusions about the American political system. They tended to stress the unique, not the general, aspects of their subject.

In the new style of organizational history these boundaries are disappearing, dissolved by a set of generalizations drawn primarily from the work of Max Weber and other sociologists. The organizational historians who use the Weberian model have a tendency to stress the universal, not the particular, qualities of their subject.[6] In the model which Weber and the organizational historians share, major emphasis is placed on the hierarchical, bureaucratic structure of authority; this form of organization normally involves precise definitions of responsibility and an emphasis upon relatively impersonal decisions made by a staff of experts filling positions which (theoretically, at least) do not change when the personnel does.[7] Other behavioral tools of analysis, such as the concept of role, have also helped these historians break out of the older categories.[8] The result of this new orientation is the beginnings of an historical synthesis which focuses on the modern organization, qua organization.

Scholarly emphasis on these kinds of large-scale organizations as a central phenomenon of modern society is certainly not new. James Burnham's famous study of *The Managerial Revolution* first appeared twenty-eight years ago, and bureaucratization became a major interest in the 1950s. In 1952, John Kenneth Galbraith suggested that the workings of our economy could, and the management of our polity should, be formulated in terms of a theory of countervailing organizational power. Galbraith's ideas were rooted in the premise that large-scale organizations had drastically and irrevocably transformed the capitalistic economy of the present century.[9] One year later, Kenneth E. Boulding published *The Organizational Revolution*, which also focused attention on the "great rise in the number, size, and power of organizations of many diverse kinds." A similar theme was developed in William H. Whyte's popular treatment of *The Organization Man*. All of these studies, and many others as well, centered on the rise of complex bureaucracies as the most important characteristic of modern America.[10]

These books were not written, however, to serve the special purposes of history. A number were policy oriented. They employed historical data and insights, and in many cases provided ideas which historians could use. But their purpose was to re-structure our view of the present, not the past.[11] They did not offer a detailed study of the historic roots of the organizational revolution. This distinguishes them from the historians who are the primary concern of this article.

A number of the new breed of organizational historians have come out of the fields of business and economic history. This is not just a coincidence. One of the concomitants of this type of history is a shift in emphasis from public policy as a central theme to the underlying modes of socio-economic organization. In order to accomplish this transition, historians first broke down the progressive categories which for years had isolated businessmen, leaving them an essentially negative role as opponents of the reform measures which (in the liberal view) shaped our modern society. Numerous historians—including Arthur H. Cole, Allan Nevins, Harold F. Williamson, Ralph and Muriel Hidy, and Arthur M. Johnson—have contributed to this task.[12] Especially important, however, was the recent work of Robert H. Wiebe, Alfred D. Chandler, Jr., and Thomas C. Cochran.

In his first book, *Businessmen and Reform: A Study of the Progressive Movement*, Wiebe used liberal history as a target. Instead of a monolithic, conservative business community, he discovered businessmen with varied forms of opinion and influence on reform measures. They opposed some laws, favored others, and influenced the content of almost all of the new economic regulations. Wiebe found the progressive era to be "An Age of Organization." But he did not employ bureaucracy as a major, positive theme, as he did in his second book. In this latter study Wiebe portrayed businessmen as confused participants, along with most other Americans, in a quest, a search for order. Instead of omnipotent robber barons, the author described businessmen who were "trapped by the present scurrying where they appeared to stalk."[13] When at last they solved their problems through a new bureaucratic order, this was, after all, the same solution that most urban Americans achieved—even the reformers. Wiebe had thus completely transformed the businessman's historical role.

Chandler took a different tack. From the first, he focused on the organizations and the organization builders, largely ignoring progressive history and its value judgments. In several influential articles and books, Chandler asked when, how, and why the modern corporation developed as it did.[14] In a recent book, he concentrated upon an important organizational innovation: the strategy of diversification as implemented by the new style of the decentralized firm.[15] Most of this work stayed well within the confines of economic history; Chandler's contribution was to emphasize the importance of bureaucratic institutions and to demonstrate the value of studying their historical evolution. Recently, however, he has shown how the bureaucratic techniques developed in the private sector of the economy had a significant influence upon public policy during World War II. In this case, the methods of business forecasting employed by General Motors and other large corporations were (with modifications) used in the government's Controlled Materials Plan. The government devised this plan, along with the Component Schedule Plan, in order to coordinate the flow of war materials through America's complex, industrial economy.[16] Chandler, like Wiebe, was describing the interaction of business and non-business organizations in ways far more complex than the style of conflict which dominated progressive history.

Cochran recently summarized and extended these new viewpoints in his presidential address to the Organization of American Historians.[17] He concluded that scholars had broken down an artificial barrier which had existed between business institutions and the rest of society. Now, he said, historians were at last able to show the influence that business had exerted "on educational development, on the writing and preaching of the clergy, on the settlement of new communities, and on all levels of politics—in a word on the other major American institutions." While Cochran did not stress the importance of bureaucratic business in particular—as Wiebe and Chandler did—he emphasized the need for "inter-institutional history" of the sort which characterizes the organizational school.

If the conclusions reached by these economic and business historians were correct, then it followed that the organizational aspects of domestic politics needed some serious re-examination. Indeed, this work has been under way for some years now. Richard Hofstadter long ago called attention to the importance of organizational questions during the progressive period.[18] Recently, Robert Cuff has explored American mobilization during World War I; his studies pointed to the importance of the organizational context in shaping wartime policies.[19] In *Conservation and the Gospel of Efficiency*, Samuel P. Hays showed that liberal conservationists and the leaders of large corporations shared many values, particularly a dedication to the rational and efficient employment of natural resources. More often than not, the corporations and the conservationists were united in their opposition to small enterprises and individual entrepreneurs who sought a free hand to exploit the nation's wealth in the haphazard style of the nineteenth century.

Efficiency was also the theme which Samuel Haber used to link scientific management and progressive politics. As Haber illustrated, the business policy of systematic management appealed to many liberals. They translated these ideas, often uncritically, into the political realm. Goals such as the strong executive, apolitical administration, and non-partisanship held out the promise of a more efficient, businesslike polity. The price was a less democratic government, but Haber (like Hays) concluded that many progressives were far more interested in efficiency than in government by the people.[20]

Cuff, Hays, and Haber limited their studies to the years before 1920, but their conclusions could well be extended to cover subsequent periods of American history. The organizations and the ideas which they examined became more, and not less, important during the 1920s, the New Deal, and World War II. New problems arose. New leaders took power. But the evolving politico-economic bureaucracies which had begun to take shape at the turn of the century provided a relatively constant dimension to the nation's political history.

Foreign, as well as domestic, affairs have been analyzed from an organizational point of view. For a number of years, diplomatic history was isolated from some of the major trends in American historiography, but this is no longer the case.[21] A few students of diplomacy have already begun to study the relationships between bureaucracy and foreign policy. In his Albert Shaw lectures at the John Hopkins University, Ernest R. May examined in some detail the formulation of American policy vis-a-vis the

Washington Naval Conference of 1922. One of the most important groups
shaping that policy was, May said, the State Department bureaucracy, the
second tier of officials, men who had been systematically ignored by most
historians. May suspects that the British and Japanese bureaucracies might
have exerted a similiar influence upon their respective national policies.
Robert Wiebe has attempted to apply a similiar thesis to the entire range of
American foreign relations, 1877-1920. In this instance, his generalizations
seemed to suffer from the lack of previous monographic research along the
lines of May's lectures.[22] But nonetheless, his chapters on this subject
indicated that the organizational aspects of America's foreign relations need
more attention from historians.[23]

These organizational themes appearing in the political and economic
history of modern America dictate a similar approach for the more diverse
field of social history. When organizations such as the new bureaucracies
achieve a substantial measure of wealth and power, their interaction with a
wide variety of other social institutions must be of interest to the historian.
Three different studies illustrate that organizational analysis has indeed
invaded social history. Philip Gleason's research on German-American
Catholics emphasized two major themes: the process of Americanization,
and the relationship between that process and the immigrant group's attitude
toward political reform. In developing these subjects, however, the author
also offered some provocative insights into the group's organizational history. One of the strongest German-American organizations was the Central
Verein, a federation of mutual aid societies. Gleason found that one of the
factors shaping the Verein's position on reform was the organization's need
to remain viable by adopting new goals. This special kind of organizational
imperative helped to shape the content of the group's political efforts. The
reform orientation could not be fully understood in terms of the membership's rationalistic response to a problem. An important, indirect influence
was exerted by the particular requirements of their organizational context.[24]

Roy Lubove's volume on the social workers, 1880-1930, goes one step
further in the direction of organizational history.[25] Lubove made progressivism a minor subject. His major concern was the emergence of a profession
and of professional organizations. He concludes that: "Specialization and
the idealization of expertise, the growth of an occupational subculture, and
bureaucratization were instrumental in shaping the character of twentieth-
century social work. These typical features of an urban-industrial society

have affected not only the professional but most spheres of life, and their controlling influence will undoubtedly remain potent.'' Similar ideas were advanced in Gibson Winter's perceptive article on religious organizations in America.[26] Winter found that the nation's churches have undergone a special brand of organizational revolution in the present century. This transformation involved the growth of complex agency bureaucracies which performed special functions related ''to human rights, economic life, political development, international concerns, welfare structures, educational activities, and mass media.'' The agencies have had different effects on the Protestant, Catholic, and Jewish faiths; but on all three, these new bureaucracies have exerted an important influence.

Winter's essay and the books by Lubove and Gleason hint at even broader applications of organizational concepts in social history. If bureaucratization is as multi-faceted and omnipresent as these scholars have indicated, then we need to examine in greater detail the relationship between the new organizations and a variety of other institutions: the family, the school, and the local community. It seems likely that large-scale organizations have influenced all of these institutions, and could perhaps provide social history with a new type of centralizing theme.

This hypothesis is strongly supported by the work of Robert H. Wiebe, the only historian who, to my knowledge, has attempted a general survey of modern American history along organizational lines. Wiebe recast the entire history of the years 1877 to 1920 in organizational terms. He described a nation which in the 1880s and 1890s was confronted with a severe social crisis stemming from the breakdown of local and regional systems of power and status. As a result, Americans sought a new set of guidelines, a new ''order'' for society. Agrarian reform failed to provide an answer. But the urban-based progressive movement advanced a more appealing program: ''The heart of progressivism was the ambition of the new middle class to fulfill its destiny through bureaucratic means.'' Bureaucracy, and its concomitant values, provided the nation with a new, twentieth-century order. By the end of World War I, ''the realignments, the reorientations of the progressive era had been translated into a complex of arrangements nothing short of a revolution could destroy.''

Wiebe's book represented a significant breakthrough, and the volume's weaknesses, as well as its strengths, set benchmarks for future organizational historians. As was already observed, the chapters on foreign policy seem relatively weak. Then, too, the author's attempt to link sophisticated philosophical systems, such as pragmatism, with the emerging bureaucratic culture appears strained. An organizational synthesis is probably far better suited for analyzing general value systems than for explaining the thought of Thorstein Veblen—let alone John Dewey. The author also slights the bureaucracies themselves. Curiously, the intricacies of organizational change receive very little attention, even though bureaucracy provides the moving force in Wiebe's view of history.

The survey's positive contributions are, however, impressive. Wiebe's framework effectively combines a wide range of political, social, and economic developments. The breadth of the synthesis is one of the book's most outstanding qualities. Within this general framework, the author's treatment of the cultural environment is most persuasive. In Wiebe's view, bureaucracy was far more than a set of formal organizations. The process of bureaucratization involved a fundamental shift in values. The new orientation stressed efficiency, continuity, systematic controls, and group action. These were the guiding norms of the new bureaucratic middle class and, by the end of the 1920s, of most urban Americans.

If historians follow the lead of Wiebe and the other scholars mentioned, they will elaborate and extend a new synthesis in modern American history. On the basis of the work already completed, one can perhaps chance a guess as to what some of the major characteristics of the organizational school will be. Organizational history will, no doubt, stress the role of environmental forces acting on the individual. Less emphasis will be placed on the individual's efforts to shape his own historical context. In part this will be a product of behavioral models which tend to fix one's attention on the more general, environmental factors instead of the unique individual.[27] Historians who draw upon Weberian sociology will find it difficult to escape this bias.

With the organizational synthesis should come new attempts at periodization. Historians in this field will doubtless abandon the progressive categories of Populism, Progressivism, the New Deal, and After. Wiebe has already broken with the familiar view of World War I as a watershed between a progressive era and a distinctive interlude during the 1920s. While any precise chronology awaits further research, it already seems clear that a crucial period in organizational terms will be the years from around 1890 to 1910. During these two decades, the modern corporation, the modern craft union, and a variety of other forms of large-scale organization underwent decisive changes. Future historians may find these organizational developments of more lasting importance than even the New Deal innovations which have heretofore loomed so large in our concept of the immediate past.

By developing an organizational analysis of modern America, historians could also produce some new ideas about earlier periods in the nation's history. If one assumes that the era of large-scale organizations began to take shape in the 1870's and 1880's, then one common characteristic of all previous periods is that they were non-bureaucratic. In this sense, the American experience from the seventeenth through the middle of the nineteenth centuries had a common element, something which distinguishes it from the modern age. Similarly, if the focal point of modern history becomes the underlying patterns of social, political, and economic organization—as opposed to particular political events or ideologies—then perhaps the same assumption would be applicable to research on the colonial and ante-bellum years. Ultimately, this type of work might suggest some modifications in the traditional categories of our national history. Such speculations are hazardous, of course, especially at a time when the organizational synthesis of modern American history has only begun to emerge.

Even more difficult to predict are the values, the moral judgments, which will be adopted by the students of bureaucracy. It is possible that they will follow Wiebe and write a relatively amoral brand of history. If so, they will abandon the heroes and villains of the progressive synthesis and the New Left. Explicit or formal ideology will receive less attention, as historians employ a McLuhanesque emphasis on the organizational medium instead of the political message. Men who are portrayed in this type of history will solve or fail to solve problems. Society will change, without moving the nation or any part of it toward a rendezvous with destiny.

It is equally possible, however, that the dominant theme will be a negative judgment on modern organizations. An air of pessimism and fatalism pervades much of the sociology of large-scale organizations, and this may influence organizational historians.[28] If this is true, the historians of bureaucracy may be attracted by the New Left's condemnation of big business and the military-industrial complex. Organizational analysis could blend with New Left ideology to produce a synthesis which would appeal to those scholars who demand that history be "relevant" in some precise and immediate way.

On the other hand, some historians may find it impossible not to surrender their own judgment to the pragmatic and self-serving viewpoints expressed by their organizational subjects. The experience of business history suggests that this could be a major problem. Although my own interest is in Wiebe's style of analysis, it seems impossible at this time to even guess which of these three courses will become most popular. The choice seems certain, however, to create difficulties for scholars working in this field.

Such problems arise for all historians, however, and they cannot override the conclusion that the organizational synthesis offers much to the student of modern America. The chief strength of the organizational approach is a mode of analysis which blends the traditional tools of historical thought with ideas from the behavioral sciences. Organizational history spreads a very broad net.[29] Ultimately, this synthesis may enable historians to combine many elements in our past which cannot be accommodated to the New Left or the liberal view. At any rate, in a society in which bureaucracies play such a commanding role as they do today, it seems likely that more and more historians will explore the new field of organizational history in the years ahead.

Notes

1.   Two recent analyses of the progressive synthesis are: John Higham, *et al.*, *History* (Englewood Cliffs, 1965), 221-30, and Samuel P. Hays, "The Social Analysis of American Political History," *Political Science Quarterly*, LXXX (September, 1965), 373-94. The liberal framework still exercises some authority among historians of the New Deal: Arthur M. Schlesinger, Jr.'s, *The Coming of the New Deal* (Boston, 1958), and *The Politics of Unheaval* (Boston, 1960), carry forward the progressive tradition in brilliant style. Even the historiography of the 1930's has been touched by revisionism, however, and an excellent example of the newer approach is provided by Barry D. Karl's perceptive analysis of *Executive Reorganization and Reform in the New Deal* (Cambridge, 1963).

2.   Richard Hofstadter, *The Progressive Historians* (New York, 1968), xv, comments on the essentially negative quality of revisionism during the past two decades.

3.   This viewpoint is brilliantly analyzed in Isaiah Berlin's study of *The Hedgehog and the Fox* (New York, 1957).

4.   Irwin Unger, "The 'New Left' and American History," *American Historical Review*, LXXII (July, 1967), 1237-63. For a harsh indictment of the New Left, see David Donald's review of Barton J. Bernstein (ed.), *Towards a New Past*, in ibid., LXXIV (December, 1968), 531-33.

5.   I prefer "organizational" to the other terms which scholars have used. John Higham, *et al., History*, 231, refers to "the new institutionalism," but this expression lacks precision and threatens to create unnecessary confusion between the new brand of history and the institutional school of economists. "Institutionalism" does not identify the particular type of institution, the large-scale, modern organization, which plays the leading role in the new synthesis. Robert H. Wiebe, *The Search for Order, 1877-1920* (New York, 1967), uses "bureaucratic." This term has the advantage of being even more precise than "organizational," but bureaucracy carries a heavy pejorative connotation which historians might eventually find burdensome.

6.   This general question is discussed in Kai Erickson, "Sociology and the Historical Perspective," the MacIver Lecture, given at the Southern Sociological Society (Atlanta, 1968). As devotees of historicism will recognize, this difference in emphasis can be of crucial significance. See R. G. Collingwood, *The Idea of History* (New York, 1956), especially 199 ff., for a superb argument against the behavorial orientation in history.

7.   Max Weber, *The Theory of Social and Economic Organization* (Glencoe, 1947), 324-41.

8.   Edward N. Saveth (ed.), *American History and the Social Sciences* (Glencoe, 1964), 357-69.

9.   *American Capitalism* (Boston, 1952).

10.   Other studies developing closely related ideas include: C. Wright Mills, *White Collar* (New York, 1951), and *The Power Elite* (New York, 1956); Peter M. Blau, *Bureaucracy in Modern Society* (New York, 1956); R. K. Merton, *et al.*, (eds.), *Reader in Bureaucracy* (Glencoe, 1952); Edward S. Mason (ed.), *The Corporation in Modern Society* (Cambridge, 1959); Adolf A. Berle, Jr., *The 20th Century Capitalist Revolution* (New York, 1954); W. Lloyd Warner, *The Corporation in the Emergent American Society* (New York, 1961); and W. Lloyd Warner, *et al., The Emergent American Society*, I (New Haven, 1967).

11.   Some of the essays in W. Lloyd Warner's *The Emergent American Society* provide an exception to this rule; see, for example, Gibson Winter, "Religious Organizations," I, 408-91. This volume has received less attention from historians than it probably deserves.

12   Arthur H. Cole, *Business Enterprise in its Social Setting* (Cambridge, 1959); Allan Nevins, *John D. Rockefeller* (2 vols., New York, 1941); Harold F. Williamson and Orange A. Smalley, *Northwestern Mutual Life* (Evanson, 1957); Ralph W. and Muriel E. Hidy, *Pioneering in Big Business* (New York, 1955); Arthur M. Johnson, *The Development of American Petroleum Pipelines* (Ithaca, 1956).

13.   Wiebe, *Search for Order*, 18.

14.   Alfred D. Chandler, Jr., *Henry Varnum Poor* (Cambridge, 1956); "Management Decentralization: An Historical Analysis," *Business History*

Review, XXX (June, 1956), 111-74; "The Beginnings of 'Big Business' in American Industry," *Business History Review*, XXXIII (Spring, 1959), 1-31; "Recent Developments in American Business Administration and Their Conceptualization" (with Fritz Redlich), *Business History Review*, XXXV (Spring, 1961), 1-27; *Giant Enterprise: Ford, General Motors, and the Automobile Industry* (New York, 1964); *The Railroads: The Nation's First Big Business* (New York, 1965); "The Railroads: Pioneers in Modern Corporate Management," *Business History Review*, XXXIX (Spring, 1965), 16-40; "The Coming of Big Business," in C. Vann Woodward (ed.), *The Comparative Approach to American History* (New York, 1968).

15.   *Strategy and Structure: Chapters in the History of the Industrial Enterprise* (Cambridge, 1962).

16.   "The Large Industrial Corporations and the Making of the Modern American Economy," in Stephen E. Ambrose (ed.), *Institutions in Modern America* (Baltimore, 1967), 91-94.

17.   "The History of a Business Society," *Journal of American History*, LIV (June, 1967), 5-18. Cochran's attitude toward the progressive synthesis has not remained static over the years; compare this essay and his volume on *The American Business System* (Cambridge, 1957), with Thomas C. Cochran and William Miller, *The Age of Enterprise* (New York, 1942).

18.   *The Age of Reform* (New York, 1955), 215-71.

19.   "Bernard Baruch: Symbol and Myth in Industrial Mobilization," *Business History Review*, XLIII (Summer, 1969), 115-33.

20.   Samuel Haber, *Efficiency and Uplift: Scientific Management in the Progressive Era, 1890-1920* (Chicago, 1964).

21.   Charles E. Neu, "The Changing Interpretive Structures of American Foreign Policy," in John Braeman, *et al.* (eds.), *American Foreign Policy in the Twentieth Century* (forthcoming at the Ohio State University Press).

22.   *Search for Order*, 224-85.

23.   Professor Jerry Israel is now working on a study along these lines; he is examining scientific management in the State Department, 1906-1924.

24.   Philip Gleason, "An Immigrant Group's Interest in Progressive Reform," *American Historical Review*, LXXIII (December, 1967), 367-79; and *The Conservative Reformers: German-American Catholics and the Social Order* (Notre Dame, 1968), 24, 74, 80-83, 90-91.

25.   *The Professional Altruist: The Emergence of Social Work as a Career, 1880-1930* (Cambridge, 1965).

26.   "Religious Organizations," in Warner, *Emergent American Society*, I, 408-91.

27.   Even Wiebe apparently finds this tendency disturbing. In a paper delivered before the Dallas meeting of the Organization of American Historians (1968),

he called upon scholars to stress the role of the individual in history—a theme which is certainly not very prominent in either of his books.

28.   This is discussed in Alvin W. Gouldner, "Metaphysical Pathos and the Theory of Bureaucracy," *American Political Science Review*, XLIX (June, 1955), 496-507.

29.   No synthesis has ever included with equal facility every aspect of a complex nation's history. The organizational framework will probably not be very useful to the scholars studying the history of the Negro or to those who are working on many facets of immigrant groups in the American past. In effect, this synthesis will probably trade some of the emotional facets of history for a better understanding of how the highly organized sectors of society actually functioned.

THE STRUCTURE OF
THE ECONOMY

After increasing in the early decades of the twentieth century, the degree of concentration in most industry groups in the United States over the last fifty years has remained remarkably stable. As a rule, those industries now characterized by an *oligopolistic* market structure—that is, one dominated by a few firms—in fact became oligopolistic soon after their birth. In contrast to the stability of relationships with competitors, however, large firms underwent several stages of internal administrative development during this half century, with many of them reaching maturity in terms of their formal management structures only after WW II.

The period from 1870 to 1920 was the seedtime for the giant industrial firm and the development of strong primary organizations. Virtually all of the successful big business enterprises were either in very new fields of economic activity—for example, petroleum and electricity—or in older industries, such as iron and steel, that were dramatically changed by new technology. Traditional industries, like textiles, leather working, and wood working, where technology had little impact, remained competitively fragmented despite occasional efforts at consolidation. The key factor accounting for the eventual emergence of the very large corporation was the possibility of economies of scale within a given industry, either in the production or, quite often, in the marketing stage of business activity. Initially, in industries where technology and markets made possible economies of scale, firms faced problems of overproduction and, as a consequence, falling prices and profits. In their effort to exert greater control over the business environment, they employed a series of tactics designed, at the very least, to reduce competitive pressures and, ideally, to create conditions approaching monopoly. An early tactic was the formation of voluntary pooling agreements within an industry which divided markets among competitors and tried to maintain stable prices and the general status quo. Invariably, pooling failed; some firms tried by subterfuge to increase their share of sales, but sooner or later these violations were detected. Meanwhile the other participants in the pool were unable to enforce the provisions of the original agreement in the courts because under American law, as opposed to the laws in many European nations, these pacts among competitors were illegal.

With pooling eliminated as a practical alternative, the stronger firms in an industry often bought out or merged with their former competitors. In 1889 New Jersey enacted a general incorporation law permitting the formation of holding companies. By allowing one corporation to buy and hold the stock of other firms, it facilitated the process of legal consolidation. Thus many nineteenth-century businessmen attempted through consolidation with competitors to create a near monopoly position in certain markets and to exercise a fair degree of control over the volume of production and, thereby, prices. In this category, the Standard Oil Company was among the most successful and certainly the most notorious of American monopolies; at one point in the early 1880s, John D. Rockefeller's firm owned approximately 90 percent of the nation's petroleum refining capacity.

Small businessmen, farmers, and reformers generally raised an outcry against the efforts of industrial and transportation firms to gain monopoly power, and they increasingly demanded government action to halt and to reverse, if possible, the trend toward tighter concentration. The mild and vague Sherman Anti-Trust Act was adopted in 1890. Ironically, the courts initially interpreted the law in a manner that outlawed agreements among formerly independent competitors but permitted their wholesale consolidation into giant holding companies. The latter outcome was not the intent of the original sponsors of the act. In retrospect, it is clear that those who protested so loudly in the late nineteenth century were generally on the mark when they pointed to the trend toward increasing concentration within many of the leading sectors in the American economy. While pure monopoly positions were rarely achieved, and even more rarely sustained, the realization of that goal was one of the prime aims of many nineteenth-century businessmen.

By the early twentieth century, however, the goals of big business leaders began to change. A few years of experience had shown that an oligopolistic market structure was a satisfactory—and in many ways a superior—form of industry organization. First, it was difficult to maintain a high degree of control over a given market, for the existence of substantial profits in a particular industry attracted fresh entrepreneurs intent on disrupting the market unless the dominant firm paid them an unjustifiably high price for their new production facilities. When one enterprising entrepreneur succeeded in selling his "nuisance" plant to aspiring monopolists, it only encouraged others to engage in the same kind of industrial blackmail. Secondly, the continued pursuit of monopolistic control in a period of limited, but potentially radical, reform was politically questionable. Meanwhile, the Supreme Court ruled in the Northern Securities case in 1904 that the recent consolidation of the two leading Northwest railroad networks was illegal. The ruling set a new tone for the enforcement of antitrust legislation: normally the law would not be used to dismantle the large firms already in existence—exceptions were provided by Standard Oil, American Tobacco, and Du Pont—but the Justice Department could henceforth be expected to prevent the merger of two or more giant firms. Thus economic and political forces combined to make oligopoly the normal form of market structure. The effort of one big firm to drive all competitors large and small permanently out of the market was too expensive, and after the first decade of the century the wholesale merger of firms within the same industry was politically and legally dangerous.

An oligopolistic market—one dominated by a few large corporations with some smaller firms on the periphery—had most of the advantages of monopoly. Prices and profits were normally stable, and there was a tacit recognition by big businessmen and government alike of the competitive status quo. A new class of salaried professional managers assumed control of many of the newly created giant corporations, and in contrast to the earlier family oriented owner-managers, the new professionals were more attracted by the possibility of earning a better than average rate of profit over the long run than by the maximization of profit in the short run.

Securely placed in an oligopolistic market, professional managers turned their attention toward the internal functioning of their organizations. They hoped to build a more efficient enterprise through the better coordination of its various parts. The internal control of the corporation now had priority over efforts to control the external, competitive environment. In order to satiate their appetite for additional growth, and as an outgrowth of their efforts to rationalize business operations, corporate leaders increasingly sought expansion through vertical integration rather than horizontal combination with other firms performing similar functions. Thus, big firms found it advantageous to acquire ownership of a secure source of raw materials and to assume greater responsibility for the final marketing of their products.

In the three articles that follow, the evolution of the twentieth-century economic structure is described in greater detail. In the first article, Harold C. Livesay and Glenn Porter succinctly trace the course of vertical integration, focusing on the factors that led some firms to move backward toward raw materials while others integrated forward in the direction of sales. Alfred D. Chandler, Jr., in the second selection, examines the shift toward greater product diversification during the 1920s and the accompanying administrative changes. Finally, Jon Didrichsen, citing the case histories of numerous American corporations, reviews the general pattern of diversification.

VERTICAL INTEGRATION IN AMERICAN MANUFACTURING, 1899-1948

By Harold C. Livesay and Glenn Porter

As part of a long-range project compiling data and source materials for American business history, we recently completed an extensive examination of vertical integration in a cross section of American manufacturing firms in the period 1899-1948. The purpose of this examination was to determine when, where, and why vertical integration occurred in the period after the giant mergers and before the conglomerates. . . .

We obtained our sample of firms by making a collated list of the one hundred largest American industrial firms in 1899, 1909, 1919, 1929, 1935, and 1948. This list was compiled from A. D. H. Kaplan's *Big Enterprise in a Competitive System* and contains all firms listed by Kaplan except those mining, transportation, finance, realty, motion picture, and publishing companies which we excluded as non-manufacturing. . . .

Reprinted with permission from *Journal of Economic History* (September 1969). Copyright © 1969 by The Economic History Association.

In the period 1899-1948 there was a general trend toward greater vertical integration in American manufacturing. The prevailing direction of vertical integration was forward, as manufacturers chose more often to integrate forward into wholesaling and retailing than backward toward raw materials. See Table 1.

Percentage	1909[a]	1919	1929	1935	1948
Integrating forward	21	11	26	18	18
Integrating backward	9	7	6	3	7

[a]The previous sample year in this case is 1899.

Most of the vertical integration which took place in the period was apparently motivated by a desire to rationalize flows by assuring efficient facilities for sales and distribution or assuring needed raw materials rather than from any widespread tendency to add the profits of suppliers or distributors to the profits of manufacturing. Backward integration was essentially a defensive strategy designed to protect firms which feared that raw material supplies might become controlled by competitors or independent suppliers. In general this meant firms whose inputs came from mineral deposits, forests, or overseas sources. Most firms in the lumber and paper; chemical; petroleum; rubber (until the advent of synthetics); stone, glass, and clay; and primary metals industries (all of them dependent on such raw materials) integrated back to raw materials early in the period, and the trend throughout was to increase such control.

In industries where the supply of raw materials was diffuse and plentiful there was little tendency to integrate backward. Thus firms in the food, tobacco, textile, leather, machinery, fabricated metal, electrical machinery, and transportation equipment industries rarely attempted to control supplies of manufacturing inputs. Such backward integration which took place in these fields was usually confined to those inputs originating in mine, forest, or overseas. Meat packers such as Swift and Armour controlled phosphate supplies for their fertilizer production but never engaged in cattle raising.

American Sugar Refining owned timber lands, stave mills, and barrel factories at a time when it owned no sugar-producing lands. United Fruit built its Central American empire to insure its banana supply. Leather firms bought hides in the open market but often controlled tanbark forests.

Some firms found integration a useful method of avoiding exploitation by independent suppliers. International Harvester's ownership of iron ore properties, blast furnaces, and rolling mills was an effective lever against United States Steel despite the small capacity of International furnaces. Sears, Roebuck bought stock in some of its suppliers for similar reasons. In such cases, backward integration could play a major role in controlling input factor costs, even if the capacity of the integrated facilities was small in proportion to the total output of all firms operating on the integrated level. In general, however, it is obvious that most firms saw no need to achieve integrated control of inputs produced by American agriculture, or by the primary metals industry.

Forward integration on the other hand usually began as an offensive competitive strategy. Manufacturing firms first entered wholesaling and/or retailing only when the existing distribution network proved inadequate. This usually occurred for one of the following reasons: the existing mercantile system was unable to provide the mass distribution facilities demanded by mass production; the complexity of the product required technical expertise not available in mercantile houses; the high unit costs of products required consumer credit which exceeded financial capabilities of independent distributors; the product was a new one for which no relevant distribution system existed.

All these limitations were bottlenecks in the flow of goods from producers to consumers. Some firms encountered more of these problems than did others, depending on the nature of their products. The evidence indicates that forward integration is therefore very complex, for a single multiproduct firm often employed several methods of distribution simultaneously. General Electric, for example, maintained sales offices in large cities staffed with specialists in each of its major product lines. This was necessary because customers required expert technical assistance when buying expensive and highly complex electrical machinery. At the same time, however, General Electric continued to market simple consumer products such as light bulbs through independent wholesale houses in areas of the country where volume was small. In general, then, a manufacturer integrated forward only in those product lines or geographic areas in which constrictions in distribution flows made it necessary. Once one manufacturer in an industry moved forward, others rapidly followed suit in order to remain competitive. Firms in most industries found it unnecessary to integrate beyond the wholesaling level, for in industries such as lumber and paper, textile mill products, chemicals, primary metals, fabricated metal products, machinery, and electrical machinery, the majority of products were producers' goods which required no retail distribution. In those industries associated with the older, agrarian economy—food, tobacco, and leather goods—change came slowly. The long-established retail network adjusted to increased volume and provided adequate outlets. No manufacturer in these industries integrated into retailing.

In only two groups of industries did firms find it necessary to engage in large-scale retailing. The first and more important group was associated with the automobile, a new product for which no adequate means of distribution existed. Ford, Durant, and others built nationwide dealer networks to provide volume distribution, consumer financing, and parts and service. The huge new market created by the automobile led rubber firms to establish first wholesale, then retail outlets to distribute tires. Before the advent of this new market, rubber manufacturers had engaged in no forward integration. The petroleum industry also built dealer networks for the retail distribution of gasoline.

The other group of industries which engaged in extensive retailing were those which manufactured technically complex and expensive consumer durables. The classic examples of this were the typewriter, sewing machine, and harvester makers, who met the problems of consumer credit, parts, and service by establishing chains of dealerships in a pattern later adopted by automobile firms. In these industries, as in others, forward integration began as an offensive strategy devised by one firm to eliminate obstacles in the flow of its products to the consumer. Other manufacturers in the field then followed suit in self-defense.

The evidence indicates that the dynamic at work in the growth of vertical integration is the firm's need to stabilize and minimize costs by rationalizing flows of raw materials and finished products. The velocity and limits of integration are determined by the specific market conditions faced by a particular industry and by the need to remain competitive within that industry. Since changing technologies and markets affect various industries at different times, it is understandable that, as our study shows, the general trend toward increased vertical integration proceeded at a very uneven pace within individual industries in the manufacturing sector. Throughout the period studied, our sample of firms included both highly integrated and relatively unintegrated firms; however, we never found these coexisting within the same industry. All firms within a single industry group were similarly integrated at any point in time, while wide variations existed between the average integration levels of whole industry groups.

Industry conditions were a far more important determinant of integration than firm size. In order to test the proposition that vertical integration is a function of size, we obtained the assets of all sample firms active in 1948 from *Moody's Industrials*. Comparison of assets to integration levels shows that (1) variations in integration levels which do exist within industry groups are not, in general, proportionate to the size of the firms in the group, and (2) small firms in highly integrated industries are usually more highly integrated than giant firms in unintegrated groups. For example, American Ice, with assets of $12 million, was operating on . . . seven . . . integration levels in 1948, while American Tobacco with assets of $687 million was operating on only two levels.

This is not to say that size plays no part in determining the degree of integration, for clearly the small, marginal firms in any industry group must concentrate on a single-function, single-product operation. It is apparent, nevertheless, that the firms in both the "peripheral" and "center" economies behave in a manner similar to the other firms in the same industry.[1]

Using data compiled in other studies we checked for correlations between concentration and integration and found no general relationship. Nor did we find, as Michael Gort has suggested, that there is an inverse relationship between integration and diversification. This does not seem to have been generally true between 1899-1948. American Tobacco also serves as an example here, for in 1948 it operated in a highly concentrated industry, and was neither highly integrated nor diversified.

Our findings show that it is difficult to make generalizations about vertical integration in the manufacturing sector of the economy as a whole. The phenomenon can be most profitably studied within the context of specific industry categories or groups of similar categories. It seems reasonable, however, to conclude that the overall trend of increased forward integration among American manufacturing firms is evidence that success in the complex American economy continues to depend more on solving the problems of mass distribution than on developing integrated facilities for mass production.

Notes

1.   These terms are Robert T. Averitt's. The center economy includes those firms which are large, diversified, integrated, decentralized competitors in national and sometimes international markets. Firms in the center economy are rich in managerial and technical talent and financial resources. The peripheral economy is composed of relatively small firms with narrower horizons, a small line of related products, centralized management, poorer credit, and a tendency to focus on short-run problems. See R. T. Averitt, *The Dual Economy* (New York: W. W. Norton, 1968), pp. 1-2.

THE STRUCTURE OF AMERICAN INDUSTRY IN THE TWENTIETH CENTURY: A HISTORICAL OVERVIEW

By Alfred D. Chandler, Jr.

In describing the industrial structure of their country, American economists have rightly focused on the concentration of productions and distribution by a few large firms within individual industries, and on the growth of the large firm itself. Economists including Morris A. Adelman, A. D. H. Kaplan, Adolph Berle, Gardiner C. Means, Willard Thorp, Warren G. Nutter, Ralph L. Nelson, Michael Gort, and John Kenneth Galbraith have pointed out that American industry is highly concentrated, that concentrated industries are dominated by large firms, and that concentration has not increased significantly in recent years. Only a few of these scholars, however, have emphasized that concentration came in some industries and not in others, and still fewer have suggested why these differences occurred. Nor have they studied, as a historian would, the changing developments within industries and within the large firm decade by decade since 1900. They have, for example, failed to analyze the ways in which multi-industry enterprises emerged from the vertically integrated companies. Moreover, these economists have used various industrial classification systems and different criteria in measuring concentration. Therefore, it is often difficult to make comparisons between their findings. . . .

By 1960, the large American enterprise had become multi-industrial. The firms which were the first to diversify were those in the most technologically advanced industries—chemicals, rubber, electrical, and transportation machinery. They were followed by others with less complex technologies including food, metals, other machinery, and even oil. In the 1960's, the latter still remained less diversified than the former. As these large enterprises which began in concentrated industries started to diversify, they often went into unconcentrated industries. Just as often they moved into other concentrated industries and so made such industries more competitive. . . .

The industrial sector of the American economy, like that of any modern technologically advanced nation, grew out of two different types of industries. There were those industries with a history, those which had long been involved in processing goods for an older, predominantly agrarian economy. And there were the new chemical and machinery industries which, based on modern engineering and science, only began to develop in the late nineteenth century.

During much of the nineteenth century, American manufacturing was primarily involved in the processing of products of field and forest, with relatively small-scale production of metals, chemicals, and stone, glass and clay products. These older industries had long been characterized by small family businesses in much the same way as had agriculture, mining, and pre-railroad transportation. Even as late as 1909, the older industries produced the largest share of product value in American industry (65 per cent even if primary metals were excluded). . . . On the other hand, by 1909 concentration was already significant in the new machinery and chemically-oriented, as well as many older metals industries whose production had been revolutionized by high-volume-output techniques based on modern metallurgical sciences. And these metal, machinery, and chemical industries were the basis of the modern economy.

Before the great merger movement at the turn of the century, the large firm had made its appearance largely in those industries where manufacturers were required to develop extensive distribution networks. In the older industries based on agricultural products, this had been true for the processors of perishable goods like meat, beer, bananas, and tobacco which required refrigeration, quick transportation, or careful storage for high volume distribution. In the newer machinery groups concentration of production in the hands of a few large firms had occurred primarily where the manufacturers, using a complex technology, also needed a national or international sales organization in order to provide initial demonstrations, consumer credit, and service and repair. This occurred in such industries as agricultural machinery, sewing machines, cash registers, and electrical machinery.

During and after the price decline that followed the depression of the 1870's, the small, non-integrated manufacturers in most industries had joined associations or alliances which attempted to control price and production. Until the merger movement at the turn of the century, however, very few of these associations or cartels followed the example of John D. Rockefeller's Standard Oil Company, which converted the alliance into a centralized manufacturing organization and then integrated forward, to control partially its own marketing, and backward to control partially its own raw materials.

Only after the merger movement which began in early 1890's and culminated in the years 1897 to 1903 did the modern structure of American industry begin to appear.[1] In those years mergers occurred more frequently and were more successful in the modern metals, and the new machinery and chemically-oriented industrial groups, than in the older, longer established ones. . . .

Shaw Livermore's article written in 1935 examined the fate of mergers by classifying 146 of them into three main categories: failures, partial failures, and successes.[2] This list emphasized that more failures came in older industries and more successes in the new industries and in primary metals. In textiles he shows ten failures and one partial success. In the leather industry all five mergers were failures. In fabricated metals there were six failures, three successes, and two partial successes. Among the food firms, the score was about even with eleven failures, eleven successes, and two partial successes. But in chemicals, stone, glass and clay, primary metals, machinery, electrical machinery, and transportation vehicles, there were more successes and partial successes than failures.

These studies indicate that in the older industrial groups, except for primary metals, glass, and some foods, size and concentration of production in the hands of few firms did not provide long-run economic advantages. In the more modern chemically-oriented and machinery industries, the large firm could develop and improve complex technological processes and make the most of new administrative techniques. It could create an extensive purchasing organization for the buying of scarce and often distant raw materials in high volume and at lower costs, and in the case of some consumer goods, it could benefit from a widespread distribution network.

In these industries and in the primary metals, size of course provided its class advantage. Heavy initial investment and continuing large operating costs were necessary to obtain the high volume production that would substantially reduce unit costs. The resulting lower unit cost made it difficult for firms with smaller output to stay in competition. At the same time, the high initial investment protected the company from the entrance of new firms into the industry. In much the same way, the creation of an extensive distribution network and heavy advertising expenses protected firms in some foods and tobacco and other consumer goods industries from new competitors.

For the makers of textiles, clothing, leather, and paper goods, and even the manufacturers of simple fabricated metals like structural steel, sheet metal, stampings, bolts, nuts, hardware, wire, and pipe, size did not provide these advantages. Nor did size offer significant economies to machinery and chemical firms which were not involved in complex production technology, did not have heavy fixed and operating costs, and did not produce for a relatively high-volume market. For example, such industries as machine tools (including machine cutting, metal forming, and metal work tools), pumps and compressors, dies and patterns, paints, fertilizers, and certain acids and salts did not secure such economies. These industries remain unconcentrated, and in them the large firm was rarely a continuing success. So too in the food industries the successful large firms were those such as producers of meat, breakfast cereals, biscuits, and distilled liquors which could benefit from the establishment of large distribution networks and the extensive use of advertising; or those few high-volume producers using relatively complex and costly refining techniques, as in the case of sugar and some corn products; or those like sugar and chocolate firms whose large buying organization gave them advantages in purchasing a raw material that came from overseas.

Livermore's lists and the detailed studies of Livesay and Porter suggest that in the first years of the century the successful mergers began quickly to expand by completing their lines by vertical integration. Many of these horizontal combinations consolidated their factories into a single manufacturing department, created their own wholesaling and in some cases retailing organization, developed their own purchasing, and often moved back to take at least partial control of parts and accessories firms and semi-finished and raw materials. Growth through integration helped preserve concentration. The cost, technological, and administrative advantages of size became even more pronounced. Entrance by new firms into the industry became even more hazardous and competition by existing small non-integrated enterprises even more difficult. At the same time it may have helped oligopoly replace monopoly or duopoly in some important cases; for, as different horizontal combinations controlling a large share of the production at one stage of an industrial process integrated backward and forward, they gave new competition to the combination controlling the other stages in the process. This happened when primary steel manufacturers moved into fabrication and fabricators into making of sheet steel or gray iron, and when crude oil producers moved into refining and refiners moved into the production of crude oil, or when the cartridge makers decided to produce their own powder or the powder companies decided to go into chemicals.

For the successful mergers completed at the turn of the century, the primary strategy of growth continued to be vertical integration until the 1920's. Most firms developed marketing and purchasing organizations shortly after they combined manufacturing activities. The patterns of further integration differed, however, from industry to industry. Nearly all primary metals firms obtained some control of supplies of ore and fuel, and a number moved forward into the fabrication of simple metal products. Almost none, however, went so far as producing machinery, because this involved them in a very different technology of production and different marketing requirements. The machinery companies, on the other hand, particularly those using interchangeable-parts manufacturing, moved back to obtain for themselves the parts and accessories needed to assure a continuous flow of materials for their assembly lines. Such backward integration, like that in metals, was essentially defensive. However, machinery firms only rarely moved still further backward into building their own blast furnaces once the supply seemed fairly assured, for the cost of such production was very high and the technology of production and the market needs were very different.

In the chemically-oriented industries those making a single major product (such as gasoline or tires for the consumer market) tended to obtain some control of all the processes involved, from the production of raw materials to retailing to the final customer. By World War I, the leading rubber companies had already purchased rubber plantations in the Far East and had begun to build their own retail-tire outlets. The story was more dramatic in the oil industry where the coming of the automobile, the opening of the new fields, and the breakup of the old Standard Oil Company in 1911 led to a spate of mergers in the second decade of the century. The old Standard Oil firms, which were largely refining and distribution companies, moved backward into the production of crude; those based in the new oil fields— such as Texaco, Gulf, and Phillips—moved forward into refining and distribution. In the chemical industry the large fertilizer and salt firms secured control of raw materials as did Du Pont. Unlike Du Pont, however, their processing techniques were simple, raw materials ample, and initial investment and operating costs were relatively low. These older industries, therefore, never became concentrated. After Du Pont moved into chemicals, and as Union Carbide and the other modern chemical companies grew, they tended to integrate backward to assure themselves of basic materials; but they rarely moved forward into the production of consumer goods, largely because of the very different marketing organization needed. . . .

By the 1920's the first stage of growth of the large enterprise in the United States was essentially complete. The large firm had come primarily in the newer and most technologically complex industries where size had real economic advantages, and where the necessity of assured supplies had encouraged vertical integration. These were precisely the industries which, as the century progressed, became increasingly critical to the continuing strength and growth of the national economy. In his recent book, *The Dual Economy*, Robert T. Averitt has identified such key industries by using eight criteria: technological convergence, capital goods production, industrial interdependence, price/cost effect on other industries, leading growth sectors, research and development, wage setting demand effect, and full employment bottleneck industries. Averitt identified forty-one such key industries. In 1919, the top 100 firms operated in all but two of these key industries. These two were machine tools and mechanical measuring devices. Furthermore, these key industries (with the exceptions of machine tools, measuring devices, construction machinery, and one or two of the chemical industries) had become quite concentrated by 1919.

Since 1920, concentration in American manufacturing has remained relatively stable—growing in such industries as glass, paper, and textiles where the production and distribution processes became more costly and complicated, and declining, though not until after World War II, in those areas that were already concentrated. And since 1920, the large firms have increasingly followed a strategy of growth by diversification rather than by vertical integration. Indeed there are indications that, because firms found it difficult to both diversify and integrate, integration in American manufacturing may have declined. . . . Diversification, that is the development of dissimilar products based on similar technological and production processes (or as in the case of the food industries, new products using similar distribution facilities), has made for the greatest change in the profile of American industry during the last thirty or forty years.

The pioneers in the new strategy of diversification were those firms which had the technological and research skills to develop new products and the administrative experience to produce and distribute them at high volume for national and international markets. Not only did technology give them a greater opportunity to develop new products and processes than had other firms, but in addition, their size and technological and managerial know-how continued to protect them from new competitors in their basic fields. Moreover, since their volume of operations tended to assure higher profits than those of smaller firms, they had more capital available (particularly during the years of the Great Depression) to carry on the costly research and development work required to bring the new products to market. Understandably, then, the large chemical and electrical-machinery firms were the first to embark on a strategy of diversification, and understandably, too, they were followed by makers of automobiles, other machinery, rubber, glass, instruments, and some food industries, and to a lesser extent by primary metals and oil firms.

More than technological opportunity, however, was needed to bring most of these firms to a strategy of diversification. It took the economic pressure created by the slowing down of the economy in the 1920's and its miserable performance in the 1930's to turn these technically sophisticated enterprises to the new strategy of expansion. Precisely because these firms had accumulated vast resources in skilled manpower, facilities, and equipment, their executives were under even greater pressure than those of smaller firms to find new markets as the old ones ceased to grow. In the 1920's, the chemical companies, each starting from a somewhat different technological base, began to widen their product lines into new industries. In the same decade the great electrical manufacturers—General Electric and Westinghouse—

which had concentrated primarily on the manufacture of light and power equipment, diversified into production of a wide variety of household appliances. They also entered electronics production with radios and x-ray equipment. During the depression General Motors (and to a lesser extent other firms in the automobile industry) moved into diesels, appliances, tractors, and airplanes. Some makers of primary metals, particularly aluminum and copper, turned to consumer products like kitchenware and household fittings, while rubber firms developed the possibilities of rubber chemistry to compensate for declining tire sales. In the same period food companies employed their existing distribution organizations to market an increasing variety of products.

Where the depression pushed firms into diversification, the war encouraged the adoption of this strategy by opening new opportunities for the production of new products. The huge synthetic rubber program, for example, caused both rubber and petroleum companies to make far greater use of chemical technologies than they had ever done before. Radar and other electronics equipment carried the electrical, radio, and machinery firms further into this new field. The production of tanks, high-speed aircraft, and new drugs all created skills and resources which large enterprises were anxious to put to use after the war ended. The post-war boom, which was characterized by pent-up demand and by a rapid expansion of the amount of government funds for research and development, gave an impetus to the great spread of diversification in the late 1940's and 1950's. Nevertheless, most makers of primary metals, some machinery manufacturers, and oil companies have remained less diversified than the producers of chemical, electrical, electronic equipment, and transportation vehicles (including aircraft engines and airframes). . . .

The enterprises that followed the strategy of diversification in the most technologically sophisticated industries were also those that developed an effective new type of administrative organization, the decentralized structure. This form was initially fashioned by Du Pont to meet the needs arising from operating in several industries and markets. Its adoption in turn made easier the process of moving from one industry to another. The decentralized structure consisted of autonomous operating divisions and a general office. The operating divisions each handled all the functions involved in producing a line of products for a major market. The general office, manned by staff and general executives, evaluated the performance of the divisions and made the critical decisions as to the allocation of the enterprise's resources, including capital, plant and equipment, and technological and administrative skills. By 1960, the large majority of diversified firms had adopted this structure.[3]

The decentralized structure effectively institutionalized the strategy of diversification. The research department of such an enterprise developed new products and tested their commercial value. The executives in the general office, freed from nearly all routine duties involved in the output of specific goods, determined whether the new product could use enough ᴐf the firm's resources or could aid in building enough new ones to warrant its large-scale production and sale. If the executives agreed on its profit potential, they then decided whether to handle the product through an existing division or to create a new one.

The diversified and decentralized industrial giant has, since World War II, taken over an increasing share of American industrial activity. In 1947, the 200 largest companies, many of which had not yet become fully diversified and decentralized, accounted for 30 per cent of the value added by manufacturing. By 1963, when most of them had adopted the new strategy and structure, they accounted for 41 per cent of value added. At the same time these companies, by moving into new products for new markets also helped to decrease concentration in the critical science-based industries. The product value produced by oligopolies has decreased in the chemical, rubber, electrical machinery, transportation vehicle, and stone, glass and clay industries, as well as in primary metals and food. (There was, however, little decrease in the petroleum industry, for while petroleum companies could move into chemicals and synthetic rubber, rubber and chemical companies have not yet developed a synthetic gasoline.)

These giant multi-industry enterprises are of central importance to the American economy. They have generated the great share of the private funds used for industrial research and development and employ by far the largest number of people who carry out the technological innovation so essential to economic growth. Moreover, they spend the greatest part of the massive funds that the federal government has allocated to research and development since World War II. These are the same firms that, according to Europeans, have moved so successfully into the Common Market—more successfully indeed than many European firms themselves. These are the corporations that the government used as prime contractors for weapons production in World War II and again in the Korean and Viet Nam conflicts.

The modern diversified enterprise represents a calculated, rational response of technically trained professional managers to the needs and opportunities of changing technologies and markets. It is much less the product of ambitious and able individual entrepreneurs or of governmental policies. Early in the twentieth century the most successful large enterprises were in those industries which had the most comnlex and costly production and distribution facilities and where, therefore, . ∴ economies of scale were most obvious. These same firms had the technological capabilities as well as the necessary funds for the development of new products and processes when the economy leveled off and faltered so badly in the 1920's and 1930's. They were the enterprises that gained the most from the development of new technological skills and resources during World War II. They were, therefore, in the best position to benefit from the post-war boom and full employment that . . . continued through the 1960's.

The individual entrepreneur did play a part in the original creation of many of these giant enterprises. Early in the century, a breed of individual manufacturers and financiers, who resembled Joseph Schumpeter's creative entrepreneur, took an important role in their formation. Nevertheless, to be successful, a business empire builder had to pick his industry carefully, avoiding those like textiles, leather, lumber, or furniture and turning instead to those like steel, chemicals, electrical machinery, or automobiles. Even within the industries where conditions favored the enterprising empire builder, technological training quickly proved its worth. In the automobile industry, for example, it is instructive to compare the outstanding record of Alfred P. Sloan, Jr., educated at M.I.T., to the disastrous one turned in by the renowned financier William C. Durant, or even to the dismal performance of the untrained manufacturer, Henry Ford, after the industry began to reach maturity. In chemicals, a similar comparison can be made with the performance of M.I.T.-trained Du Ponts to that of financier Orlando Weber of Allied Chemical.

Furthermore, strategies of diversification were rarely if ever carried out by individual financiers or owner-executives. They were undertaken by professional managers, anonymous bureaucrats whose names are not even known to the most conscientious student of American business history. These men were executives who, precisely because of their educational background and their experience in the management of the large, vertically integrated enterprises, had developed the necessary technological and administrative skills to initiate and execute a new and complex strategy of expansion. Such skills were rare in the small-unit clothing, furniture, or lumber industries, or even in the textile or publishing and printing industries. Such skills, so vital to industrial innovation and economic growth, still appear to be in short supply in the rest of the world, even in the old industrial countries of western Europe.

Governmental policies appear to have had even less effect on the development of the large firm or the overall structure of industry than have had individual entrepreneurs. Before World War II the policies of the federal government that most affected American industry were those involving anti-trust regulation, taxes, and tariffs. Clearly the needs and requirements of changing technologies and markets rather than anti-trust policies have played the major role in determining changes in concentration in American industries. Anti-trust had nothing to do with keeping the clothing industry diffuse and transportation vehicles concentrated. It was research and development, not anti-trust that led to the lessening of concentration in the electrical machinery, chemical, and rubber industries after World War II. For a brief period the breakup of Standard Oil affected concentration in the petroleum industry, but the coming of a huge new market—the automobile—and the opening of new oil fields were equally significant. Tariffs and taxes may have played a more important role, but tariffs were generally as protective on products of industries that remained diffuse and operated through small firms as they were on the products of those industries where a few firms came to dominate. Tax policies in the 1930's undoubtedly influenced the reinvestment of profits for research and development. The undistributed profits tax did not, however, prevent diversification in those industries where firms had technological opportunities for product development.

Since the 1930's, however, the federal government has played a larger role in the American economy, and while not directly affecting the structure of industry in any significant way, it has strongly influenced the environment in which industry operates. Committed to assuring full employment, the government has helped in maintaining aggregate demand and assuring a stable and even increasing market. Of more direct importance to American industry the government has made available vast amounts of money for research and development. Through its control of the allocation of these resources the federal government has and can continue to guide the direction which research and development of new products and processes takes. At the same time, the growing concentration of production of these technologically advanced products by a few hundred large, multi-industry enterprises would seem to facilitate the coordination of long-range planning between the government and private enterprises. Such coordinated planning of the use of technological skills and resources, combined with effective policies for maintaining aggregate demand, may ultimately make it possible for Americans to meet the continuing challenges of successfully managing the technologically advanced industrial economy. Even if such sensible cooperation fails, these giant enterprises will undoubtedly continue to play as decisive a role in the American economy during the remainder of the twentieth century, as they have during the years of this century that have already become history.

Notes

1.   I will not consider in this paper the reasons for the coming of the merger movement as my views on this important subject are summarized in "The Large Industrial Corporation and the Making of the Modern American Economy," Stephen E. Ambrose, editor, *Institutions in Modern America* (Baltimore, 1968), 76-82, and in "The Role of Business in the United States, a Historical Survey," *Daedalus*, 98 (Winter, 1969), 23-40.

2.   Shaw Livermore, "The Success of Industrial Mergers," *Quarterly Journal of Economics*, 50 (November, 1935), 68-96.

3.   Alfred D. Chandler, Jr., *Strategy and Structure* (Cambridge, 1962).

THE DEVELOPMENT OF DIVERSIFIED AND CONGLOMERATE FIRMS IN THE UNITED STATES, 1920-1970

By Jon Didrichsen

The 1920's saw the emergence of the large, diversified, multi-divisional firm in the United States. In the years which have passed since that decade, the strategy of diversification rather than that of integration, and the multi-divisional as opposed to the functional organization have become dominant characteristics of many large firms in American industry. In the early 1950's the conglomerate firm has grown extremely rapidly to become a significant element in American industrial structure.

The appearance and growth of diversified and conglomerate firms can be properly understood only as a continuation of the evolution of the American industrial firm over the period of the last hundred years or more. That evolution has been synthesized and presented by Alfred D. Chandler, Jr., in a book and several articles. The present article makes an attempt to continue that work by focusing in particular on the development of the diversified firm in the most recent period of time, the last fifty years. My research indicates that in becoming diversified, the large firms have rather consistently followed one of a few predominant diversification strategies. The strategy chosen reflected certain corporate characteristics while at the same time it put its imprint on the evolving character of the firm. . . .

Diversification began to emerge in the earliest part of this century as a result of a desire of the firms to be able to supply entire lines of interrelated products. Diversification came most rapidly in industries which were faced with a declining or stagnating demand for their primary product. Beginning in the 1920's diversification was increasingly the result of an effort in research and development which more and more came to be directed towards finding entirely new products and not just improving old ones.

The diversified firm brought increasing complexities due to the variety of technologies, manufacturing processes, channels of distribution, and managerial tasks facing a large firm. In response to this, the decentralized, multi-divisional organization was developed. It was pioneered by Du Pont and General Motors in the 1920's and was soon accepted by firms in the chemical, motor vehicle, and electrical industries. Somewhat later it spread to processors of agricultural products and the oil and rubber industries, but basic metals and materials industries were hesitant about accepting it. . . .

Research conducted by Leonard Wrigley shows that of *Fortune's* 500 largest manufacturing firms in 1970, 86 per cent were multi-divisional companies.[1] . . . The overall conclusions one can draw from Wrigley's research are that the majority of large American firms (or about 80 per cent) are diversified, and the vast majority are multi-divisionally organized. . . .

The purpose of the research reported below was to explore the process whereby large industrial firms became diversified and how the present product-market posture developed. Also, when constituent parts of that product-market posture did not seem to have an inherent logic to them, a historical explanation was sought. Certain strategies of diversification soon emerged and were found to be related to the firms' particular competence, in other words, the kinds of activities at which they were most proficient.

Selecting only diversified firms for study helped focus the research on the development of diversification in the group which makes up the vast majority of large American business firms. By concentrating on the development of diversification as it took place over time and by making a concerted effort to recognize a broad range of ways in which corporate activities can be related (not only through the technical likeness of products), I hope to have avoided some of the weaknesses of early studies. . . .

The research was undertaken in the academic year 1970-1971 and consisted of a library study of published data on large diversified firms. Excluding firms producing a single, or predominantly a single product or product line as well as integrated companies unless they were at the same time diversified, fifty manufacturing firms among the 200 largest in sales in 1970 were chosen. Originally I intended that all diversified firms among the 200 largest would be studied. When very consistent patterns were found, however, the research was terminated after fifty companies. The sample is not random; instead, care was taken to have all major industries and kinds of companies represented.

The study is based on the companies' annual reports for the entire period in which they were published. Depending on the company in question, that period varied between less than ten years and more than a century. I supplemented the annual reports with magazine articles and a few visits to two of the large conglomerate firms. . . .

Conglomerate diversification began about 1953. One can only speculate about the reasons for the timing of the appearance of conglomerates, and it is a question which requires much more investigation. Expecting a depression, many firms came out of World War II with vastly expanded productive capacity and capabilities in various technologies. The government had supported research and capital investment, and these factors combined to give birth to new industries such as aerospace and electronics and to greatly expand the scope of others such as chemicals.

Firms which became diversified through internal development commonly started with a competence either in a broad technology or in a narrow specialty. The former could be called the extensive central technology and the latter branching technology. The firm which relied on a central technology had developed an extensive competence in a major industry such as electronics or organic chemicals. There are unlimited opportunities for the development of new products within such comprehensive fields. Through a major effort in research and development, a firm may achieve great diversity, and the end-products of the research effort may sometimes seem completely unrelated, especially when they are by-products of this research and development. Reliance on branching technology was as common as the former pattern. The typical firm did not have a competence in a major technology, but started from a narrow base and the research effort was then allowed to branch into a variety of fields. Contiguous steps in the branching process may be related, but a comparison of the starting point with the products and technologies the firm was involved in many years later conveys an impression of a total lack of relation. The firms which rely on internal development will almost always diversify into areas which are related at least in one way. Occasional exceptions may emerge, for instance, when basic research has accidentally yielded a new and entirely unrelated product.

Du Pont is an excellent sample of a company that has developed an extensive competence in a major technology through internal development. Du Pont's central technology was organic chemicals. Some twenty or thirty years ago it was a producer of bulk staple organic chemicals and synthetic fibers. The centralized research effort had a high degree of internal interaction and cross-fertilization. The research showed an almost self-sustained growth in a variety of directions. An increasing emphasis on fundamental research also tended to channel activity into unrelated directions.

The heart of the matter is that Du Pont thought of itself as a producer of organic chemicals and such closely related products as synthetic fibers sold to the textile industry. Research focused on improved products and processes, modified specification, slightly changed characteristics, and new uses under new conditions. The company's field of interest is still organic chemicals. But, in the process of improving their products (such as synthetic fibers) to make them, say, stronger, more heat-resistant or abrasion-resistant, or more elastic, a lot more has been achieved than just a better fiber. Du Pont gathered knowledge and skills in the area of heat-resistance, elasticity, and abrasion. From there the step was not great to new products seemingly totally unrelated to man-made fibers. Thus, Du Pont is today a producer of such diverse products as photographic film, pharmaceuticals, advanced instruments, precious metal compositions, and others.

Du Pont could have had no *detailed* long-term strategy. Their new products and markets were often accidental throw-offs from research activities, and therefore investments in new products were frequently the result of unintended commitments which Du Pont had "backed into." Lately, it has been evident that many are very profitable. As a result, there is now a more conscious pursuit of new opportunities. Here we see a growth through related product areas to a position of relatively high diversity which seems to go in the direction of even less related products. This development, which was initially quite undirected, has since increasingly become the result of a consciously planned strategy. The same impression is conveyed by the research focus which in recent years has been extended to cover radiation, graphic reproduction, magnetic materials, bio-chemistry and physics, and so on.

The company's organizational structure would seem consistent with the development of Du Pont's diversity. There has been a high degree of centralized financial and even operating control over product departments. Lately, the degree of autonomy has increased; for example, the recently acquired Endo Laboratories, a pharmaceuticals company, operates fairly autonomously.

International Harvester has also developed from a major central technology. It started out as a fully integrated manufacturer of farm equipment. Before World War I it already owned coal lands, iron ore properties, sisal plantations, timberlands, coke plants, blast furnaces, steel mills, foundries, twine mills, and saw mills. Therefore, it was considered a highly diversified company. It was diversified in a technological sense, but apart from sales of steel to outsiders, for instance, the entire effort was directed towards producing farm equipment. In other words, International Harvester was a vertically integrated rather than a diversified firm.

The major central technology in which International Harvester has remained is mechanical power based on the internal combustion engine. The development of crawler tractors and earthmoving equipment logically belongs within the same technology. Growth has been entirely internal except for the acquisition of a gas turbine manufacturer in 1960. This acquisition provided a new research and engineering capability, and introduced International Harvester to a new technology. A competence in the field of gas turbines might sooner or later become an absolute necessity for the largest producer of specialized trucks. Internal development of such a separate technology could be slow, expensive, and uncertain.

This case is very similar to the acquisition of Endo Laboratories by Du Pont in 1969. There was a realization on the part of Du Pont that a significant contribution in the pharmaceuticals field could not easily be made on the basis of internal research and development, though a few pharmaceutical discoveries had already been made by Du Pont. Therefore, a strategy of acquisition was adopted after a decision had been made to undertake a real commitment in the highly profitable field of pharmaceuticals. For International Harvester, its lone acquisition may also have had a defensive character; the firm did not want to be left out of the gas turbine field.

Uniroyal shows a similar development within the large area of rubber technology. It has made several acquisitions, but none of them diversifying. On the other hand, diversity has come from internal research with the result that Uniroyal today is engaged in the production of plastics, chemicals, and fibers. A partial result has been that Uniroyal has become more highly integrated. To the extent that it has diversified, it has moved into products with related characteristics or products which compete with its original ones.

If Uniroyal became diversified through competence in a broad technology, Minnesota Mining and Manufacturing presents a good example of diversity which branched out from a narrow technological base. The company started as a mining operation in 1902 and then became a manufacturer of sandpaper and abrasives. In response to a radical decline in the market for abrasives, 3M diversified into adhesives. From there, research has branched out, always into technologically related areas, and resulted in so many new products that 3M today produces a total of more than 30,000.

There have been innumerable, usually small, acquisitions by 3M, but still the company's diversity was primarily a creation of internal R&D. Acquisitions have mainly served to strengthen existing activities in a product area by adding to a product line, securing raw materials or a market, or filling a gap in the technology. Here is a firm which has attempted to simplify and speed up its diversification by supplementing its internal efforts with some acquisitions. The company branched out from its narrow base to become involved with products very far removed from the initial technological base, which today is only a very minor part of 3M's skills. For example, the original development of adhesive tape led to the development of electrical insulated tape, reflective materials, non-slip material, some hospital supplies, and perhaps even to heat-sealable film and magnetic tape, which in turn led to the introduction of stereo cartridge systems.

PPG (formerly Pittsburgh Plate Glass) is very similar to 3M, but its diversity is almost exclusively internally generated. While glass is still the largest single product category, chemicals and paints account for as much of the firm's sales. Some products of PPG's internal research and development are fungicides, plastics, insulation materials, solvents, and specialty fabrics. A part of its diversity has been the result of attempts at backward integration; examples are chemicals and pigments. In addition to the fact that PPG's diversity is the result of branching technology resulting in turn from expansive R&D, there is another factor which increases the commonality of the firm's business: all sales are industrial, and therefore there is homogeneity in the marketing effort. There are logical technological, production, and marketing connections between the products.

These five firms—Du Pont, International Harvester, Uniroyal, 3M, and PPG—all grew by internal development, only occasionally supplemented by acquisitions. In diversifying, they paid far more attention to technical and technological relationships than to marketing or distribution. Their new products were internally generated results of research and development. As time passed a continuing and expanding R&D effort resulted in more and more diverse products.

ACQUIRED TECHNOLOGY

A number of firms have diversified since the 1920's by acquiring companies which can supplement their technology. Those firms, nevertheless, have remained basically within one major line of business. They did not diversify into totally unrelated areas. Sometimes they followed a long-term plan which outlined a strategy step-by-step for broadening their technology. In other cases, this brand of diversification came as a response to a decline in the firms' original industry.

White Consolidated Industries is a good example. Its strategy included an element of defensiveness. In 1954, White found itself in an unprofitable industry with few growth prospects—sewing machines. Since 1956, the firm has acquired a large number of companies, all in the general area of industrial machinery and equipment and consumer appliances. The initial competence in this field was very limited, but through acquisition White has added to its expertise to such an extent that the competence today is broad and there is a surplus of transferable management. The firm's present activities are not an extension of their particular skill in the narrow base of producing sewing machines with which they started. That particular competence did not motivate the acquisition, but rather, the acquisitions contributed the skills which White may have today. If they now have a pool of management skills in industrial machinery and equipment, that has been the result of frequent acquisitions and not of continued development of a central technology.

One can compare the narrow skills of White with the broad technology of Du Pont. The latter built up slowly, entirely through internal development, a broad competence in the whole area of organic chemistry. Therefore, the two companies cannot be equated simply by saying that both have expanded from a core skill into related areas.

TRW (formerly Thompson, Ramo, Wooldridge) is the result of a combination of a producer of automotive and aircraft parts and an electronics firm in 1958. Since then the company has made frequent acquisitions initially intended to be a supplemental or economic means of achieving desired results, i.e., a reinforcement of internal growth. But even so, acquisitions have clearly added technologies related to mechanical and electronic components. TRW is active in a large number of product areas and is also a producer of entire systems (satellites, computers), which is natural, since it produces many of the components. It is also a producer of a range of products from low to high technology, which is equally natural since its customers manufacture products (such as aircraft) which contain both kinds of technology.

Continental Can, another example of acquired technology, was a manufacturer of tin cans and crown caps in 1939. During the subsequent twenty years, the firm undertook a detailed diversification program through acquisitions. It became a producer of metal, glass, plastic, and paper containers, glass closures, bottle caps, and flexible packaging material. Thus, Continental has added related, supplemental technologies. Again we have a company engaged in many product categories, but one which is in essence a producer of only one product—packaging. The ability to produce something in addition to tin cans was a necessity when profitability on cans decreased and packaging technology advanced and the needs for new types of packaging grew. Continental's diversity served to fulfill a need, though the characteristics and specifics of that need may vary, and Continental's products and production technology may be correspondingly varied.

White Consolidated, TRW, and Continental Can are counterparts to the firms which diversified by internal development. Unlike the latter, they have built up their technology primarily by acquisition. In doing that they have remained in rather well defined areas where they rely on expertise in research and development and production which they have developed over the years.

HOMOGENEOUS MARKETS

A group of large firms have diversified in recent years by acquiring companies which manufacture and sell products which use the same or similar channels of distribution, reach the same customers, and utilize the same principles and methods of advertising and promotion. Sometimes these products fill the same consumer needs or are used for similar purposes. To the companies involved, these products are related insofar as they can draw on a particular competence or set of skills in the firm's marketing and sales efforts, since the business of selling these products follows the same "rules of the game." At the same time, these products may be technically unrelated and have completely different requirements on the production side.

These are firms which have an expertise in marketing. They have several important characteristics in common. Most of them are producers of nationally advertised, mass-merchandised, branded consumer goods. Many have only been diversifying in the last few years. The emphasis on marketing is only natural. These firms simply utilize their particular competence by diversifying into areas where the demands on marketing skill are roughly the same as those for their existing products. Not surprisingly, liquor and tobacco businesses fall in this category. Furthermore, tobacco companies follow a defensive diversification strategy in anticipation of the possibility of a decline in the tobacco industry as a result of the issue of the effect of smoking on health. Good examples are American Brands (formerly American Tobacco), Liggett & Myers, and Heublein. In 1966, after many years of stagnant sales and a change in top management, American Brands diversified into pre-packaged foods and alcoholic beverages. By 1964, Liggett & Myers had suffered a decade of declining sales and chose to diversify into alcoholic beverages, pet food, cereals, and watchbands. Since 1963, Heublein has had an explicit policy of looking for acquisitions which lend themselves to its marketing techniques and channels of distribution.

Standard Brands, which is engaged in pre-packaged and convenience foods, should also be mentioned. In spite of the great variety in the firm's products, there are also production similarities in this case. When manufacturing is not uniform, then at least channels of distribution and marketing methods are the same. Most of the products go to the same ultimate consumer, are often used concurrently, and fulfill similar needs. Thus, Standard Brands operates on the basis of a uniform body of skills and knowledge, a particular competence in the pre-packaged and convenience-food business.

CONGLOMERATE STRATEGIES

In the case of the three previously discussed strategies, the relationships between the products produced and sold were reasonably clear. Firms which have followed a conglomerate strategy, however, diversified into totally unrelated areas. There are two distinguishable patterns depending on the characteristics of the company when it initiates a conglomerate strategy. The firm which is already doing substantial business in a relatively homogeneous area relies on supplemental diversification. It extends its activities into unrelated areas for either defensive or offensive reasons. In the first case, the firm is typically faced with declining prospects in its original business. It therefore finds it necessary to supplement its earnings by diversifying into unrelated and more profitable areas in order to survive. In the second case, the firm has typically operated very successfully and is looking for ways to invest excess capital.

A different strategy is followed by entrepreneurial firms. They generally start as very small companies which are the vehicles for rapid growth by acquisition of unrelated firms. This could be called true conglomerate diversification. In the extreme cases it amounts to stock market manipulation, but many of the conglomerates impart managerial skills in acquired companies and utilize sophisticated financial controls.

One example of supplemental diversification is Philip Morris. The major part of its business is still tobacco. In that area it is essentially a one-product company. Most of its acquisitions in the tobacco business have served to establish distribution in a new country. When a diversification program was initiated late in the 1950's, the guiding principle was to invest excess capital in growth opportunities. The inherently greater risk in these would be offset by the stability of earnings in the tobacco business. Recently, the possibility of a decline in sales in the cigarette industry has presented an additional rationale for diversification. Philip Morris' diversification has been conglomerate in nature. Acquired products are usually not related on the production side, and unlike such firms as Liggett & Myers and American Brands, Philip Morris has only partly utilized its marketing competence by diversifying into other branded consumer articles. The firm has thus exhibited a willingness to venture beyond its particular field of prior competence. As a result, the acquired companies have become highly autonomous subunits.

Beatrice Foods shows the same pattern without the added incentive of a threat to its original business. After World War II it moved from its original dairy products business into the related field of grocery and specialty foods. In the last few years, the firm has diversified into totally unrelated areas. These areas, such as education and recreation, were chosen specifically for their profit potential. There is evidence that Beatrice has become more profitable in recent years as a result.

PepsiCo presents very much the same picture. The company achieved an initial diversification into snacks and convenience foods, which are related to soft drinks in the marketing sense. More recently, PepsiCo has entered trucking and several fields of leasing. These diversification moves have the nature of investments in profitable opportunities. There may, however, possibly be an integrative rationale as well, because other divisions of the firm are major users of leased trucks and vans.

Unlike Philip Morris, Beatrice Foods, and PepsiCo, Textron represents true conglomerate diversification. In 1953 it began to diversify to supplement the meager earnings from its declining textile operations, which proved to have consistently low profitability and cyclical features. The company's hope that the textile business would again become satisfactory proved baseless, and the textile operations were sold, the last of them being liquidated ten years after the first diversification move. Textron depends on a formula of guiding, coaching, and counseling subunits. The group vice presidents in the firm serve an important function as internal management consultants. Textron has acquired manufacturing companies only and maintains that the problems they face are similar enough to permit an exchange of formulas for success. The divisions each have their strengths, weaknesses, and problems, but not in the same area or at the same time. Therefore, the experiences of one division might be very beneficial for others.

ITT is similar to Textron in that it began to diversify from a substantial base. In 1959, it was a telecommunications and electronics firm, which has since become a company engaged in a great variety of manufacturing and service operations. It first expanded into related areas of electronics and allied commercial products and subsequently into services, an area in which it had some basic expertise. Gulf & Western is a case where the original business was very small and only served as a springboard for conglomerate expansion. Beginning in 1957, the first diversification phase made it an integrated manufacturer and distributor of auto parts. The products were many and technically varied, but all served one market. From there a conglomerate giant was built with no central interest except engaging in virtually all industries and services.

Transamerica is a firm which, like Textron, has built up a unifying competence on a very general level. With one minor exception, it supplies only services. It started as a diversified holding company with an emphasis on financial services. In the 1960's when pressure to produce growth and earnings increased, the company identified the most promising areas of services as being education, medicine, and leisure time. Services are a relatively rapidly growing area of the economy, and there were underlying fundamental forces which made the services Transamerica had chosen especially attractive.

SUMMARY AND CONCLUSIONS

It seems that a roughly equal number of firms has diversified by internal development, acquiring technology, acquiring firms in closely related markets, and, finally, following a conglomerate strategy. Firms in the first two groups emphasize R&D and technology and the functional area of production. The third group of firms stresses advertising and promotion and the functional area of marketing. The firms which follow a conglomerate strategy are financially oriented. To them a business is not primarily a product, a technology, a market, nor a consumer, but a balance sheet and an income statement.

The logic behind the strategies which the firms have followed is the manner in which these firms draw on their particular competences. The firms which rely on internal development as a vehicle for diversification mostly build on an expertise in research and production. The companies which acquire technology may sometimes have a distinctive technological expertise, but very often it is limited to a small area. Firms which expand into homogeneous markets rely heavily on their marketing skills. Even firms which acquire unrelated businesses frequently do have a body of knowledge or skill in general management or finance which they draw on in achieving their diversity.

The development of diversity in the firms analyzed here indicates how complex and multi-dimensional it really is. Despite the complexity, it has been possible to show that certain strategies were followed with a relatively high degree of consistency, and that the chosen strategies were related to the particular competence of the diversifying firm. The strategies are an explanatory and predictive aid in the analysis of diversity, because they identify the reasons for the development towards diversity and the resulting product-market structure. Organizational, technological, and personal factors are no less important, but the lack of dependable information has made the analysis of them much more cursory.

Notes

1.   Leonard Wrigley, "Divisional Autonomy and Diversification" (DBA thesis, Harvard GSBA, 1970), 52-60.

SECTION II

LABOR AND AGRICULTURE

The increased power and influence of labor unions and the penetration of corporations into agriculture are two striking features of the changing twentieth-century economy. Following years of stagnation, organized labor, after adopting new tactics and gaining the solid backing of the federal government, made a major breakthrough in the period from 1935 to 1945. In the last twenty-five years, big labor has arisen to assume a position alongside big business as one of the most powerful institutions in modern society. Meanwhile, in the post-WW II period there was a renewed effort on the part of corporate investors to discover on the farm the same kind of economies of scale that had emerged earlier in certain facets of American industry. Despite the success of corporate farming in a few specialized areas, the movement slowed significantly in the late 1960s and early 1970s; overall, it has had much less of an impact on agriculture than some of the early publicity suggested.

The history of organized labor in the United States has been quite different

Reprinted with permission from *Change and Continuity in Twentieth-Century America,* edited by John Braeman, Robert H. Bremner, and Everett Walters (*Modern America,* no. 1). Copyright © 1964 by Ohio State University Press.

from contemporaneous developments in Europe and other industrial societies. A major branch of the American labor movement in the nineteenth century rejected the Marxist view of divided social classes and pursued a program that included many aspects of liberal, humanitarian reform. Reform-minded labor leaders such as Terence Powderly of the Knights of Labor disavowed such standard employee tactics as strikes as a method of achieving their goals. Utopians at heart, they clung to the hope that someday "producers cooperatives" would emerge, in which there would be no demeaning distinctions between employer and employee. In a cooperative framework, every citizen could preserve the American tradition of self-employment within an economically independent, classless society. Under these conditions, the existing privately-owned industrial enterprises would become superfluous and disappear.

Although the reformers focused their appeal on the broad mass of workers, this wing of the labor movement, contrary to European precedents, generally disdained politics. It formed no labor party and even avoided close association with the traditional Democratic and Republican parties. Because this movement was so out of tune with the development of industrial society, reform-oriented unions had mostly collapsed by the 1890s, and it is not altogether clear why they managed to survive for so long.

More successful in the long run were union organizations that accepted the permanence of the class system, worked for the limited goals of better pay and working conditions, and relied primarily on strikes, or the threat of strikes, to achieve their aims. Led by Samuel Gompers, these trade unions also avoided ties with a single political party, choosing instead to use their votes to reward friends and punish enemies irrespective of party affiliation. Gompers and his associates decided to follow the path of slow, steady growth and not to opt for comprehensive social reform or fundamental changes in the capitalist system.

As a practical matter, the trade unions ignored the bulk of unskilled workers employed by large firms. They concentrated instead on the skilled, well-paid employee who could afford dues high enough to build a substantial strike fund, who was not easily replaced in the event of a strike, and who worked for small or medium-sized firms that had neither the financial nor the political strength to crush the union. This strategy of organizing workers along skilled craft lines in nonoligopolistic industries was viable, and it laid the basis for the foundation and survival of the American Federation of Labor. But large numbers of workers—machine operators and day laborers—employed by large firms at the heart of the industrial economy remained unorganized.

Before the 1930s, successful efforts to organize a mass labor force along industrial rather than craft lines were few. The only success was achieved in an industry—coal mining—not characterized by a concentrated market structure and which was suffering badly from overproduction and falling prices. In the first quarter century, coal was one of the so-called sick industries that was plagued by overcapacity because of competition from a new energy source—petroleum. The mine owners lacked a unified ownership and vast financial resources, and they proved vulnerable to union activity. But the success of the United Mine Workers as an all-inclusive, industry-wide organization representing every worker, skilled or unskilled, was unique.

As David Brody shows in the following essay, the aspiring industrial union faced a problem of legitimacy on three major fronts. The issue was broader than a mere dispute over wage rates; it was primarily a question of economic power. By the twentieth century, big businesses were well entrenched primary organizations anxious to preserve the status quo, and business leaders, especially the one-family owner-managers, were frequently adamant about retaining almost complete authority over the conditions of employment. The large firm had so many powerful weapons available to fight unionization that, as Gompers and his associates had determined from the beginning, only the foolhardy and ideologically motivated were induced to enter the fray.

In oligopolistic industries dominated by giants, strikes were usually ineffective. In a real contest, most large firms had sufficient financial resources to withstand strikes of undetermined length. Meanwhile, the unskilled members of the working force had little opportunity for alternative employment and, because of their low wages, they could not afford to maintain a high dues schedule and therefore had no strike fund to enable them to outwait the corporation. Employers could hire strike-breakers, recruited from distant states if necessary, along with private armies to protect them. Large firms often did not have to outlast unions, for they had a strong ally in the courts which frequently enjoined strikes or strike-related activities. Finally, many giant corporations preempted outside organizers by forming their own "company" unions, which gave workers the illusion, if not the substance, of representation.

In addition to its economic, financial, and legal powers, in labor disputes big business often had public opinion and, therefore, the nation's elected public officials in both the executive and legislative branches, on its side in labor disputes. The mass industrial union seemed to many citizens to be tainted with radicalism of one variety or another—either syndicalism, socialism, anarchism, or, especially after the success of the Russian revolution in 1917, communism. Union activities aimed at big firms frequently led to violence and bloodshed, and it was often difficult to determine which combatant initiated the trouble. The nation's newspapers expressed little sympathy for the plight of union organizers, and the public saw these men as irresponsible agitators, violence-prone, and ideologically suspect. As a result, few public officials at any level of government espoused the cause of industrial unionism.

In addition to the external problems of big business hostility and government apathy, the more conservative, nonideological champions of mass unionism met serious opposition within the labor movement itself. The traditional craft unions were unenthusiastic, and the AFL leadership had no real power to dictate policy to them. As it was, the trade unions were frequently embroiled in jurisdictional disputes over which one had the exclusive right to organize specific groups of employees along craft lines. None was anxious to authorize the creation of new industrial rivals and intensify jurisdictional problems. At the very least, the existing trade unions would face increased competition for new members, and, at worst, defections to the industrial unions. Besides, few AFL member unions believed it prudent to pour money into organizing efforts aimed at oligopolistic industries when the prospects for success seemed so dim. After demurring for years, at its annual convention in 1935 the AFL finally rejected outright the concept of independent charters for new industrial unions.

Despite all these handicaps, the diehard supporters of mass unionization thought they saw clear signs of a changing economic and political climate in the 1930s. They took advantage of the temporary financial weakness of large firms during the Great Depression and the fading public image of big businessmen, and they relied on the newly found backing of the federal government after President Roosevelt took office. Thus the advocates of industrial unions were able, in the period from 1935 to 1945, to gain for the workers in mass-production industries the recognition of their legitimate right to full, independent representation. Brody's brilliant essay explains how these changes came about so rapidly.

Like the history of industrial unionism, the history of large-scale farming in the United States was almost universally a story of failure in the nineteenth and early twentieth centuries. Prior to WW II, there were very few large, corporate farms that survived the death of their founders. The main unit of agricultural production had been and, for that matter, still remains the unincorporated family farm. The size of the individual family unit and the output per acre have expanded, however, especially in the period since 1940. Economies of scale have clearly had an impact but, except for a few specialized products, the impact has been insufficient thus far to justify the investment of massive funds in the creation of giant farms employing thousands of workers.

Before 1840, productivity increases in agriculture occurred at a slow rate. However, the two decades prior to the Civil War were a turning point in American agriculture because two severe limitations on both the possibility and practicality of increased output were almost simultaneously alleviated. In the past bottlenecks had existed in harvesting and in transporting surplus production. First, the building of canals and railroads permitted farmers in the Midwestern states, with some of the most fertile topsoil in the world, to reach distant markets at home and abroad at competitive prices. Second, the flat contour of Midwestern farmland made it ideal for the widespread use of the reaper, invented in Virginia in the 1830s, and other mechanical harvesting devices. In the past, farmers were generally able to plant and grow surplus crops, but only a limited amount of ripe, unspoiled grain could be harvested by hand with a labor force restricted largely to the immediate family. Machines pulled by horses permitted the family unit to harvest substantial surpluses. For example, the output of wheat per capita nearly doubled in the second half of the nineteenth century despite virtually no change in the average yield per acre. The later introduction of the gas-powered tractor and other new equipment has increased the harvesting capacity of the family farm. Meanwhile, the application of new knowledge from the chemical and biological fields has led to dramatic rises in yields per acre in the twentieth century.

Over the decades, the progressive increase in output per farmhand freed surplus labor in agriculture for employment in the cities and other sectors of the economy. The shift of population from rural to urban and later suburban residence has gone on continually since Colonial times; whereas approximately 90 percent of the population in 1790 lived on the farm, by 1920 the figure has dropped to around 30 percent and by 1972 to less than 5 percent. Because of the increased demand for food in the early 1970s and the sharp rise in food prices, however, there are indications that the proportion of the labor force engaged in agriculture may have stabilized recently. If the current trend holds, later historians may one day view the cessation of the rural to urban migration in the same light as Frederick Jackson Turner saw the closing of the frontier in the late nineteenth century.

The spread of corporate farming in the 1950s and 1960s can be seen in two related, but different, parts of the agricultural sector. In the first instance, the backward integration strategies of established food processors led to greater corporate involvement in farming. Yet, food processors rarely assumed outright ownership of farmland; instead they generally engaged in "contract farming." Under this arrangement, production was carried out according to conditions set forth in a contract between farmer and processor. For the processor corporation, a secure source of raw materials was guaranteed, and for the farmer an assured market. In 1970 about 22 percent of U.S. agricultural output was produced under contract, with much of it concentrated in such specialized products as sugar cane and sugar beets (100%); vegetables for processing and canning (95%); citrus fruits (85%); milk (98%); chicken broilers (97%); turkeys (54%); and eggs (40%). Crops grown under contract were normally high in value and required relatively little acreage. In contrast, only a small part of the crop land devoted to grain production for human and livestock consumption, which accounts for the vast majority of the acres harvested, was covered by contract in 1970.

Corporate ownership of production facilities has concentrated in specialty cropland—particularly fruit, nuts, and wine—and in livestock feeding. The last activity has been influenced greatly by special and quite favorable income tax regulations. Since 1951, cattle held for a sufficient length of time before sale, now 24 months, have been taxed at the capital gains rate, or one-half the standard rate for earned income, with a maximum rate of 35 percent. Before 1958 only individuals and partnerships were eligible for these preferred rates, but that year the revenue code was amended to permit small business corporations with ten stockholders or less to be taxed as partnerships. This amendment made it possible for stockholders to report income from the sale of livestock as capital gains. In order to take advantage of this tax ruling, wealthy individuals in high income tax brackets—many of whom probably never set foot on a farm—invested heavily in corporations involved in livestock production. By limiting to ten the number of stockholders in any corporation eligible for partnership taxation, the law has, of course, precluded the possibility that giant firms will emerge in this field (although overlapping ownership does occur). Nevertheless, these new organizations and new patterns of investment have caused significant changes in this sector of American agriculture.

In the last part of his informative review of the rise of agri-business in the twentieth century, Philip M. Raup discusses agricultural change using the organizational framework advanced by Chandler and Galambos in the concluding essay in this book. Always at the mercy of uncontrollable market forces, farmers were one of the first large special interest groups to seek government assistance in stabilizing prices, and thus they fostered new attitudes about the legitimacy of the government's role in guiding and regulating economic activity. Given the highly competitive nature of the market, secondary organizations involved in coordinating activities matured early and have had a great impact on American agriculture. The dominance of secondary organizations is likely to continue, Raup feels, because with the exception of a few specialized crops and in the absence of special tax breaks for certain forms of livestock production, the expanded family farm manned by two or three able workers can still realize most of the gains associated with an increased scale of operations.

THE EMERGENCE OF
MASS-PRODUCTION UNIONISM

By David Brody

At the coming of the New Deal, American organized labor was an arrested movement. Membership was slightly under three million in 1933. The unionized portion of the non-agricultural labor force—one-tenth—remained unchanged after thirty years. It was not only a matter of numbers. Labor strength was limited to the needle trades, public utilities (excluding communications), coal-mining, building construction, and the railroads. A vacuum existed in manufacturing, above all, in the mass-production sector. Organized labor had not breached the industries characterized by the giant firm; by multiplant operation for a national market; by an advanced technology involving mechanization and division of labor; and by a work force composed primarily of unskilled and semi-skilled men. The mass-production core—iron and steel, non-ferrous metals, rubber, electrical products, chemicals and petroleum, and food-processing—seemed impervious to trade unionism.

The great breakthrough occurred after 1935. A decade later, most of the mass-production industries had experienced thorough unionization. The consequences were, of course, profound. It was, as Walter Galenson said, "a fundamental, almost revolutionary change in the power relationships of American society." The accomplishment had its origin in the 1930's. But the favoring climate of that decade failed to carry the new unionism to its conclusion. Ultimately, permanent success came from the very events that ended the Great Depression and the New Deal.

The unionization of the mass-production industries still requires explanation; that is the purpose of this preliminary essay.

The achievement began with the changing labor movement. The central fact, obviously, was the creation of the Congress of Industrial Organizations (initially, the Committee for Industrial Organization) as the unionizing agency for the basic industries. Several related questions claim our attention here. What was the necessity that split organized labor? What did the CIO bring to bear that had been lacking in the American Federation of Labor approach to the unionizing of mass production? And, finally, was the union effort decisive in accounting for the organization of the mass-production sector?

The irreconcilable issue seemingly was a matter of structure: industrial versus craft unionism. Industrial organization—the inclusion of all workers in an industry within one union—was a choice closed to the AF of L for several reasons. Foremost was the numerical dominance of the craft unionists: since theirs were the interests to be injured, industrial-union resolutions had never mustered a majority in AF of L conventions. The Federation was also in a constitutional bind. Jurisdiction was exclusive; only one union could hold rights to a given category of workers. And it was absolute: a union did not have to organize its jurisdiction in order to maintain its right. The craft unions had a kind of property interest within the basic industries. Beyond that was the immovable fact of trade autonomy; the locus of power rested with the national unions. The AF of L was a voluntary institution, William Green observed, and therefore had "no power to compel any union or person to do anything." Even the passage of an industrial-union resolution, Philip Taft has pointed out, "would not have forced any craft union to surrender its jurisdiction, nor compelled unions to amalgamate with each other." There was, finally, the subtle role of *macht-politik* within the labor movement. Themselves lacking power, Federation officers respected it in other hands. The power realities ordinarily favored the craft interests, and so, therefore, did the inclination of the AF of L leadership.

These considerations remained binding during the historic debate over structure that took place in the mid-1930's. At the AF of L convention of 1934 in San Francisco the issue was joined over the question of chartering national unions in the automobile, cement, aluminum, and other unspecified mass-production fields. Industrial-union sentiment, stimulated by recent events, forced the convention to recognize that "a new condition exists requiring organization upon a different basis to be most effective." But the convention also wanted "to fully protect the jurisdictional rights of all trade unions organized upon craft lines. . . ." This second statement carried more weight. The Executive Council, to which the actual choice was left, excluded tool-, die-, and machine-making workers and parts plants from the jurisdiction of the new United Automobile Workers and maintenance and machine-installing men from the United Rubber Workers. The fateful Atlantic City convention of 1935 ratified the decision against industrial unionism.

It was a choice that John L. Lewis and his supporters could not accept. They insisted, as Charles Howard of the Typographical Union said, that "in the great mass-production industries industrial organization is the only solution." The aftermath of the 1935 convention was independent action that turned rapidly into dual unionism.

It has been hard to hold the momentous events of 1934-35 in perspective. The debate then was couched in the terminology of industrial unionism, and the outcome was the creation of a group of strong industrial unions. So it seemed to follow that the conflict over structure was the key to the formation of the CIO. That conclusion misplaces the emphasis.

The AF of L did not lack an alternative arrangement. No less than his critics, Samuel Gompers had seen the inappropriateness of the original craft structure for emerging American industrialism. Over the years, there had developed a response to mass production. Gompers had early accepted the need "to organize our fellow workers in unskilled labor."

> With the invention of new machines and the application of new forces, the division and subdivision of labor, many workers who had been employed at skilled trades find themselves with their occupations gone. . . . Thus we see the artisan of yesterday the unskilled laborer of today.

The essential device was the federal labor union. Gathered first into these mixed local bodies, the unorganized would be drawn off by occupation into the appropriate national unions or into local trade unions affiliated, as were the federal unions, directly with the AF of L. The federal labor unions, said Gompers, were "the recruiting ground for the trade union movement."

Besides organizing non-craft workers, the Federation tried to alter the existing structure to make room for them. Charters were granted to national unions covering the unskilled and semi-skilled within single industries; for instance, the Hod Carriers in construction and the Tin Plate Workers in tin plate manufacture. But Gompers' preference was for the less skilled to find a place within the "primary unions," that is, national unions covering the occupations specific to an industry.[1] To that end, the AF of L urged unions to amalgamate or to accept broader jurisdictions. The optimum result was a national union covering all occupations specific to an industry, irrespective of the skills involved, plus common labor. Such residual jurisdictions in fact were operative at some time in practically every mass-production industry before the 1930's. The craft unions were not victimized thereby. Defining its position in the Scranton Declaration of 1901, the AF of L adhered as closely to the "fundamental principle" of craft organization "as the recent great changes in methods of production and employment make possible." Primary jurisdictions would not normally encompass such inter-industry occupations as teamsters, carpenters, machinists, and similar trades.

Co-ordination, finally, was encouraged. The primary and craft unions had to act together in the basic industries. As early as the Scranton Declaration, the suggestion had been made of "closely allying the subdivided crafts" through "the organization of district and national trade councils. . . ." Much of the subsequent co-operation, particularly in joint organizing drives, was on an informal and sporadic basis. During and after World War I, national unions in meat-packing joined together only when faced with the need for common decisions. In steel, on the other hand, twenty-four national unions acted in 1918-20 through the permanent National Committee for Organizing Iron and Steel Workers. At the district level, local unions had formal bodies in the Schenectady plant of General Electric for over a decade after 1911, in meat-packing centers from 1901 to 1904 and again in Chicago from 1917 to 1920, and in steel during the union upsurge of the war period. The departments of the AF of L also promoted joint union activity. The Metal Trades Department chartered local councils and mounted co-operative organizing drives, for instance, in the automobile industry in 1914 and 1927. Inade quate though most of these ventures were, they did not show that organizational unity was unattainable under the primary-craft structural arrangement for the mass-production fields.

The AF of L was adhering to this established plan in 1935. Its advocates insisted that the formula was workable. The separation of craft workers would not, after all, be numerically important in mass production. The rubber industry was a case in point. Its labor force, according to a breakdown in the census of 1930, was composed of the following:

559	carpenters
395	compositors, linotypers, and typesetters
915	electricians
1,206	mechanics
1,148	stationary engineers
482	millwrights
4,665	machinists
805	plumbers
300	toolmakers
1,267	truck drivers
456	painters and glaziers
80,835	operatives
29,123	laborers

Jurisdiction over the last two categories would give a rubber workers' union nearly 90 per cent of the labor force in the industry. William Hutcheson of the Carpenters could not see why organization would be impeded by separating "a comparatively small number as compared to the total number employed in the rubber industry." And co-ordination could surely be made to work. John Frey was convinced that "joint negotiations and joint agreement reached through the [Metal Trades] Department forms the most effective answer to . . . the so-called industrial form of trade union organization . . . enabling an employer to negotiate but one agreement which will cover all his employees. . . ." In September, 1934, this policy had been adopted for the metal and building trades. Both AF of L departments entered negotiations on this basis with the Anaconda Copper Company.

If not the optimum solution, the AF of L alternative nevertheless seemed adequate and reasonable. The primary-craft formula could not be ruled out as unworkable on the basis of past experience. While deprecated by Lewis adherents, it could not by itself drive the breach in the labor movement.

Nor, for that matter, could the appeal of industrial unionism. "Much has been said about principles in the war between the C.I.O. and the A.F. of L.," commented the informed labor consultant Chester M. Wright in 1939. "As I see it, the whole dispute is one involving tactics and practices. I fail to find any principles involved at any point." Earlier, industrial unionism had involved fundamental differences. Its advocates had been mainly Socialists and others seeking to make the labor movement a vehicle for political action and/or basic social change. That was not the case in the 1930's. Industrial unionism then was directed only at the mass-production industries, not, as in the amalgamation movement of the early 1920's, at the entire economy. The ideological groundwork was mostly gone. John L. Lewis himself had opposed the amalgamationists of the postwar period. His emergence as industrial-union leader in the early New Deal period presumed that the debate over structure did not reflect basic differences about the role of the trade-union movement.

The antagonists were not doctrinaire even on the narrow structural issue. Bitter opponents of Lewis as they were, the Carpenters, Machinists, and Electrical Workers were themselves asserting industrial jurisdiction over limited areas between 1934 and 1936. For his part, Lewis was not rigid on industrial unionism. When the AF of L Executive Council was considering in February, 1935, what craft groups to exclude from an auto workers' union, Lewis pleaded that the "cavilling be deferred until in the light of what accomplishment is made in the objective we can take up the question of dividing the members, that contention over the fruits of victory be deferred until we have some of the fruits in our possession." While he retained hope in the AF of L, Lewis did not commit himself to industrial unionism.

It was not in itself of importance. Lewis was a pragmatist in the dominant tradition of American trade unionism. Labor leaders responded, as William Green said, to "the fact, not a theory but a situation actually existing. . . ." The formation of the CIO was a drastic measure which, from Lewis' standpoint, had to yield a commensurate return. The structural reform of industrial unionism was not such a return. Nor, in fact, was it absolutely precluded from the pragmatic labor movement. Industrial unions could find a place—as did the United Mine Workers of America itself—within the AF of L. The Butcher Workmen had put the fact neatly back in 1922 when the issue over requesting industrial jurisdiction in meat-packing arose. It would be better, the convention decided, first to unionize the industry "and then by reason of the strength that would accompany such an organization, take and retain control over all men of whatever craft employed in the industry." The obstacles to that first point—not the second—were the operative ones in 1935.

What excited Lewis and his adherents was a concrete objective: the organization of the mass-production industries. That accomplished, the structural issue would resolve itself and would, in any case, not be of great moment. "The fundamental obligation is to organize these people," Lewis insisted. The resulting problems should be considered "after we had accomplished organization and not before, after the fact of organization has been accomplished [,] not tie on reservations that will in themselves deter an effective campaign." This revealed the heart of the crisis: would the AF of L take the measures necessary for the organization of mass-production workers?

Industrial unionism fitted into this larger context. The immense influence of the idea sprang from the contemporary assessment of the psychology of industrial workers. "I know their state of mind," William Green asserted, speaking of the automobile workers. . . . "If you tell them to go here, you here and you there, you will never get anywhere. They are so closely related and inextricably interwoven they are mass minded." In her perceptive *Industrial Valley*, Ruth McKenney described the problem as she saw it in Akron rubber plants.

> . . . The machinists and the electricians kept coming to the Federal local meetings. [The AF of L organizer] could never make them understand they were supposed to stay away, supposed to belong to a separate union. He could never teach them that their interests were different from the common ordinary rubber-worker. Stubbornly and stupidly they clung to the Federal locals.

Industrial unionists had here an explanation for the failure to hold the thousands of industrial workers who had flocked into the AF of L federal unions in 1933. Sidney Hillman noted, for example, that during the NRA period over 40,000 rubber workers had been organized. Then the AF of L "started to divide those workers among the different unions claiming jurisdiction over them. As a result of that procedure, the membership of the rubber workers union fell as low as 3,000."

The problem was *tactical*. Since industrial labor was "mass minded," the first stage of organization had to be on a mass basis. "Vice President Lewis said there is a psychology there among the men . . . ," read the minutes of the February, 1935, meeting of the AF of L Executive Council.

"What he has in mind [is that] the time to quarrel over jurisdiction is after we organize the men rather than before." William Green shared Lewis' view. The mass-production industries should be organized "as best we can, then after they are organized if the question [arises] on the jurisdiction of an international union, perhaps by education we can bring about respect among these workers of the jurisdiction of the national and international unions."

That reasoning explained the hopefulness following the San Francisco convention of 1934. The objectives then enunciated seemed irreconcilable: to protect craft jurisdictions and to organize mass-production fields on "a different basis." But an apparent accommodation had emerged from the many hours of talks off the floor of the convention. The Executive Council was "directed to issue charters for National or International Unions"—the instructions did not specify precise jurisdictions. Second, "for a provisional period" the chartered unions should be under AF of L direction "in order to protect and safeguard the members of such National and International Unions as are chartered. . . ." Both these points—temporary AF of L control and an undefined jurisdiction—were included in John L. Lewis' seven-point program for an automobile union which was presented to the Executive Council in February, 1935. And there was a final point:

> That all questions of overlapping jurisdiction on the automobile parts and special crafts organizations encountered in the administration policy be referred to the Executive Council for consideration at such time as the Council may elect to give these questions consideration.

"This proposal is in strict conformity with the action of the A. F. of L. convention of 1934," Lewis explained, "and in proposing it I intend that if this policy does an injury to any international union that the union thus affected will have the right to take up these questions with the Executive Council of the American Federation of Labor and I assume that judgment will be rendered in conformity with . . . the record of the previous actions of the Council."

Confronting the proposal, the craft leaders could not accept it. Dan Tobin of the Teamsters saw "some merit" in Lewis' view and was willing to permit a "dispensation for six months or so in the hope he will unscramble them later on. . . ." But others, above all Wharton of the Machinists, had higher stakes in the automobile field. They were responding to the realities of the American labor movement: could they successfully exert their juris-dictional rights *after* organization had occurred on an industrial basis? In fact, they had grown critical even of the standard AF of L practice of placing skilled recruits in federal unions because these recruits then became reluctant to transfer to the appropriate craft unions. William Hutcheson of the Carpenters thought the jurisdictional question "should be straightened out now to avoid trouble." The Executive Council so decided: specific groups were excluded from the jurisdiction of the Auto Workers and, at the next Council meeting, of the Rubber Workers. In essence, the craft unions were refusing to gamble—at long odds—their vested rights in order to unionize mass-production workers. Tobin put the fact bluntly: "We are not going to desert the fundamental principles on which these organizations have lived and are living to help you organize men who have never been organized."

The jurisdictional problem was only the most visible of the obstacles to effective action. National unions with old-line leadership had primary jurisdiction in a number of basic industries—most importantly, the Amalgamated Association of Iron, Steel and Tin Workers. The industrial bloc agreed with Green's view that "the officers of the Amalgamated cannot organize these workers with their own resources or with the set-up as is. . . . The change has been taking place but the Amalgamated has been standing committed to its old tradition policy." Lewis urged the chartering of another national union with jurisdiction over steel. The craft unionists refused to abrogate the sacred rights of an autonomous union, as William Hutcheson said, "even if it was in bad straits." They were willing to permit others to mount a steel campaign, but the bulk of the steelworkers would have to go into an organization which had amply proved its incapacity. Exclusive jurisdiction and trade autonomy seemed to be immutable principles.

Finally, the necessary resources were not being directed to the organization of the basic industries. The income of the labor movement accumulated in the national unions, not in the Federation. President Green was able to augment his organizing staff by only fifteen in the critical year 1933. The affiliated unions were unwilling either to raise the per capita going to the AF of L or to expend adequate funds directly in the organizing effort. (The response to Green's appeal in March, 1936, for funds for a steel drive totaled $8,625 from five unions.) The flabbiness of the financial support could be gauged by the later reaction to the CIO threat: AF of L organizing expenses during 1937-39 were triple those of 1933-35. Nor were the unions with jurisdiction in the basic industries roused to a common effort. No joint drives were mounted in 1933-34 that would compare to those of earlier years in steel, autos, textiles, and meat-packing. The AF of L convention of 1934 instructed the Executive Council not only to charter national unions in mass-production industries but to inaugurate a union drive in steel. The Council had done nothing beyond passing a resolution by the time of the fateful convention of 1935.

At bottom, the AF of L was experiencing a crisis of will. Lewis bitterly commented in May, 1935, "that some six months have gone by since we adopted that resolution in San Francisco and there still remains the fact that there has been no administration of that policy, no execution of the promissory note that this Federation held out to the millions of workers in the mass-production industry. . . . Neither do I understand there is any immediate desire to carry out that policy. . . ." The choice rested with the controlling craft unionists. And they were not really committed to organizing the mass-production workers. Dan Tobin of the Teamsters, for instance, spoke contemptuously of "the rubbish that have lately come into other organizations." A widespread feeling was, as Mathew Woll said in 1934, that the industrial workers were "perhaps unorganizable." Tobin was saying in February, 1936, that "there isn't a chance in the world at this time to organize the steelworkers."

To John L. Lewis, the basic obstacle was the indifference of the craft leaders. They were the object of his plea at the 1935 convention:

> Why not make a contribution to the well-being of those who are not fortunate enough to be members of your organizations? . . . The labor movement is organized upon a principle that the strong shall help the weak. . . . Is it right, after all, that because some of us are capable of forging great and powerful organizations of skilled craftsmen in this country that we should lock ourselves up in our domain and say, "I am merely working for those who pay me"?

The AF of L had to choose between becoming "an instrumentality that will render service to all of the workers" and resting "content in that comfortable situation that has prevailed through the years. . . ." Convinced at last that the craft bloc preferred the second path, Lewis saw independent action as the only remedy to "twenty-five years of constant, unbroken failure."

Mass-production unionization merged with industrial unionism only when hope was lost in the AF of L. Actually, this began to happen months before the Atlantic City convention of 1935. Lewis started to shift his ground after the defeat of his program for an auto union at the February meeting of the Executive Council. At the May meeting, he did not try to apply his compromise formula to the Rubber Workers. Rather, he wanted "the jurisdiction granted to the organization to cover all workers employed throughout the rubber industry." Nothing was said at the subsequent convention either in Lewis' arguments or in the Minority Report about the postponement of jurisdictional questions until after the achievement of mass-production organization (although there were such intimations in the speeches of Lewis' supporters Charles Howard and Sidney Hillman). The full commitment to industrial unionism became evident in Lewis' offer of $500,000 toward an AF of L steel-organizing fund on February 22, 1936. One condition was that "all steel workers organized will be granted the *permanent* right to remain united in one international union."

Having opted for independent action, Lewis had every reason to espouse industrial unionism: it was a desirable structural reform; it would draw in unions such as the Oil Workers and the Mine, Mill and Smelter Workers that were having jurisdictional troubles within the AF of L; and, above all, it would serve as a rallying cry in the union rivalry and in the organizing field. But industrial unionism remained a subordinate consideration. When the occasion demanded, it was sacrificed to the necessities of the organizing task and to the inevitable ambitions for the CIO as an institution. Nor did industrial unionism fulfill the expectations of earlier advocates. No real transformation was worked in the objectives of the labor movement. Differing in some ways, the rival federations were, as Chester Wright insisted, "brothers under the skin," and the passage of twenty years was time enough to permit them to join in a merger.

The CIO had been created with the fixed purpose of organizing the mass-production industries. Liberated from past practice and vested interest, the effort could be made with optimum effectiveness. Starting fresh, the CIO thoroughly exploited its opportunity.

The previous restrictions were immediately thrown off. The separation of skilled men no longer, of course, constituted an impediment to organization. Funds in massive amounts were now injected in some areas. The Steel Workers Organizing Committee received in six years $1,619,613 from outside sources, as well as the services of many organizers who remained on the payrolls of other unions. In part, the money came as direct contributions from affluent CIO affiliates. The Mine Workers and the Clothing Workers, frankly anxious for the organization of industries related to them, directed most of their assistance to steel and textiles, respectively. The rest of the CIO income came from a high per capita tax of five cents a month. Proportionately, the investment far surpassed what had been possible within the AF of L (although, it should be noted, the latter in response was doing likewise). Finally, the CIO was able to build the new industrial unions, particularly those which first took the form of organizing committees, free from the restricting hand of the past. There were instances, notably in steel and textiles, where AF of L unions with old-line leaders came over to the CIO, but they were held to subordinate roles. Able officials were recruited from men rising from the ranks or, as in the case of steel, from experienced unionists elsewhere in the CIO.

The job of organizing was meanwhile changing radically. First, mass-production workers were bursting with militancy. The upsurge of NRA-inspired unionism, for instance, was very largely spontaneous. At the time, it seemed to William Green "a sight that even old, tried veterans of our movement never saw before." Another official believed it would surpass in "numbers, intensity, and duration" the union experience of World War I. Even before the CIO, popular militancy was expressing itself in internal resistance to AF of L policies and/or in independent unionism, and in rank-and-file strikes such as that of the Toledo Chevrolet plant in April, 1935. The second change followed from the Wagner Act. For the first time, workmen had the legal right to express through majority rule their desires on the question of union representation. On the counts of both rank-and-file sentiment and federal law, success came to depend on the union appeal, hitherto of secondary importance to the workingmen. To this requirement, the CIO responded brilliantly.

The ingredients of success were unremitting effort and a mastery of the techniques suited to the special conditions of the mass-production industries. A pool of effective organizers for this work could be drawn from CIO affiliates, above all, the Mine Workers; from left-wing groups; and from militants within the industrial ranks. In addition to using the standard methods, CIO organizers emphasized rank-and-file participation. These were the instructions to a group of adherents in Fort Worth on how to organize their Armour plant:

> It takes Organizers inside the plant to Organize the plant.
> The Committee that organized the Oklahoma City plant was a voluntary committee established inside the plant.
>
> You cannot wait for the National Organizer to do all the work. . . . You people here can have a Union, but you will have to work to build it.

Typically, an intricate network of unpaid posts was established in CIO plants, so that "more men are given responsibility, and our organization becomes more powerful and more closely knit." The aim was to avoid "bureaucratic" rule by putting the leadership, as one organizer said, not in a few hands, but in "the whole body, in one, acting as one."

Another significant CIO tactic arose out of sensitivity to the deep-seated resentments of the workers. At the plant level, grievances characteristically received aggressive support. When the men saw "how the CIO was fighting to protect workers' rights . . . ," a Packinghouse Workers' official explained, they flocked into the organization. Direct action was another expression of CIO militancy. Sudden strikes and slowdowns, although often against official policy, were frequently encouraged by local officers. For, as one functionary observed of the stoppages at the Armour Chicago plant, they "demonstrated to all, union members and non-union members, that the CIO had plenty of stuff on the ball and that there was no such thing as waiting for something to happen."

The effectiveness of the CIO had another dimension. The basic industries had drawn the newcomers and underprivileged of American society. Eastern Europeans and then, when the flow of immigrants was stopped by World War I, migrants from the South filled the bottom ranks of mass-production labor. The colored workers had unquestionably been among the chief obstacles to earlier union efforts. William Z. Foster, who had taken a leading part in the AF of L drives of World War I, admitted that "we could not win their support. It could not be done. They were constitutionally opposed to unions, and all our forces could not break down that opposition." The problem was of diminishing magnitude in the 1930's. Negro workers, mostly new arrivals from the South fifteen years before, had gone through a lengthy adjustment. In addition, racial tensions had largely abated. There would be no counterpart to the Chicago race riot of 1919 which had disrupted the union drive in the stockyards. Yet the Negro workers still required special treatment.

Here again the CIO capitalized fully on the opportunity. It became an aggressive defender of Negro rights. After a foothold had been gained in the Armour Chicago Plant, for example, one of the first union victories was to end the company practice of "tagging" the time cards of colored employees: "the Stars will no longer offend the Negro workers of Armour & Co." The initial informal agreement at the Swift plant included a company pledge to hire Negroes in proportion to their numbers in the Chicago population. The AF of L could not match these zealous efforts. From the start, Gompers had insisted on the necessity of organizing the colored workers, not out of concern for "social or even any other kind of equality," but to insure that they would not "frustrate our every effort for economic, social and political improvement." This view prevailed, before as well as during the New Deal, wherever the membership of Negroes was essential to the success of a union. But many craft affiliates could afford to exclude or segregate such workers, and the Federation reluctantly accepted what it could not prevent. Besides being tainted by discrimination, the AF of L failed to crusade even where it favored racial equality. Doing so, the CIO swept the Negroes in mass production into its ranks. The same sensitivity to non-economic factors marked the CIO approach to immigrant and female labor and to the fostering of public support through political work and such communal activities as the "back of the yards" movement in the Chicago packing-house district.

The labor movement thus generated an effective response in the basic industries. A further question remains: Was this the decisive change? It does not seem so. More than the incapacity of organized labor had prevented earlier success. Had everything else remained constant, the CIO effort alone would not have resulted in permanent unionization of the mass-production sector—nor, for that matter, would it even have been attempted.

The sense of urgency was significant. At his last AF of L convention, John L. Lewis told Powers Hapgood that a union drive in the basic industries in the past "would have been suicide for organized labor and would have resulted in complete failure. But now, the time is ripe; and now the time to do those things is here. Let us do them." The American system of industrial relations was being profoundly shaken during the mid-1930's. "Conditions as they exist now," Charles Howard told the Atlantic City convention, "make it more necessary, in my opinion, for effective organization activity than at any time during the life of the American Federation of Labor."

In retrospect, employer resistance looms largest in accounting for the long years of union failure in mass production. The sources of that hostility need not be explored here. Suffice it to say that American industrialists found compelling reasons and, more important, adequate means for resisting labor organizations. Lewis noted the "great concentration of opposition to the extension and logical expansion of the trade union movement."

Great combinations of capital have assembled great industrial plants, and they are strong across the borders of our several states from the north to the south and from the west in such a manner that they have assembled to themselves tremendous power and influence. . . .

". . . there is no corporation in America more powerful than these corporations—General Motors and Ford," William Green said respectfully. "Everybody knows their financial strength. . . . It is a fact we have always recognized." No real possibility of countering the resources and advantages available to industry had earlier existed; the power balance had been overwhelmingly against labor.

In the 1930's, a new legal framework for industrial relations emerged. In the past, the right to organize had fallen outside the law; unionization, like collective bargaining, had been a private affair. Within normal legal limits, employers had freely fought the organization of their employees. Now that liberty was being withdrawn. World War I had first raised the point. The National War Labor Board had protected workers from discrimination for joining unions and thus contributed substantially to the temporary union expansion of the war period. The lesson was inescapable. Unionization in the mass-production industries depended on public protection of the right to organize. The drift of opinion in this direction was discernible in the Railway Labor Act of 1926 and the Norris-LaGuardia Act of 1932. But the real opportunity came with the advent of the New Deal. Then key union spokesmen, notably Green and Lewis, pressed for the insertion of the famous section 7a in the National Industrial Recovery Act. After an exhilarating start, section 7a foundered; loopholes developed and enforcement broke down long before the invalidation of the NRA. But the intent of section 7a was clear, and it soon received effective implementation.

"If the Wagner bill is enacted," John L. Lewis told the AF of L Executive Council in May, 1935, "there is going to be increasing organization. . . ." The measure, enacted on July 5, 1935, heavily influenced Lewis' decision to take the initiative that led to the CIO. For the Wagner Act did adequately protect the right to organize through a National Labor Relations Board clothed with powers of investigation and enforcement. Employer opposition was at long last neutralized.

The Act made it an unfair labor practice for an employer "to interfere with, restrain, or coerce employees in the exercise" of "the right of self-organization." This protection unquestionably freed workers from fear of employer discrimination. Stipulation cases required the posting of such notices as the following at a Sioux City plant:

> The Cudahy Packing Company wants it definitely understood that . . . no one will be discharged, demoted, transferred, put on less desirable jobs, or laid off because he joins Local No. 70 or any other labor organization. . . . If the company, its officers, or supervisors have in the past made any statements or taken any action to indicate that its employees were not free to join Local No. 70 or any other labor organization, these statements are now repudiated.

Even more persuasive was the reinstatement with back pay of men discharged for union activities. The United Auto Workers' cause at Ford was immensely bolstered in 1941 by the rehiring of twenty-two discharged men as the result of the NLRB decision which the company had fought up to the Supreme Court. By June 30, 1941, nearly twenty-four thousand charges of unfair labor practices—the majority involving discrimination—had been lodged with the NLRB. More important in the long run, vigorous enforcement encouraged obedience of the law among employers. Assured of their safety, workers flocked into the unions.

The law also resolved the knotty problems of determining union representation. During the NRA period, company unions had been widely utilized to combat the efforts of outside organizations. The Wagner Act now prohibited employers from dominating or supporting a labor union. Legal counsel at first held that "inside" unions could be made to conform with the law by changing their structure, that is, by eliminating management participation from the joint representation plans. The NLRB, however, required the complete absence of company interference or assistance. Few company unions could meet this high standard, and large numbers were disestablished by NLRB order or by stipulation. In meat-packing, for instance, the Big Four companies had to withdraw recognition from over fifteen company unions. Only in the case of some Swift plants did such bodies prevail over outside unions in representation elections and become legal bargaining agents. Besides eliminating employer-dominated unions, the law put the selection of bargaining representatives on the basis of majority rule. By mid-1941, the NLRB had held nearly six thousand elections and cross-checks involving nearly two million workers. Given a free choice, they overwhelmingly preferred a union to no union (the latter choice resulting in only 6 per cent of elections in 1937 and, on the average, in less than 20 per cent up to the passage of the Taft-Hartley Act). Having proved its majority in an "appropriate" unit, a union became the certified bargaining agent for all employees in the unit.

An unexpected dividend for union organization flowed from the Wagner Act. In the past, the crisis of mass-production unions had occurred in their first stage. Rank-and-file pressure normally built up for quick action. Union leaders faced the choice of bowing to this sentiment and leading their organizations into suicidal strikes—as happened on the railroads in 1894, in the stockyards in 1904, and in steel in 1919—or of resisting the pressure and seeing the membership melt away or break up in fractional conflict—as occurred in meat-packing after World War I. The Wagner Act, while it did not eliminate rank-and-file pressures, eased the problem. A union received NLRB certification on proving its majority in a plant. Certification gave it legal status and rights which could be withdrawn only by formal evidence that it lacked majority support. Defeat in a strike did not in any way affect the status of a bargaining agent. Restraint, on the other hand, became a feasible policy. The CIO unions as a whole were remarkably successful in resisting workers' demands for national strikes in the early years, although not in preventing local trouble. The resulting dissidence could be absorbed. The Packinghouse Workers Organizing Committee, for instance, was in continual turmoil from 1939 to 1941 because of the conservative course of Chairman Van A. Bittner; but internal strife did not lead to organizational collapse there or elsewhere. NLRB certification permitted labor leaders to steer between the twin dangers—external and internal—that earlier had smashed vigorous mass-production unionism.

Years later, the efficacy of the Wagner Act was acknowledged by an officer of the most hostile of the major packing firms: ". . . The unions would not have organized Wilson [and Company] if it had not been for the Act." That judgment was certainly general in open-shop circles.

Yet the Wagner Act was not the whole story. For nearly two years while its constitutionality was uncertain, the law was virtually ignored by anti-union employers. And after the Jones and Laughlin decision in April, 1937, the effect was part of a larger favoring situation. John L. Lewis was not reacting to a single piece of legislation. He saw developing in the mid-1930's a general shift toward unionization.

The change was partly in the workers themselves. Their accommodation to the industrial system had broken down under the long stretch of depression. The resulting resentment was evident in the sitdown strikes of 1936-

37, which involved almost half a million men. These acts were generally not a calculated tactic of the union leadership; in fact, President Sherman Dalrymple of the Rubber Workers at first opposed the sitdowns. Spontaneous sitdowns within the plants accounted for the initial victories in auto and rubber. Much of Lewis' sense of urgency in 1935 sprang from his awareness of the pressure mounting in the industrial ranks. A local auto-union leader told Lewis in May, 1935, of talk about craft unions' taking skilled men from the federal unions. "We say like h—they will and if it is ever ordered and enforced there will be one more independent union." Threats of this kind, Lewis knew, would surely become actions under existing AF of L policy, and, as he warned the Executive Council, then "we are facing the merging of these independent unions in some form of national organization." That prophecy, Lewis was determined, should come to pass under his control. The CIO succeeded in large measure because it became the vehicle for channeling the militancy released by the Great Depression.

The second factor that favored union organization was the impact of the depression on the major employers. They had operated on a policy of welfare capitalism: company paternalism and industrial-relations methods were expected to render employees impervious to the blandishments of trade unionism. The depression forced the abandonment of much of this expense and, beyond that, destroyed the workers' faith in the company's omnipotence on which Swift and Company said, industrialists had to admit that grounds existed for "the instances of open dissatisfaction which we see about us, and perhaps with us. . . ."

The depression also tended to undermine the will to fight unionization. Anti-union measures were costly, the La Follette investigation revealed. The resulting labor troubles, in addition, cut deeply into income. The Little Steel companies, Republic in particular, operated significantly less profitably in 1937 than did competitors who were free of strikes. Economic considerations seemed most compelling, not when business was bad, but when it was getting better. Employers then became very reluctant to jeopardize the anticipated return of profitable operations. This apparently influenced the unexpected decision of U.S. Steel to recognize the Steel Workers Organizing Committee. In 1937 the Steel Corporation was earning substantial profits for the first time during the depression; net income before taxes that year ultimately ran to 130 million dollars. And the first British purchases for defense were just then in the offing. During the upswing, moreover, the competitive factor assumed increasing importance. Union firms had the advantage of avoiding the disruptions incident to conflict over unionization. Certainly a decline of 15 per cent in its share of the automobile market from 1939 to 1940 contributed to the Ford Company's retreat of the following year.

Finally, the political situation—the Wagner Act aside—was heavily weighted on the side of labor. Management could no longer assume governmental neutrality or, under stress, assistance in the labor arena. The benefits accruing to organized labor took a variety of forms. The Norris-LaGuardia Act limited the use of injunctions that had in the past hindered union tactics. A federal law prohibited the transportation of strikebreakers across state lines. The *Thornhill* decision (1940) declared that antipicketing laws curbed the constitutional right of free speech. Detrimental governmental action, standard in earlier times of labor trouble, was largely precluded now by the emergence of sympathetic officeholders on all levels, from the municipal to the national. Indeed, the inclination was in the opposite direction. The response to the sitdown strike illustrated the change. "Well, it is illegal," Roosevelt commented. "But shooting it out and killing a lot of people because they have violated the law of trespass . . . [is not] the answer . . . . There must be another way. Why can't those fellows in General Motors meet with the committee of workers?" This tolerance of unlawful labor acts, as sitdowns were generally acknowledged to be, could not have happened at any earlier period of American history. These were negative means of forwarding the labor cause.

But political power was also applied in positive ways. The La Follette investigation undermined anti-union tactics by exposure and, among other ways, by feeding information on spies to the unions. At critical junctures, there was intercession by public officials ranging from President Roosevelt and Labor Secretary Perkins down to Mayor Kelly of Chicago. Governor Frank Murphy's role in the General Motors controversy is only the best known of a number of such mediating contributions to the union cause. At the start of the CIO steel drive Pennsylvania's Lieutenant-Governor Thomas Kennedy, a Mine Workers' officer, announced that organizers were free to move into steel towns and that state relief funds would be available in the event of a steel strike. The re-election of Roosevelt in 1936 no doubt cast out lingering hopes; many employers bowed to the inevitable after F.D.R.'s smashing victory with labor support.

These broader circumstances—rank-and-file enthusiasm, economic pressures on management, and the political condition—substantially augmented the specific benefits flowing from the Wagner Act. In fact, the great breakthrough at U.S. Steel and General Motors in early 1937 did not result from the law. The question of constitutionality was resolved only some weeks later. And the agreements themselves did not accord with the provisions of the Wagner Act. The unions dared not utilize procedures for achieving certification as bargaining agents in the auto and steel plants. Lee Pressman, counsel for the SWOC, later admitted that recognition could not then have been won "without Lewis' brilliant move" in his secret talks with U.S. Steel's Myron C. Taylor.

> There is no question that [SWOC] could not have filed a petition through the National Labor Relations Board . . . for an election. We could not have won an election for collective bargaining on the basis of our own membership or the results of the organizing campaign to date. This certainly applied not only to Little Steel but also to Big Steel.

Similarly, the *New York Times* reported on April 4, 1937: "Since the General Motors settlement, the union has been spreading its organization rapidly in General Motors plants, which were weakly organized at the time of the strike." The NLRB could not require either U.S. Steel or General Motors to make agreements with unions under those circumstances. Nor did the companies grant the form of recognition contemplated in the Wagner Act, that is, as *exclusive* bargaining agents. (This would have been illegal under the circumstances.) Only employees who were union members were covered by the two agreements. These initial CIO victories, opening the path as they did for the general advance of mass-production unionism, stemmed primarily from the wider pressures favorable to organized labor.

The Wagner Act proved indecisive for one whole stage of unionization. More than the enrollment of workers and the attainment of certification as bargaining agent was needed in unionization. The process was completed only when employers and unions entered bona fide collective bargaining. But this could not be enforced by law. Meaningful collective bargaining was achievable ultimately only through the interplay of non-legislative forces.

The tactics of major employers had shifted significantly by the 1920's. Their open-shop doctrine had as its declared purpose the protection of workingmen's liberties. "We do not believe it to be the wish of the people of this country," a U.S. Steel official had said, "that a man's right to work shall be made dependent upon his membership in any organization." Since the closed shop was assumed to follow inevitably from collective bargain-ing, the refusal to recognize unions was the fixed corollary of the open shop. The argument, of course, cut both ways. Open-shop employers insisted that their employees were free to join unions (whether or not this was so). The important fact, however, was that the resistance to unionism was drawn tight at the line of recognition and collective bargaining. That position had frustrated the attempt of the President's Industrial Conference of October, 1919, to formulate principles for "genuine and lasting cooperation between capital and labor." The union spokesmen had withdrawn in protest against the insistence of the employer group that the obligation to engage in collec-tive bargaining referred only to shop committees, not to trade unions. In effect, the strategy was to fight organized labor by withholding its primary function.

Federal regulation of labor relations gradually came to grips with the question of recognition and collective bargaining. During World War I, the NWLB only required employers to deal with shop committees. Going further, the NRA granted employees the right to "bargain collectively through representatives of their own choosing. . . ." This was interpreted to imply an obligation of employers to deal with such representatives. The major failing of section 7a was that the NRA did not implement the interpre-tation. In practice, determined employers were able, as earlier, to escape meaningful negotiation with trade unions. It seems significant that the permanent union gains of the NRA period came in those areas—the coal and garment industries—where collective bargaining did not constitute a line of employer resistance. Profiting by the NRA experience, the Wagner Act established the procedure for determining bargaining agents and the policy of exclusive representation and, by the device of certification, withdrew recognition from the option of an employer.

But recognition did not mean collective bargaining. Section 8 (5) did require employers to bargain with unions chosen in accordance with the law. Compliance, however, was another matter. In the first years, hostile em-ployers attempted to withhold the normal attributes of collective bargaining. When a strike ended at the Goodyear Akron plant in November, 1937, for example, the company insisted that the agreement take the form of a "memorandum" signed by the mediating NLRB regional director, not by company and union, and added that "in no event could the company predict or discuss the situation beyond the first of the year." (Although the Rubber Workers' local had already received certification, it would not secure a contract for another four years.) Westinghouse took the position that collective bargaining "was simply an opportunity for representatives of the employees to bring up and discuss problems affecting the work force, with the final decision reserved to the company. It rejected the notion of a signed agreement because business conditions were too uncertain. . . ." Some companies—for instance, Armour in April, 1941—unilaterally raised wages while in union negotiations. The contractual forms were resisted: agreements had to be verbal, or take the form of a "statement of policy," or, if in contractual terms, certainly with no signatures. These blatant evasions of the intent of section 8 (5) were gradually eliminated: a series of NLRB and court rulings prohibited the refusal to negotiate or make counteroffers, the unilateral alteration of the terms of employment, and opposition to incorporating agreements into written and signed contracts.

The substance proved more elusive than the externals of collective bargaining. "We have no trouble negotiating with Goodyear," a local union president observed, "but we can never bargain. The company stands firmly against anything which does not give them the absolute final decision on any question." The law, as it was interpreted, required employers to bargain "in good faith." How was lack of good faith to be proved? The NLRB tried to consider the specific circumstances and acts, rather than the words, of the employer in each case. That cumbersome procedure was almost useless from the union standpoint. Delay was easy during the case, and further evasion possible afterward. Barring contempt proceedings after a final court order, moreover, the employer suffered no penalties for his obstruction; there was no counterpart here for the back-pay provisions in dismissal cases. The union weakness was illustrated at Wilson & Co. The Cedar Rapids packing plant had been well organized since the NRA period, but no agreement was forthcoming from the hostile management. In 1938 the union filed charges with the NLRB. Its decision came in January, 1940, and another year was consumed by the company's unsuccessful appeal to the Circuit Court. The negotiations that followed (uninterrupted by a strike which the union lost) led nowhere because, a union official reported, Wilson "as always . . . tried to force the Union to accept the Company's agreement or none at all." The contract which was finally consummated in 1943 resulted neither from an NLRB ruling nor from the free collective bargaining that was the aim of the Wagner Act. Clearly, "good faith" was not to be extracted from recalcitrant employers by government fiat.

The collective-bargaining problem has a deeper dimension. The bitter-enders themselves constituted a minority group in American industry. For every Westinghouse, Goodyear, Ford, and Republic Steel there were several major competitors prepared to abide by the intent of the law and enter "sincere negotiations with the representatives of employees." But, from the union standpoint, collective bargaining was important for the results it could yield. Here the Wagner Act stopped. As the Supreme Court noted in the Sands case, "from the duty of the employer to bargain collectively . . . there does not flow any duty . . . to accede to the demands of the employees." No legal force sustained the objectives of unions either in improving wages, hours, and conditions or in strengthening their position through the union shop, master contracts, and arbitration of grievances.

The small utility of the law in collective bargaining was quickly perceived by labor leaders. The CIO packing-house union, for instance, did not invoke the Wagner Act at all in its three-year struggle with Armour. The company, in fact, objected to the intercession of Secretary of Labor [Frances] Perkins in 1939 on the ground that the union had not exhausted, or even utilized, the remedies available through the NLRB. The dispute actually did involve issues which fell within the scope of the Wagner Act. But the union clearly was seeking more effective ways—federal pressure in this case—of countering Armour's reluctance to negotiate and sign contracts. For the prime union objective was a master contract covering all the plants of the company organized by the union, a concession which could only be granted voluntarily by the company. Collective bargaining, both the process itself and the fruits, depended on the working of the other advantages open to the unions in the New Deal era.

Where negotiation was undertaken in "good faith," there were modest initial gains. The year 1937, marking the general beginning of collective bargaining in mass production, saw substantial wage increases as the result of negotiations and/or union pressure. In steel, the advances of November, 1936, and March, 1937, moved the unskilled hourly rate from 47 cents to 62½ cents. In rubber, average hourly earnings rose from 69.8 cents to 76.8 cents; in automobiles, from 80 to 93 cents. Other gains tended to be slender. The U.S. Steel agreement, for instance, provided the two major benefits of time-and-a-half after eight hours and a grievance procedure with arbitration. The vacation provision, on the other hand, merely continued an existing arrangement, and silence prevailed on many other questions. The contracts were, in contrast to later ones, very thin documents. Still, the first fruits of collective bargaining were encouraging to labor.

Then the economy faltered again. In 1938 industrial unions had to fight to stave off wage cuts. They succeeded in most, but not all, cases. Rates were reduced 15 per cent at Philco after a four months' strike. Less visible concessions had to be granted in some cases. For example, the SWOC and UAW accepted changes which weakened the grievance procedure at U.S. Steel and General Motors. The mass-production unions were, in addition, hard hit by the recession. Employment fell sharply. The UAW estimated that at the end of January, 1938, 320,000 auto production workers were totally unemployed and most of the remainder of the normal complement of 517,000 were on short time. The union's membership was soon down to 90,000. It was the same story elsewhere. In the Chicago district of the SWOC, dues payments fell by two-thirds in the twelve months after July, 1937 (that is, after absorbing the setback in Little Steel). Declining membership and, in some cases, internal dissension rendered uncertain the organizational viability of the industrial unions. And their weakness in turn further undermined their effectiveness in collective bargaining. They faced a fearful choice. If they became quiescent, they would sacrifice the support of the membership. If they pressed for further concessions, they would unavoidably become involved in strikes. By so doing, they would expose their weakened ranks in the one area in which labor legislation permitted the full expression of employer hostility—and in this period few even of the law-abiding employers were fully reconciled to trade unionism.

Collective bargaining was proving a severe obstacle to the new mass-production unions. The Wagner Act had little value here; and the other favoring circumstances had declining effectiveness after mid-1937. Hostile employers were evading the requirement of negotiating in good faith. For the larger part, the industrial unions achieved the first approximation of collective bargaining. But from 1937 to 1940 very little more was forthcoming. The vital function of collective bargaining seemed stalled. The situation was, in sum, still precarious five years after the formation of the CIO.

John L. Lewis had made something of a miscalculation. The promise of the New Deal era left mass-production unionism short of permanent success. Ultimately, two fortuitous circumstances rescued the industrial unions. The outbreak of World War II finally ended the American depression. By

1941, the economy was becoming fully engaged in defense production. Corporate profits before taxes leaped from 6½ billion dollars in 1939 to 17 billion in 1941. The number of unemployed fell from 8½ million in June, 1940, to under 4 million in December, 1941. It was this eighteen-month period that marked the turning point for the CIO. Industry's desire to capitalize on a business upswing, noted earlier, was particularly acute now; and rising job opportunities and prices created a new militancy in the laboring ranks. The open-shop strongholds began to crumble. Organization came to the four Little Steel companies, to Ford, and to their lesser counterparts. The resistance to collective bargaining, where it had been the line of conflict, was also breaking down. First contracts were finally being signed by such companies as Goodyear, Armour, Cudahy, Westinghouse, Union Switch and Signal. Above all, collective bargaining after a three-year gap began to produce positive results. On April 14, 1941, U.S. Steel set the pattern for its industry with an increase of ten cents an hour. For manufacturing generally, average hourly earnings from 1940 to 1941 increased over 10 per cent and weekly earnings 17 per cent; living costs rose only 5 per cent. More than wages was involved. Generally, initial contracts were thoroughly renegotiated for the first time, and this produced a wide range of improvements in vacation, holiday, and seniority provisions and in grievance procedure. Mass-production workers could now see the tangible benefits flowing from their union membership. These results of the defense prosperity were reflected in union growth: CIO membership jumped from 1,350,000 in 1940 to 2,850,000 in 1941.

The industrial unions were arriving at a solid basis. That achievement was insured by the second fortuitous change. American entry in the war necessitated a major expansion of the federal role in labor-management relations. To prevent strikes and inflation, the federal government had to enter the hitherto private sphere of collective bargaining. The National War Labor Board largely determined the wartime terms of employment in American industry. This emergency circumstance, temporary although it was, had permanent consequences for mass-production unionism. The wartime experience disposed of the last barriers to viable collective bargaining.

For one thing, the remaining vestiges of anti-unionism were largely eliminated. The hard core of resistance could not be handled summarily. In meat packing, for instance, Wilson & Co. had not followed Armour, Swift, and Cudahy in accepting collective bargaining. In 1942 the NWLB ordered the recalcitrant firm to negotiate a master contract (Wilson was holding to the earlier Big Four resistance to company-wide bargaining). Years later in 1955, a company official was still insisting that Wilson would not have accepted "a master agreement if it had not been for the war. Such an agreement is an unsatisfactory arrangement; today or yesterday." Subsequent negotiations having yielded no results, a Board panel itself actually wrote the first Wilson contract.

Beyond such flagrant cases, the NWLB set to rest an issue deeply troubling to the labor-management relationship in mass production. With few exceptions, the open shop remained dogma even after the acceptance of unionism. "John, it's just as wrong to make a man join a union," Benjamin Fairless of U.S. Steel insisted to Lewis, ". . . as it is to dictate what church he should belong to." The union shop had been granted in auto by Ford only; in rubber, by the employers of a tenth of the men under contract; in steel, by none of the major producers (although they had succumbed under pressure in the "captive mines"). The issue was profoundly important to the new unions. The union shop meant membership stability and, equally significant, the full acceptance of trade unionism by employers. The NWLB compromised the charged issue on the basis of a precedent set by the pre-war National Defense Mediation Board. Maintenance-of-membership prevented members from withdrawing from a union during the life of a contract. Adding an escape period and often the dues checkoff, the NWLB had granted this form of union security in 271 of 291 cases by February, 1944. The CIO regarded maintenance-of-membership as a substantial triumph. And, conversely, some employers took the measure, as Bethlehem and Republic Steel asserted, to be a "camouflaged closed shop." Among the expressions of resentment was the indication in contracts, following the example of Montgomery Ward, that maintenance-of-membership was being granted "over protest." This resistance, however, was losing its force by the end of the war. The union shop then generally grew from maintenance-of-membership.

The war experience also served a vital educational function. A measure of collective bargaining remained under wartime government regulation. Both before and after submission of cases to the NWLB, the parties involved were obliged to negotiate, and their representatives had to participate in the lengthy hearings. From this limited kind of confrontation, there grew the consensus and experience essential to the labor-management relationship.

Wartime education had another aspect. The wage-stabilization policy, implemented through the Little Steel formula by the NWLB, tended to extend the issues open to negotiation. Abnormal restraint on wages convinced labor, as one CIO man said, that "full advantage must be taken of what leeway is afforded" to achieve "the greatest possible gains. . . ." As a result the unions began to include in their demands a variety of new kinds of issues (some merely disguised wage increases), such as premium pay, geographical differentials, wage-rate inequalities, piece-rate computation, and a host of "fringe" payments. Thus were guidelines as to what was negotiable fixed for use after the war and a precedent set that would help further to expand the scope of collective bargaining. The collapse of economic stabilization then also would encourage the successive wage increases of the post-war rounds of negotiation. However illusory these gains were in terms of real income, they endowed the industrial unions with a reputation for effectiveness.

Finally, the wartime restrictions permitted the groping advance toward stable relations to take place in safety. The danger of strikes that might have pushed the parties back to an earlier stage of hostilities was eliminated. Strikes there were in abundance in the post-war period, but these could then be held to the objectives of the terms of employment, not the issue of unionism itself. Nothing revealed more of the new state of affairs than the first major defeat of an industrial union. The packing-house strike of 1948 was a thorough union disaster in an industry traditionally opposed to trade unionism. Yet the United Packinghouse Workers of America recovered and prospered. As one of its officials noted with relief, it was the first time in the history of the industry that a " 'lost' strike did not mean a lost union."

Unionization thus ran its full course in mass production. The way had been opened by the New Deal and the Great Depression. The legal right to organize was granted, and its utilization was favored by contemporary circumstances. John L. Lewis seized the unequalled opportunity. Breaking from the bounds of the labor establishment, he created in the CIO an optimum instrument for organizing the mass-production workers. These developments did not carry unionization to completion. There was, in particular, a failure in collective bargaining. In the end, the vital progress here sprang fortuitously from the defense prosperity and then the wartime impact on labor relations. From the half-decade of war, the industrial unions advanced to their central place in the American economy.

Notes

1.   For lack of an apt term in the literature, I have coined the phrase "primary union" to describe organizations with residual jurisdiction in mass-production fields. It should be noted that the local unions of these nationals tended to be organized around trades or departments rather than plants, as would be the case with industrial unions.

CORPORATE FARMING
IN THE UNITED STATES

By Philip M. Raup

Corporate farming is not new in the United States. The companies of "gentlemen adventurers" setting out in the seventeenth century to establish settlements in the New World were not corporations in a modern sense, but in organizational form and motivation they bear a striking resemblance to corporation-farming ventures of recent decades. The twin lures of short-run profits and long-run capital gains have been major forces in shaping land-use patterns and institutional structures throughout America's history. For over 300 years repeated efforts were made to use large-scale organizational forms to reap these rewards in agriculture. Up to 1950 the record was one of almost consistent failure.

Among early failures were two farms established in 1833 near present-day

Reprinted with permission from *Journal of Economic History* (March 1973). Copyright © 1973 by The Economic History Association.

Dupont and Toledo, Washington, by the Puget's Sound Agricultural Company, a subsidiary of the Hudson's Bay Company. Both in genesis and demise, this venture was prophetic of future corporate-farming trends. The farms were created to enable the Hudson's Bay Company to supply wheat, livestock and dairy products under contract to Russian fur-trading posts in Alaska. After a few years of early success, the farms steadily lost money. The company was unable to compete with encroaching small settlers, whose activities "raised the price of labor and made it more difficult to maintain a disciplined labor force." The company sold its land to the United States Government and liquidated in 1870, having paid only seven dividends in 32 years.

Examples of successful corporate farms can be found before 1950 among fruit and vegetable farms of California, sugar and pineapple farms of Hawaii, and ranching and land-holding corporations in Arizona, Texas, the Mountain States, the Gulf Coast and Florida. A distinction must be made between corporate ownership of rural land, and corporate farming. There has always been a significant area of land owned by large business firms or corporations in the United States and especially since the railroad land giants were inaugurated in 1850. Corporate holdings figured prominently in the Florida land boom of the 1920's. A 1945 study of land ownership in the United States reported 5.6 percent of all land in farms as owned by corporations but many of these were not farm-operating corporations. No national data exist prior to 1968 on the actual extent of corporate farm operation in the United States.

The first national attempt to measure corporate farms as a class was in 1968. In that year the U.S. Department of Agriculture estimated that there were 13,313 farming corporations, comprising 1 percent of all commercial farms, operating 7 percent of all farm land, and accounting for 8 percent of gross sales of farm products.

There are wide variations among states and regions. Florida and California had one fifth of the total number of corporate farms. They accounted for 31 percent of the land in farms in Florida, 28 percent in Utah, 22 percent in Nevada, and 19 percent in California. They were most prominent in field and specialty crop areas of Florida and California, in ranching areas of the Great Plains and Mountain States, in the Massachusetts-Rhode Island-Connecticut area, in Washington and Oregon, and in the Mississippi Delta States. They occupied one percent or less of the land in farms in most of the Middle West. . . .

What happened after World War II to stimulate a sudden expansion of interest in corporation farming? In answering this question it will be helpful to ask another: Why did corporate farming fail to develop in parallel with the rapid expansion of agricultural mechanization in the 1920's and 1930's? It was not for lack of effort. One of the best publicized attempts was made by the Wheat Farming Corporation of Topeka, Kansas, organized in September, 1927. With holdings in excess of 65,000 acres in Northwestern Kansas, the corporation mobilized large-scale mechanized equipment, land and capital in the specialized production of wheat. "There will be no surplus," was one of the headings used in literature developed to promote stock sales in 1929. "Every cent decrease in the average level of wheat prices brings white bread within the reach of hundreds of thousands of hungry Orientals."

The timing could not have been worse. Within three years the collapse of wheat prices led to dissolution of the corporation. The political reaction stimulated the Kansas legislature in 1931 to enact a law prohibiting farm corporations from "producing, planting, raising, harvesting, or gathering wheat, corn, barley, oats, rye or potatoes or the milking of cows for dairy purposes." This experience was dominated by a faith in economies of large-scale production that has been one of the major themes in the history of corporation farming. And it illustrates one facet of the evolution in interpretation of Frederick Jackson Turner's thesis regarding the role of the frontier in American history.

It has been difficult to sustain the "labor safety valve" version of the Turner thesis by reference to Eastern industrial labor or wages in manufacturing. It is easier to support the Turner thesis by reference to agricultural labor. As long as free land was available on the frontier it was difficult to hold hired labor in agriculture. The desire to create large farms has been continuously present in America, but capacity to hold a labor force was available only under slavery in the South. In the Middle West, the larger-than-family farm had to compete with the frontier in the nineteenth century and with the rapid expansion of industry in the twentieth century for its labor supply.

Until the advent of efficient tractors in the 1920's, and in large numbers in the 1930's, there was little opportunity to substitute capital for labor in agriculture on a scale that could offset the added costs of wage-labor supervision. The early tractors were primarily substitutes for horses and mules, but not at first for men.[1] The grain combine was much more a substitute for men. In wheat areas, the potential for large scale or corporate farms increased greatly after combines came into general use. This helps explain the flurry of experiments with corporate and large-scale farms in the Great Plains in the late 1920's.

The Depression of the 1930's put an end to most of these undertakings. As the Depression was ending, World War II made it difficult to mobilize either labor or equipment to operate a large or corporate farm. Fear of a repetition of the farm price collapse of 1920-1921 following the end of World War II also inhibited large-scale investment of non-farm capital in agriculture in the immediate post-war period.

Until the middle of the twentieth century, conditions were never favorable for the growth of large-scale and corporate farms in the Middle West and Great Plains. It seems reasonable to assign a part of the cause to the lagged influence of the frontier, which had retarded the build-up of redundant agricultural labor supplies. It was a labor supply, and not capital, that was a critical variable in the development of large and corporate farms in the period prior to World War I, when capacity to substitute machines for men was limited. Mechanization created a technological potential for large-scale agricultural enterprises which was well-developed by the end of the 1920's. Delay in exploiting it must be explained in terms of price and market relationships, and the dislocating effects of wartime.

A major change in the economic climate occurred after World War II. The war generated relatively favorable price-cost relationships but farmers, and prospective farm investors, entered the post-war period with the history of 1920-21 clearly in mind. The response of prices after 1945 did not lessen their apprehension. An upward surge in 1945-47 reflected short-run demands for food for areas devastated by war, but by the end of the 1940's the thrust of this demand had eased. Wheat prices fell $1.00 per bushel from January, 1948 to July, 1949. The Korean war gave a temporary fillip to all commodity prices including farm products. By 1953 this was dissipating but there was no disastrous collapse. Land prices reflected these trends. It is significant that, in the entire period from 1939 to 1972, the index of United States farmland prices declined only in the years 1950 to 1954.

The early 1950's stand out as a major turning point in American agricultural history. It slowly became apparent that there was not going to be a repetition of the farm-prices disaster of 1920-21 or of the associated destruction of capital values in land. A policy base was thus created for a reappraisal of investment possibilities in farming. Land prices were relatively low, farm prices cushioned against collapse, and a rich storehouse of new technology was available. There was an opportunity for strategically-placed investors to capture a unique capital gain.

As Donald A. Nichols has emphasized, "A change in the rate of [economic] growth leads to a once and for all capital gain for land holders. This is because the returns to land are capitalized at a rate equal to the marginal product of capital minus the growth rate, or alternatively, because the future returns to land can be expected to be larger with a high growth rate than with a low one."

One explanation for the increased interest in corporation farming after the mid-1950's was a realization that a basic change in the rate of growth of agricultural output was in process. Those fortunate enough to be landowners at the time of this change would be able to capture a part, at least, of a resultant one-time capital gain. A fundamental shift in the production function was under way.

Two seemingly minor institutional changes in the 1950's also had a significant impact on the development of corporation farming. One was a change in the Internal Revenue Code in 1958, permitting corporations having only one class of stock, no more than ten shareholders, who must be individuals or estates, and meeting other conditions, to be treated for income tax purposes as if they were partnerships. In these "Subchapter S" corporations, income can be "passed through" the corporations and taxed only to the shareholders, thus avoiding double taxation. An even more important feature for many non-farm investors is that capital gains can be passed through to the shareholders, where they will be taxed at favorable rates. Similarly, a corporate operating loss can be passed through, permitting the shareholder to take his share of any carryforward or carryback deductions for corporate net operating losses.

This increased the attractiveness of farm incorporation as an alternative to farm-family partnerships and helps explain the fact that 19,716 of the 21,513 corporate farms enumerated in the 1969 Census of Agriculture had no more than ten shareholders. Not all of these are Subchapter S corporations, and many are simply incorporated family farms or ranches, but many are much larger than family-size operations. Available data do not permit a separation.

The second institutional change was an alteration in the Internal Revenue Code in 1951 permitting farmers to treat livestock held more than twelve months for draft, breeding, or dairy purposes as "property used in trade or business." As we will see, the effect was to make livestock breeding highly attractive to non-farm investors in high-income brackets. A corporate form of business was usually advantageous if non-farm investors were to exploit this windfall. This explains much of the recent corporate activity in ranching areas, and in livestock breeding generally.

The stage was set in the 1950's for an increase in corporation-farming activity. The consequences can be read from data on the pace of incorporation. Of all farming corporations surveyed in 1968 by the Department of Agriculture, 50 percent had begun farming operations in 1960 or later. In the Northern and Southern Plains states, just under 70 percent of all 1968 farming corporations started operation in the 1960's. Together with the Mountain States, these were the three regions in the United States in which over half of all farming corporations were engaged in beef-cattle breeding and ranching. The other area of rapid corporate-farm expansion after 1960 involved soybeans in the Delta States of Mississippi, Arkansas and Louisiana. Extensive land-clearing operations were carried out in these states in the 1960's and the corporation farm was a favored organizational device for these activities.

Two major and interrelated economic arguments are used to explain and justify the growth of corporation farming: economies of size, and provision of capital. Given a history of small family-sized farms and rapid technological change, it is understandable that a part of the national farm folklore includes a faith in bigness. "Expand the size of your farm business" has been the advice to farmers for over fifty years, from agricultural universities, experiment stations, extension services and their supporting agencies in the U.S. Department of Agriculture. The market-development activities of farm-equipment manufacturers and supply industries have been at least as effective. Virtually the entire educational and promotional apparatus of American agriculture has focused on size. Up to a point the argument has had merit.

It is being increasingly questioned in recent years. Virtually all current studies of economies of size in agriculture yield the same conclusion: In all but a few types of farming, well-managed one- and two-man farms can obtain most of the gains to be had from increased size, as measured by decreases in cost per unit of output.[2] . . .

All available evidence indicates that agriculture in the 1960's was better supplied with capital than at any time since the First World War.

> Forty years ago, by any reasonable measure, the farm sector was disadvantaged in the money markets. But at least since World War II, there has apparently been discrimination in favor of agriculture in the national allocation of money. . . . A result of this "favorable" money policy is the overcapitalization of the farming sector relative to other sectors of the economy and relative to the true productivity (in a social sense) of marginal capital allocation to the farm sector.[3]

The capital supplied by the federal government to create the various components of the cooperative Farm Credit System (Federal Land Banks, Production Credit Associations, Banks for Cooperatives) had all been repaid by 1968 and the system is now fully owned by its farmer borrowers. Reflecting this shift in the relative supply of capital, life insurance companies began to withdraw capital from agriculture after 1965. From 1940 to 1965, life insurance companies had annually made from 16 to 21 percent of all new farm mortgage loans in the U.S.; in 1965 the figure was 19 percent. By 1970 this had declined to 4 percent.

The recent cycle in the formation of large-scale corporation-farming enterprises reached its peak in 1965-70. This was not a response to a capital shortage in agriculture. The driving force came from non-farm investors seeking tax shelters, quick returns from new technology, and capital gains through land-value appreciation.

Incentives rooted in tax policy were reinforced by the nature of government farm-price support programs. These have played a key role in promoting corporation farming in field crops, especially wheat, feed grains and cotton. With benefits a function of historical-acreage base, an incentive was created for farm-size enlargement. Farm-program payments also provided financial leverage that could be exploited by large or corporate farms but was not equally available as a credit base for small farms.

Urban expansion, population concentration and threats of a world food shortage also help explain the flowering of interest in corporation farming in the 1960's.

Large numbers of us are apparently Malthusians at heart. We seem transfixed by the simplicity of the proposition that population continues to expand while the surface of the earth is fixed. This argument has appeared in virtually all of the promotional literature aimed at prospective investors in corporate farms. When coupled with recent attention to the population explosion and environmental deterioration, the result was the creation of a climate of opinion in which food production emerged as a safe long-run growth industry. Fear of inflation provided powerful reinforcement. Beginning slowly in the mid-1960's and accelerating with the Viet Nam war, investors were increasingly susceptible to the argument that they should move some of their money into land. "Owing to the increase in population, particularly in farm-rich places like California, arable land has been growing critically short. . . . In the opinion of many experts, arable land is bound to grow scarcer."

The retreat from Malthusianism was rapid after the first impact of the "Green Revolution" in the late 1960's. India was almost self-sufficient in wheat and rice by 1971; Japan was exporting rice; and the world trading community no longer accepted the inevitability of famine-induced demands for farm products. It became clearer that investments in corporate-farming ventures would have to be justified primarily by domestic market potentials and not by prospective foreign demand.

There are types of farming for which capital requirements and economies of size are often beyond the reach of single-proprietor or family-type farms. Heading this list are integrated poultry and egg enterprises, mechanized orchards, citrus and nut groves, large-scale beef-cattle feed lots, pineapple and sugar cane, and vegetable crops for canning or processing. It is likely that corporation-farming activity will remain strong and even expand in these types of farming. The most vulnerable sectors are beef breeding and certain types of fruit and nut crops. Tax policy has attracted non-farm capital into these sectors to an extent that defeats any attempt to argue the case for corporate or large-scale farming on the basis of conventional tests of efficiency or economies of size. The greatest stimulus arises from capital-gains tax provisions and from the opportunity for non-farm investors to use farm losses to offset non-farm income. These are under increasing attack in the Congress, and could easily be altered by a policy change. A significant part of corporate-farm activity in tree-crop and ranching areas has been initiated by non-farm investors seeking tax shelters.

For corporate-farming sectors less flagrantly stimulated by farm-price supports or tax policy, there has been a tendency to forecast growth by drawing analogies from industrial history. Although the corporate era arrived late in farming, the usual assumption is that the course of its development has been charted by the industrial corporation, and the only doubtful feature is timing. There is in the literature virtually no discussion of the possibility that corporate farming may not trace out the same sequence of growth stages that characterized industry.

In tracing the growth stages of large-scale economic organizations in America, Chandler and Galambos characterize 1870 to the early 1930's as the first stage, in which firm growth was confined to horizontally or vertically integrated units within traditional product lines. A steel mill grew by absorbing other steel mills or by integrating coal, ore and transport components in steel-making. And in the early corporate firms, family control played a major role.[4]

This seems superficially to fit the pattern of recent development in corporation farming. Family-farm corporations can be likened to early stages in the emergence of industrial corporations almost a century earlier. One leading farm-management consultant has concluded that, in agriculture, "Many family corporations will 'go public' when they are transferred to the next generation. The desire will be there for further expansion and this will be the natural route."

What reasons are there to question this vision of the growth cycle in corporate farming? Chandler and Galambos point out that the first stage from 1870 to the 1930's involved the rapid growth of primary industrial organizations, or "large-scale complex organizations which were essentially concerned with the job of organizing people in order to provide goods or services." This first period witnessed a much slower growth of "a second kind of large-scale organization which was largely concerned with coordinating the activities and with communicating between other organizations. These secondary organizations included trade associations, union federations, and some governmental agencies." After the 1930's this was reversed in industry, and secondary organizations grew much more rapidly.

In agriculture, the large-scale secondary or coordinating organizations came first. The emergence of corporate agriculture has thus occurred in the "second stage," with agriculture well supplied with coordinating organizations. Among them are agricultural cooperatives, farm political organizations, and a complex structure of informational and governmental organizations, including universities, experiment stations, extension services, the Soil Conservation Service, the Farm Credit Administration, crop and livestock statistical-reporting services, market-news and weather-reporting services, the Rural Electrification Administration, a structure of demarcated milk sheds governed by Market Orders, and a variety of related secondary organizations.

The institutional infrastructure of agriculture is highly developed. Many services that a large-scale primary organization might provide are now available to American agriculture through large-scale secondary organizations. This applies significantly to the functions of research and development, and dissemination of information. In industry, the ability of private firms to control information flows and dominate research and development activities has frequently been decisive. These opportunities are greatly reduced in agriculture. If a flow of capital can be maintained, it is not at all clear that large-scale industrial-type corporation farms are essential to continued agricultural development.

A closely related point concerns the attitude of workers toward their jobs. Our industrial corporate world developed in an era in which no serious attempt was made to answer Marglin's question: ''. . . is alienating work the price we must pay for material prosperity?'' This question is relevant in a plantation economy, or in migrant labor camps. It is not relevant in a system of proprietary businesses or family farms. Is alienation less likely to emerge in corporation farming? Or is it likely to be intensified by constant exposure to a capital structure that was once owned by the workers?

It is difficult for a worker in a textile mill, a steel mill, an oil refinery, or an airline to imagine himself the owner of the capital with which he works. This identification is much more plausible in agriculture. A corporate-farm structure in the last quarter of the twentieth century must struggle with the alienation question. It seems likely that the solution will not involve corporate forms we know in industry. This conclusion is reinforced by the high fraction of total farm capital that must be invested in land and livestock. As long as price-support programs, tax policy, and depreciation rules favor non-farm investors, we can expect a derived demand for corporations in farming to facilitate exploitation of these advantages. But if land must be held for production only and not for speculation, the capital costs may be too high for non-family types of farming corporation. They cannot afford to immobilize capital in a factor of production that will be carried by family farmers at rates of return on capital that large corporations find intolerable.

One result is a shift to types of contract farming in which land and working capital remain largely in the hands of family-size farms. Large corporate processing firms can contribute to the control of product quality and standardization but many have found land ownership and direct farm operation unrewarding. One reason is the decline in rate of growth in agricultural efficiency in the late 1960's. From 1954 to 1960 agricultural output per unit of input increased at an annual rate of 3.0 percent. From 1965 to 1970 it was virtually zero. When the recent corporate farm boom reached its peak in the late 1960's the major impact of the post-World War II surge in efficiency of resource use in agriculture had been dissipated.

Farm corporations that began operation after 1965 were too late to capture big operating gains from rising efficiency, and just in time to encounter inflated land costs. Add to this the costs of pollution control on big farms, plus the success of Cesar Chavez in organizing farm labor in California and Florida, and it is not surprising to find a flight out of farming by corporations that a few years earlier were extolling a new farming era. . . .

Farming corporations can play a useful role in agriculture, and particularly for family businesses that in an earlier day would have been loosely described as partnerships. It is difficult to justify most types of large corporations in farming by conventional economic tests of efficiency in resource use and management. Those we now have are largely a consequence of farm-price support and tax policies, which were aimed at family farmers and badly missed the target.

Notes

1.   For an account of large-scale farming experiments at the dawn of mechanization see Hiram M. Drache, *The Day of the Bonanza* (Fargo, N.D.: North Dakota Institute for Regional Studies, 1964).

2.   J. Patrick Madden and Earl J. Partenheimer, "Evidence of Economies and Diseconomies of Farm Size," *Size, Structure, and Future of Farms*, A. Gordon Ball and Earl O. Heady, eds. (Ames: Iowa State University Press, 1972), pp. 100-104. Their conclusion is that "Problems of coordination and uncertainty may place a practical upper limit on farm enlargement." (p. 106).

3.   John E. Lee, Jr., "The Money Market—Is It Adequate for the Needs of Today's Agriculture," *Agricultural Finance Review*, USDA-ERS, Vol. 32, August 1971, 2-3.

4.   A. D. Chandler and L. Galambos, "The Development of Large-Scale Economic Organizations in Modern America." [The last essay in this volume.]

SECTION III

BUSINESS, GOVERNMENT, AND THE MILITARY

The connecting thread of the following five articles dealing with a variety of subjects in twentieth-century American history is their focus on organization. In this section we examine numerous instances where business, the civilian branches of government, and the military intersect and interact. Two of the essays—the first and the last—deal with the origins of the so-called military-industrial complex, which President Dwight D. Eisenhower (who is the topic of the fourth essay) warned against in his farewell message to the American people in January, 1961.

In the course of their development, all three institutions—big business, government, and the military—had to come to terms with organizational concepts and administrative problems. Big business and the military met the challenge more successfully, in part because the goals were clearer and narrower—profits in one case and military victory or the maintenance of a strong defense in the other—but also because the continuity of leadership was much greater. For government the basic goals and standards of perfor mance were less obvious, and both were subject to frequent change. Except for the unprecedented tenure in office of FDR, no administration held power for longer than eight years.

Adversity or a serious new challenge often stimulated institutions to consider significant organizational reforms. In response to the post-war recession of 1920-21, the interconnected Du Pont and General Motors firms were among the first large manufacturers to revamp administrative structures. Unable to adjust quickly to the sudden fall in demand after the war, huge losses spurred both firms to fresh thinking about the most effective management structure for the large, diversified corporation. The challenge of two world wars within a span of just over two decades produced similar responses in the civilian government and the military services. Previously, both had been limited in size because of the traditional outlook of Americans, who saw great virtue in small government and a minimal peacetime army; however, the world wars multiplied the amount of public spending and created complex organizational difficulties that were resolved only through restructuring agencies and altering the chains of command.

The first four selections that follow relate the efforts of Bernard Baruch, Alfred Sloan, Herbert Hoover, and Dwight Eisenhower—all in very different circumstances—to deal with matters that were at least partly organizational in nature.

First, Robert D. Cuff examines the administrative confusion surrounding the mobilization of American armed forces in WW I and the prominent role played by Bernard Baruch, a Wall Street financier turned government bureaucrat.

When Europe was plunged into conflict in 1914, the nation had not been engaged in a major war for half a century. The Civil War was fought at the dawn of industrialization in the United States; by 1917 the country was an industrial giant, with the largest and most complex economy in the world. To aid in the war preparations, a group of "dollar-a-year" men came to Washington—executives who had been released by business firms to serve in government administrative posts while continuing to draw their former pay from the private sector. Initially, regular government bureaucrats, military men, and even President Wilson were suspicious about the motives and capabilities of these businessmen transformed into mobilizers. But as problems of supply and coordination mounted, these executives, with wide experience in the management of large, complicated organizations, demonstrated their ability to outperform the regular government and military personnel in matching industrial production with the material requirements of the armed services. Previously, many historians were led to believe that these efficiencies were the result of the "dictatorial rule" of the wartime "economic czar" Bernard Baruch, who had assumed leadership of the War Industries Board in March, 1918. But Cuff shows that this view of Baruch's power and position in Washington must be substantially modified.

Given the absence of precedents, it is surprising that mobilization proceeded so smoothly, although, as Cuff indicates, the unique mix of centralized and decentralized authority, which arose with little forethought as a matter of expediency, was largely responsible for the outcome. When the war ended in late 1918, the rationale for the existence of this sophisticated organizational system ended as well, and it was quickly dismantled. But, according to the argument advanced by Chandler and Galambos in the final essay, the lessons of that experience were not entirely wasted, because administrators applied them in the 1940s, when the United States again became involved in a global conflict. Meanwhile, in their effort to discover the best combination of centralized and decentralized responsibility and authority, Baruch and his associates engaged in discussions that soon had a counterpart in the boardrooms of some of the nation's largest industrial firms, such as Du Pont and General Motors.

In the excerpt from his autobiography, Alfred P. Sloan, who became the chief executive officer of GM in 1923, gives a firsthand account of how these organizational concepts were developed and applied. Before his association with GM, Sloan was the owner-manager of an independent manufacturer of automotive parts. In 1916 Sloan sold his firm to GM for $13.5 million, and he immediately became the head of GM's parts and accessories division. Under the leadership of William Durant, GM's founder and chief executive officer, Sloan's division, like the others under the GM umbrella, operated autonomously. Sloan received little advice or direction from above. With the market for automobiles growing rapidly, Durant was primarily interested in expanding production facilities, and he gave slight attention to organizational matters.

The postwar depression brought the du Ponts into GM management. The close links between GM and Du Pont, which persisted until the successful prosecution of an antitrust suit in the 1950s, originated in 1917. The du Ponts, seeking a promising investment outlet for their substantial earnings from the sale of gunpowder to the Allies, purchased a large block of GM common stock. In the crisis of 1920-21, Durant was forced to retire, and

Pierre du Pont, motivated strongly by a desire to protect the family's outside investments, became the head of the automobile firm. During the time in the early 1920s that he was chairman of the board of both Du Pont and GM, he was surely one of the most powerful men in the American economy.

Drawn to Alfred Sloan in part because his approach to organizational problems paralleled the ideas that had emerged independently at the Du Pont Company, Pierre du Pont soon designated Sloan as the man to inherit control of GM. Pierre du Pont held the presidency only about two years, long enough to oversee the implementation of the original Sloan reorganization plan. Sloan describes for us the evolution of his thoughts on sound business administration and their translation into a new management structure for the giant automaker.

In contrast to the problems facing his contemporaries in big business, Herbert Hoover as Harding's and Coolidge's Secretary of Commerce had the difficult task of convincing government officials and the general public of the positive role that secondary, coordinating agencies might play in fostering a stronger and more efficient American society. Hoover, as Ellis W. Hawley's article shows, had to overcome a strong bias in Washington against direct government involvement in the promotion of business activity. His programs ran against the ingrained American belief in limited government. Except for the close relationship between business and government during WW I—which most considered an aberration—and the passage of a few mild regulatory acts in the Progressive period, the ideology of laissez-faire still set the tone for government economic policy in the 1920s. Thus, Hoover's task was not merely to demonstrate that his programs were practical and beneficial, but also to show that the rationale for their existence was reasonably in harmony with prevailing views about the proper role and function of government.

A comparison of the educational backgrounds and later careers of Herbert Hoover and Alfred Sloan reveals some intriguing similarities. Both men graduated as engineers in 1895, Sloan from M.I.T. and Hoover from Stanford (in the first graduating class). Probably from their engineering training, these men—and many others like them after the turn of the century—identified with programs designed to eliminate or at least minimize waste and inefficiency, whether in the physical world or increasingly in the less exacting realm of human institutions. Sloan was clearly more successful in reaching this goal, as witnessed by the steady profits he achieved for GM over the long run. Hoover's obstacles were vastly more formidable. According to Hawley, the Commerce Secretary was attempting to move beyond the essentially negative reform thrust on Progressive politics by educating the public to the realities of the bureaucratic, organizational forces that increasingly were shaping modern society. Hoover hoped to demonstrate to his fellow citizens how these forces could be harnessed by the federal government for the general welfare.

In this article we do not see Hoover as he is so often pictured—as a tragic figure, or a defender of the status quo, or a reactionary who was ideologically and emotionally unable to cope with the demands of the twentieth century. Instead, we see the picture of a Hoover who was aggressive, forward looking, and probably more in tune with the general movement of events than any individual in government service. Indeed, from this perspective, he appears to have been one of the best qualified presidents in the nation's history. Although the Great Depression severely tarnished Hoover's public reputation, it is noteworthy that his political peers did not forget his more positive accomplishments. In his later years, he was called back to Washington by Presidents Truman and Eisenhower to head commissions charged with the task of recommending new ways to improve the efficiency of government through a restructuring of the executive branch.

The military services also were influenced by organizational forces. As American military leaders became deeply involved in planning for WW II, defining the nature and scope of the command structure was a top priority. General George C. Marshall, then Chief of Staff, selected Dwight D. Eisenhower, at the time one of the Army's lower ranking senior officers, to draft a comprehensive plan for an innovative, unified theater structure that would combine under one supreme commander the army, navy, and air force of the United States and of another sovereign nation—Britain—as well. When it came time to choose the supreme commander, the author of the plan ended up with the top post. Eisenhower followed the same path to power as Sloan at General Motors.

As explained by Alfred D. Chandler, Jr., in the editor's introduction to the Eisenhower papers, many of the problems Eisenhower dealt with as Supreme Commander of Allied Forces in Europe were similar to those encountered by the leaders of large public and private organizations in the twentieth century. He too sought to find the right mix of centralized authority and local initiative. Overall planning of war operations rested squarely in the hands of the staff officers at headquarters, but Eisenhower saw to it that once the fighting began, his commanding officers in the field had sufficient latitude to make on-the-spot tactical decisions. In addition to maintaining good rapport with the large number of military officers under him, the Supreme Commander also had to pay close attention to his relations with the political figures directly above him, men who ultimately determined Allied grand strategy. By the 1940s, most corporate chief executives had found ways to make their boards of directors mere rubber stamps, but Eisenhower did not have this luxury. He was continually asked to explain and justify his actions to the Roosevelt administration in Washington and sometimes to Prime Minister Winston Churchill, a leader who often perceived events in a much broader context than the ones defined by strictly military demands.

Baruch, Sloan, Hoover, and Eisenhower, as leaders of large, complex modern bureaucracies, discovered that, while a rational and formal administrative structure was vital, the maintenance of close personal contact with their immediate associates was also important for success in the long run. Although all these men had the authority to issue orders and take action without fully revealing their reasons to subordinates, they soon found that the most effective method of gaining solid backing for their policies was through the power of persuasion—which became a two-way street.

The careers of these four unusually able men indicate that the successful leader of a modern organization is not an autocrat issuing directives from on high, but rather a masterful coordinator with the ability to select talented senior associates and encourage them to cooperate and achieve common goals. If, for example, the early eulogizers of Bernard Baruch had fully understood the actual role of leaders in large, modern institutions, it is unlikely they would have so badly miscast him as wartime economic czar or dictator. These leaders who shared many personal characteristics and faced many of the same difficulties, probably had more in common with each other than with their nineteenth-century counterparts: Baruch with Lincoln's Secretary of War Edwin M. Stanton, Sloan with Carnegie and Rockefeller, and Eisenhower with Generals Lee and Grant. Hoover, who had no equivalent as Commerce Secretary in the previous century, had a more difficult task than the others, for he had to practice the art of persuasion not only on superiors and subordinates but also on the general public.

The last article focuses again on the interrelatedness of the political, military, and business systems. After WW I demobilization had proceeded unimpeded, and the same process began in 1945 and 1946. As Donald J. Mrozek reveals, however, President Truman's chief defense advisers ly perceived the importance of a permanent state of preparedness in an atomic age and the necessity of maintaining U.S. technological superiority in a period of rapid scientific advances. They urged closer ties between the military services and the nation's major aircraft manufacturers. Between 1940 and 1945, in response to wartime requirements, the aircraft industry had grown from a relatively small, almost marginal business into one of the country's largest employers, with an enormous investment in new plant and equipment.

At the end of the war, many firms hoped that the market for commercial planes would expand and provide a substitute for the diminishing market for fighters and bombers. When the commercial demand failed to materialize, the aircraft companies were left with acres of unused plant and large teams of highly trained, but idle engineers. Although they had initially feared excessive reliance or outright dependence on government contracts, most aircraft executives had concluded by the end of the decade that the alternatives had narrowed to increased defense work or bankruptcy; not surprisingly, all of them chose the former.

By the early 1950s, the call for a strong, permanent defense force was unanimous from the executive and legislative branches of the federal government, local officials and small businessmen in the vicinity of defense installations, the military leadership, and the aircraft companies. But, as Mrozek emphasizes, this union of the public interest and private profit was by no means predetermined nor was it the work of any single special interest group in or out of government. It was in part a product of the new age of organizations—an age in which organizational imperatives frequently shaped the destinies of governments, private firms, and most of the citizens of the United States.

BERNARD BARUCH:
SYMBOL AND MYTH IN
INDUSTRIAL MOBILIZATION

By Robert D. Cuff

The appointment of Bernard M. Baruch as chairman of the War Industries Board on March 4, 1918, completed one of the outstanding success stories of the Great War. From a virtually unknown Wall Street speculator, Baruch emerged in the process of industrial mobilization as the best known of the "dollar-a-year men," the major symbol of business-government cooperation during World War I. Even though the memory of the Board has faded, the image of Bernard Baruch the "industrial dictator" of World War I remains.

The persistence of this textbook image owes a great deal to the standard account of the WIB, Grosvenor B. Clarkson's *Industrial America in the World War*, the source of most brief accounts. The book has many heroes, but none looms larger than Bernard Baruch. Indeed, at one point in the

Reprinted with permission from *Business History Review*, 43 (Summer 1969). Copyright © 1969 by The President and Fellows of Harvard College.

narrative the author's enthusiasm moved him to say: "He [Baruch] had helped build the machine [the WIB of March, 1918] in every part from the earliest days, and the general plan had been originated by him."
Clarkson's work is a valuable contribution, but it must be read with care as both history and memoir. The author had long admired the men who managed America's corporate system, and turning this sentiment into a livelihood, he had done some public relations work in the prewar years. An account with the automobile industry led him to Howard E. Coffin, vice-president of the Hudson Motor Car Company, who persuaded him to direct publicity for an industrial-preparedness campaign in 1916. In company with Ivy Lee, Edward Bernays, and other practitioners of a burgeoning art, Clarkson subsequently lent his talents to the war effort as secretary and then director of the Council of National Defense.

After the war, Clarkson sought to tell, and sell, the story of industrial mobilization, and in 1920 he finally found a man who was willing to subsidize his efforts. "I will say frankly," he informed Bernard Baruch, his new client, "that the controlling factor with me in undertaking this history will be the simple justice that I believe to be due in the way of recognition to the great business battalions that you and your associates called to the side of the government for the prosecution of the war. I believe that that recognition has been unjust, not only to the elements involved but to the country as well." Clarkson received $38,000 and expenses to do the book, and he went over "every word of the manuscript" with Leland Summers, one of Baruch's right-hand men during the war.

Baruch made many contributions to economic mobilization, of which his early drive for a centralized, civilian, mobilization agency is perhaps the best known. Yet even a cursory reading of *Industrial America in the World War* shows that he was not the sole originator of the WIB; Daniel R. Beaver has underlined this point further by illustrating the way in which Newton D. Baker, Secretary of War, shaped the Board's origins and evolution.[1] Nor is "dictatorship" a very useful concept to employ in an analysis of Baruch's chairmanship, for it obscures a number of subtleties which permit a more realistic appraisal of his position.

What then are the central characteristics of Baruch's place in industrial mobilization? In an effort to separate the myth from the reality of his role, I propose in this article to comment on three interrelated points. These include, first, the particular kind of viewpoint which Baruch represented in industrial mobilization, with attention to the social bases of his ideas;

second, the extent to which his place as chairman was determined by ongoing institutional developments over which he had little control, and often little knowledge; and finally, the symbolic function he performed as head of the WIB.

The vast majority of the American people were reluctant to enter World War I, but once President Wilson reached his decision, they responded to the crisis with an outburst of patriotic fervor and a deluge of voluntary activity. A deeply embedded tradition of associational activity, a confidence in individual initiative, a suspicion of central government, and a faith in the benign presence of Adam Smith's invisible hand all helped to make the springtime mobilization an intensely decentralized, fragmented, haphazard process. While it is true that the Advisory Commission of the Council of National Defense, formed in October, 1916, and the General Munitions Board, formed in March, 1917, attempted to give some coherence and direction, they both suffered from vague mandates, advisory status, and daily conflicts with the military services. Nor could the Army and Navy offer stability and order. The services regarded each other warily, and the several Army bureaus, unable yet to deal blows to the Germans, focused their militancy on supply battles with each other.

Mobilization was swept away in a sea of independent feudalities. Many individuals and groups simply attached themselves to an agency like the Council of National Defense and tried informally to solve whatever problem interested them. Business volunteers rushed rapidly into that twilight zone between public and private status which has so often characterized their relationship with government when the public has placed a premium on community interest. Arch Shaw, the business publicist from Chicago, for example, came to Washington in March, 1917, persuaded the Administration that it needed a committee to conserve labor and scarce commodities, set up a Commercial Economy Board, staffed it with friends from the Harvard Business School, and continued to preach to businessmen the virtues of scientific management he had so long advocated in his writings. Ultimately Shaw's organization was absorbed into the WIB in March, 1918, in a way which shows both the continuity in the Board's development and Baruch's tangential relationship to much of that development. Shaw recalled:

> . . . after Mr. Baruch was appointed he asked me to come into his office, and said that he didn't understand very much about the work of the Commercial

Economy Board, but that the President had incorporated in his letter to him the function that had been performed by the Commercial Economy Board, and said that he would like to transfer that to me.

The fluidity of early mobilization offered a great opportunity for individuals like Shaw to establish their own patterns of behavior in Washington, to transform private practice into public policy. LeRoy Clark, president of a New York wire and cable company, arranged military purchases in those commodities for his industry entirely on his own initiative. He stated later: "I did not have any body whom I headed up to the first year. I was simply a little king in my own dominion. I simply got the stuff." Clark's work finally achieved a formal connection with the WIB in May, 1918, when Clark became a commodity chief for wire and cable. Walter Gifford, the statistician from the American Telephone and Telegraph Company and director of the Council of National Defense, took an interest throughout the spring in trying to formalize business-government relations. In September, 1917, he called on the United States Chamber of Commerce to organize trade associations in every industry, a plan which eventually contributed to the War Service Committees of industry which were to cooperate so closely with the WIB's Commodity Sections.

This was the kind of chaotic environment in which Baruch found himself in the spring of 1917 as the member of the seven-man Advisory Commission in charge of raw materials and metals, and he defined his own sphere of power in much the same way. For one thing he built a strong, personal organization. Baruch was keenly aware of the dictum that knowledge is power, and he created an informal group of experts for himself in subsequent months that extended the scope of his influence. Among those whom he had with him by the summer of 1917 were Leland L. Summers, an engineer-entrepreneur of great expertise in munitions and chemicals; Frederick W. Allen, a former buyer for the Simmons Hardware Company, then employed with Lee, Higginson and Company of Boston; Alexander Legge, International Harvester executive; J. Leonard Replogle, president of a small steel company with a background in sales; and Pope Yeatman, a consulting engineer, who in a Hoover-like odyssey had travelled around the world first with the John Hays Hammond engineering firm and then with the Guggenheim mining organization.

Eugene Meyer, Jr., who also joined this informal group, proved a great asset to Baruch in the early months. A Wall Street investor with whom

Baruch had floated mining stocks in the past, he now helped put Baruch's Washington office in order, and arranged deals for him with acquaintances in the mining trades. Meyer observed years later, "Baruch was a very personal operator. He wasn't a technician in any sense. He wasn't used to dealing with engineering problems. He was good at getting men, backing them and keeping his equanimity."

Baruch's decisions and opinions throughout the war were largely group decisions and group opinions; and his rise to the front ranks was the triumph of a satellite of expertise in which he was a kind of *primus inter pares*. This is not to suggest that Baruch merely accepted passively the advice given to him or that he possessed no ideas of his own. He participated aggressively in the mobilization process and vigorously contributed his suggestions to it. Nor should we regard lightly his ability to gather good men around him, and then maintain their loyalty in the competition for knowledge that marked even so inchoate a bureaucracy as the early American war administration. Yet, nevertheless, it must be emphasized that Baruch operated by means of a group of experts who provided him with expertise and distilled opinion without which his efforts could never have been so effective, or his reach so wide.

The Council of National Defense and the Advisory Commission decided early to harness the volunteerism of business groups. It encouraged the formation of small trade committees to assist civilian and military officials. Baruch stood in the vanguard of this movement. He diligently identified the "local notables" in the raw materials and metals trades under his supervision and acquainted them with the military purchasing departments. Baruch found the informal nature of these early negotiations wholly congenial to his temperament, for he consistently viewed the war effort more in terms of powerful personalities than in terms of evolving institutions. As an independent financier and speculator Baruch had achieved financial success not by moving up through the bureaucratic ranks of business corporations as Walter Gifford and others had done before the war. He had served rather as a broker among them. C. Wright Mills captures this side of Baruch's role in his discussion of the "new entrepreneurs" of the 1930's, men who infused the New Deal's bureaucratic setting with the "go-getting competition"[2] and freewheeling individualism of an earlier day. World War I is certainly a prototype of the New Deal in its dependency upon an emergent bureaucracy (although the Wilson Administration had necessarily to rely more heavily on private agencies), and in the spring of 1917, Baruch and his men charted their paths between private and public bureaus in the same kind of "uneasy but calculated rhythm" that was later to characterize the operations of Tommy Corcoran and the other bureaucratic entrepreneurs of New Deal days.

Baruch's power flowed largely from how others perceived his usefulness. His credibility with the Administration and military services depended on the kind of cooperation he received from the business elite in raw materials and metals. He had to prove to Cabinet officials and military officers that he could deliver his constituency and the goods they produced. Conversely, he had to persuade his committeemen that he spoke for their best interests; that they could gain much by cooperating with him. Baruch was more acutely aware than most of the delicate nature of the web which linked all the parties to economic mobilization, and he was more apprehensive than most lest an unpopular move by any one of them rent a gaping hole in the tenuous network.

Given his dependency on the good will of businessmen both within his personal organization and in the committees under him, it is not surprising that Baruch should regard their suggestions and complaints with great tenderness. His own predilections were reinforced and qualified in turn as he assessed the information and rumors which they passed on to him. He received business complaints about excessive competition among the military purchasing bureaus; about conflict among mobilization agencies; about intransigence among private producers; and about anxiety over the anit-trust laws. He championed a number of measures in response to these inquiries including government intervention to stabilize markets, centralized policy decisions, greater public power for his trade committees (so they could bring all members of an industry into line), and finally, an end to the anti-trust laws. All of these demands which Baruch so persistently advocated reflected the sentiment of businessmen from private industry with whom he was so intimately associated. Anything that made their work more effective helped the war effort and increased his prestige as well.

Business pressure for a rationalized mobilization process lay at the heart of the evolution and operation of the WIB; and more than any other businessman in government in the early months, Baruch spoke for this business drive to bring order out of economic chaos. Businessmen who were close to the economics of the war shared the vision of a strong, centralized, civilian agency which could develop those strategies of direction and protection which industry so sorely needed. It is ironic, of course, that Baruch should carry forward so forcefully a process of formalization and bureau-cratization which would necessarily constrict the free play of his highly personal and individualistic style.

The antipathy which Baruch and his men felt toward the armed services arose from their early experience handling military requirements. The military's adherence to traditional, competitive purchasing patterns disordered the markets they were trying so desperately to stabilize. Their refusal to purchase exclusively through the Raw Materials Committee, and the more than thirty committees of businessmen it represented, undercut the usefulness of Baruch's supply network and reduced his power as well. From the time he first arrived in Washington he urged the War and Navy departments to coordinate their purchasing activities and then go into the market for goods only through his committees. "We endeavored in every way to have both the Army and Navy formulate their programs and advise as to the materials they would require," recalled Leland Summers. "Where we could not get any action from them, we proceeded as best we could to warn the industries that large requirements might be expected and endeavored to have the industries prepare to supply these materials. . . . Many of these industries had representatives who had been abroad and almost all the industries had done business with the Allied purchasing departments, and in most instances understood the necessity even more than the Army or Navy officials."

The tension which marked Baruch's relationship with the services distinguished him from Frank Scott, the Cleveland manufacturer who became the first chairman of the WIB. Scott's own business sense of efficiency was tempered by a long admiration for the military profession and a close tie with his fellow Clevelander, Newton D. Baker. Scott had a more sympathetic and understanding attitude toward the handicaps under which military officers labored, and he struggled anxiously in the early months to help the supply departments overcome their difficulties. Unlike most businessmen in Washington, Scott had no desire to replace traditional military institutions with new governmental structures. He did not want to transfer power and legal responsibility from the military services to a civilian and predominantly business-run organization.

Baruch's immediate experience, on the other hand, supplemented by a strong drive for personal power, caused him to side with the ideas of a Ministry of Munitions which would place all supply functions, including the right to make contracts, in a single-headed, civilian agency. He stood behind this proposal when the Advisory Commission advanced it in March, 1917, and he testified on its behalf during the Congressional inquest into the war program in January, 1918. Indeed, it is often forgotten that the WIB which Baruch led after March, 1918, was not the kind of Munitions Ministry he had in mind. As Beaver and Koistinen have recently reminded us [see note 1], the WIB of March, 1918, represented a compromise for Baruch rather than a complete triumph for his position.

The WIB was formed in late July, 1917, as a subordinate agency of the Council of National Defense with Frank Scott as chairman and Baruch as Commissioner of Raw Materials. In addition to representatives of the Army and Navy, the executive also contained Robert Brookings, Commissioner of Finished Products, Robert S. Lovett, Priority Commissioner, and Hugh A. Frayne, Labor Commissioner. These men were developing functions which later came under Baruch's direction as chairman. Brookings had set up twelve Commodity Sections by January, 1918; Lovett issued the first priority order in September, 1917, and greatly expanded this segment of mobilization in the months thereafter.

It is clear that the WIB was a pluralistic organization, and that in subsequent months the whole proved a great deal weaker than its constituent parts. To summarize its history briefly, we can say that the period from August, 1917, until the spring of 1918, was simply a struggle for survival for the Board. It fought on one side against internal chaos, and on the other against the external cross currents of military, business and Congressional pressures—and the furious pace of war itself. It came near to extinction in the desperate winter of 1917-1918 and reached safety only in the following spring by the personal intervention of President Wilson, and because of the strength of its various units.

It was at this point, in March, 1918, that Baruch was made chairman and associated more closely with presidential power by virtue of his appointment. In his public letter designating Baruch chairman, Wilson gave him a number of duties of a general supervisory nature and assigned him the ultimate decision over all questions affecting the Board except the determination of prices. This subject was placed in a separate Price Fixing Committee. The President directed the Board as a whole to continue the various functions such as conservation which were already under way.

Baruch never achieved supreme power. Wilson's letter to him only symbolized centralization in Washington; it did not create it. The President specifically charged Baruch "To let alone what is being successfully done and interfere as little as possible with the present normal processes of purchase and delivery in the several departments,'' processes which Baruch had been trying to concentrate in one agency since his days on the Advisory Commission. The letter received legislative support when the Overman Act was passed in May, a law which gave the President power to reorganize his war administration at will.

Wilson had no plan for a grand reorganization in mind, however, as his letter to Baruch had already indicated. He simply made the WIB independent of the Council of National Defense. "I am afraid that great things will be expected of me by way of reorganization under the Overman Bill,'' he wrote privately, "because of the large amount of public attention it has attracted. My purposes under it are very modest.'' Even more to the point, the letter and Baruch's new position required operational definition, and in that process the Board's frustrating search for greater authority over the military departments, other war boards, and private business groups continued to the Armistice.

The Board's internal development both before and after March, 1918, added to this persistent instability. The Board continued to find difficult the integration of the conglomeration of functional groups which composed it. It remained perplexed by the process of absorbing personnel and private volunteer business groups into its extended administrative network. In April, 1918, for example, Charles A. Otis, a Cleveland investment banker, set up a Resources and Conservation Section and divided the entire country into twenty-one industrial regions. The Board faced an awesome task in integrating this regional structure into its Washington organization, and it tried to solve it by relying on the administrative arms of local chambers of commerce or regional business groups to cooperate with Otis' central office. Linking the sixty Commodity Sections also proved a problem. Some had originated primarily from business pressures for protection; others had been formed at the initiative of the Board itself. Some existed before March, 1918; others were created at various times thereafter.

Commentators have long been fascinated with the paradoxical nature of the power wielded by the WIB and its chairman. Some writers regard the Board as the apotheosis of concentrated, dictatorial power, and others portray it as the embodiment of democratic cooperation, but the predominant opinion, which is best represented by Clarkson's *Industrial America in the World War*, finds a unique combination of the two. Thus Baruch emerges as both democrat and autocrat; decentralizer and centralizer. This duality stems largely from the efforts of writers during and after the war to unite the ideology and rhetoric of a democracy at war with the imperatives of administrative control and centralized coordination. Many observers felt compelled to prove that America could wage war with the efficiency and effectiveness of an autocracy while it still retained the spirit of a democracy and the values of individual initiative and economic free enterprise associated with it. The semantic and conceptual chaos which has resulted from this attempt has served only to obscure the reality of the war experience. The argument being developed here suggests that a useful way to cut through the rhetorical mists is to concentrate attention on the organizational and structural factors of the process and hopefully observe with some precision the degree of cooperation or compulsion, centralization or decentralization in any one instance.

What deserves emphasis from this perspective is the fact that as a constellation of evolving structures, the WIB pursued a continuous search for external power and internal cohesion. Its very success as an organization, as well as the position of its chairman, depended upon the configuration of external power relationships and internal structural patterns that existed at any one time, around any one decision. Neither the Board nor a single man could control all these factors at once. When the Board managed to achieve a favorable balance among external and internal forces, then Baruch as chairman seemed to possess the power of an autocrat, especially to those who opposed a particular action. We observe this when the Price Fixing Committee and the majority of an industry or its dominant groups lined up behind a proposal, as in the latter stages of steel price fixing. But when the forces were in disarray, either through divison within the Board or strong, united opposition without, then Baruch and the Board could not act, or could do so only cautiously. Then the WIB was perceived more than ever as an agency stressing cooperation and persuasion. Concerned with the conflict of interest problem in July, 1918, for example, Baruch wrote as follows to his Director of Textiles, John Scott: "I advise you to surround yourself with as few men in the trade as possible." He expressed similar sentiments to George Peek when Peek was thinking of getting a man from the rubber industry to take charge of a Commodity Section for rubber in the WIB. But both Scott and Peek and the industries involved disagreed with Baruch, and his advice was consequently ignored. And even if Scott, Peek, and Baruch had been unanimous on this point, they could not have imposed their plan on an unwilling industry. To understand the operation of emergency war boards like the WIB requires attention to the nature of the shifting power relationships between them, and a study of how problems of structure and personnel influenced the exercise of power by a board and its chairman.

In this context it can be argued that the growing stability the WIB achieved in the spring of 1918 had less to do with the appointment of a single chairman (in place of the Board's former executive committee), a point which can be easily exaggerated, and more to do with the gradual elimination of unpredictability in the Board's external relations and with the modification of internal structural problems, processes earlier under way. Only as the military services on the one hand and business groups on the other could be relied upon to cooperate with the Board did it achieve meaningful power. Supplementing this was the increased rationalization and predictability of the Board's own internal operations. In large part, these developments waited upon the process of bureaucratization itself. Cooperation might have been proclaimed by law at an earlier stage, but only an evolutionary movement could bring it to fruition. Volunteerism gave way only slowly to bureaucratization, largely under the administrative pressure of war itself. Nor did the mobilization process ever become fully rationalized. The outcome by November, 1918, is better thought of as "fragmentalized system of bureaus"[3] than an integrated bureaucratic system.

Many of the WIB's functions were initiated well before March, 1918, and required time to develop. The big compromise with the steel industry over prices, the compromise which set the ground rules for all negotiations to follow, occurred in September, 1917, for example. By March, 1918, when Baruch took over and the Price Fixing Committee was set up, relations between the Board and the industry were already partially institutionalized. Thus, while the individual at the center of the administrative network was important after March, 1918, his role was in large degree predetermined by earlier decisions. Ultimately, concentration on the limits of his freedom of action, and not the extent of his power, provides the best perspective for understanding the position of the WIB chairman.

Unlike most of his colleagues on the WIB, Baruch's participation in industrial mobilization and ultimate appointment as chairman was only a continuation of the transformation of the private to the public man. Baruch had been in search of a more satisfying role for himself for some years before America entered the war. As part of his search he moved increasingly toward public life. For one thing he groomed himself for a position as the Wilson Administration's link with American business. In 1916, he offered Wilson advice on how to improve his image among businessmen in that election year, and he suggested the promotion of industrial preparedness as one of his tactics. The year before he had proposed formation of a "Business Man's Commission" to ready the Army for war, and he subsequently recommended its enactment along with anti-dumping legislation and a tariff board (two proposals popular among business groups), as a way by which the Administration could prove its trust and confidence in business.

The two most important bridges by which Baruch crossed over from private to public life, however, were the Democratic Party and industrial preparedness. That he had proved himself a loyal Democrat before the war was of enormous benefit in overcoming later criticism in official circles of his Wall Street background. Baruch threw himself into the preparedness effort in 1915, and made clear his willingness to organize and lead a commission of businessmen to aid the Government in purchasing supplies and arranging transportation for the Army. As a result of his desire for a public post, he carefully avoided the acquisition of munitions stocks which might compromise his future. He observed that to make such investments "might open me to criticism on the part of many small and suspicious people and might affect the great cause I have been working on for so long." Two points deserve note here. First, Baruch's own search for a congenial place in public life and his long association with the problem of industrial mobilization helps to account for his unusually strong identification with the whole concept, for there is no doubt that Baruch personally identified more strongly with the WIB than any of the over seven hundred men who staffed it. It reinforced what would have been a natural tendency as chairman to personalize the agency, to feel responsible not only for what happened to it at the time, but what happened to it in the public memory. Second, Baruch's desire to leave private business separated him from most of his colleagues on the Board who viewed public life as a temporary phenomenon. Baruch was willing to come to Washington early and to stay a long time. He never had to face the anxiety of a Daniel Willard, for example, whose desire for public service conflicted with a deep commitment to private business as president of the Baltimore and Ohio Railroad.

Students of public administration have pointed out that cultural and political myths have a vital place in the governing process. In the United States the "myth" of popular sovereignty possesses particular significance for it encourages a belief that power and authority reside solely with a populace which alone can delegate them to a ruling body. Governors gain legitimacy as they respond to the wishes of the governed. This helps to create a pattern of public administration that relies heavily on the willingness of private groups to comply with official policies, and also reinforces a belief in their ultimate right to shape these policies. Wartime experience provides a generalized model of this historic theme. Agencies like the WIB remained in continuous dialogue with the various interests who moved within their suzerainty.

According to Clarkson and other commentators, the way in which Baruch decentralized his authority was one of the truly noteworthy aspects of a generally noteworthy administration. "Having entrusted power to his chiefs and sections," writes Clarkson, "he kept out of sight. . . . Baruch in the background was the bogey man, the final repository of power, the Zeus of the Olympus of Industry . . . whose portentous potentialities were not to be lightly invoked." Yet, not only did this approach rest on a pervasive assumption about public administration, for decentralization after all permitted the mandatory negotiations between the governor and the governed, but equally important, it was dictated largely by the pressure of circumstances as the WIB adjusted to its bureaucratic and economic environments. Baruch's power was decentralized because it could not be centralized. Baruch refused magnanimously a gift he could never have. He was bounded by power relationships on all sides, with private industries, the military departments and his own internal organization. Like any chief executive, moreover, he had neither the time nor the expertise to contradict his subordinates.[4] Nor did he possess any sanctions to punish Board members, for he in no way determined the length of their stay in Washington. Similarly, the Board as an organization also found itself enmeshed in congeries of power relationships to which it had to make constant adaptations. And as far as its relationship to business is concerned, the theme of decentralization should be regarded largely as a rationalization for the Board's dependency on oligarchies of private economic power. To find in decentralization an object of praise under these circumstances is essentially to find virtue in the Board's recognition of necessity.

Furthermore, to represent the WIB or any other emergency agency as the triumph of popular sovereignty is to mistake the myth for the reality. It was easy and compelling in the patriotic euphoria of war to embellish the hard facts of power and conflict with the rhetoric of volunteerism and cooperation, but the results could be very misleading. Not untypical of the curious outcome is the perception of mobilization retained by Samuel Vauclain, vice-president of the Baldwin Locomotive Works and a dollar-a-year man who arrived early on the Washington scene. "I tell you," reminisced Vauclain in 1920,

> . . . you will go a hell of a long way before you will find men like our Americans and the way they worked together in Washington. There was no other Government that had such a crowd. You can talk about the people in Washington; you can talk about Baker, about Daniels [Josephus Daniels, Secretary of the Navy], about President Wilson; but the people who won this war and the people who managed the war and the people who were responsible for the results in this war are the common people you see walking around here everywhere engaged in all walks of life who had no hand really in the official affairs of Washington. But they regulated it by a certain force that was felt there and the[y] had to act as the people insisted on.

Dispersion of power to the outposts of the WIB did not make Baruch uncomfortable, for he had long believed that private businessmen both inside and outside the Board were sufficiently competent and trustworthy to direct industrial mobilization, and he was more than willing to offer them a full share in decision-making. His earlier attitude toward formation of the industrial committees is suggestive of the path he would later follow. "The plan was one of decentralization. So that, as long as we got cooperation, we left the interior organization and control of the particular industry to the leaders of that industry as represented by these committees." In the same spirit, Baruch rarely interfered with the Board's lower echelons where the most important decision-making occurred. It is no exaggeration to conclude, therefore, that his role vis-à-vis the WIB was essentially to legitimize the actions of his subordinates and to represent the WIB position in the higher councils of government.

That Baruch could appear independent as chairman while being largely dependent on a complex array of forces is testimony to his personal charisma. His own impressive physical presence, his air of infallibility, his confidence, all added to the mystique; his close association with the President and the very imprecise nature of his position as chairman increased it. Even more importantly, however, Baruch benefited as chairman from the widespread desire among Americans to believe that all was well with the war program in Washington, especially after the reorganization of March, 1918. The public wanted to believe that power was now centralized, and above all responsible, in government. The extent to which the public perceived

Baruch as a "dictator" is a measure of its search for security in a period of relentless uncertainty.

By the spring of 1918, then, Baruch had moved from the leading specialist in raw materials and metals to the leading generalizer of industrial mobilization. He had progressed from a practical problem-solver to an abstract public symbol, a position he would strengthen and maintain in the post-war years. Such eminence heightened his sensitivity to the public nature of his duties as chairman and increased his concern for the reputation of an agency with which his own destiny had become so intertwined. Whereas in the spring of 1917, he showed only irritation with the conflict of interest problem, and dismay with the angry Senate progressives who raised the issue, in June, 1918, he took pains to warn Scott and Peek to steer clear of it.

Baruch as symbol performed many useful functions in the later months of the war. Now the administration could argue that not only was efficient mobilization possible, but with such a strong man in charge, the forces of potential evil could be held firmly in check. Baruch as the all-powerful public protector would see that the public interest was not lost in the scramble among selfish business groups. Even though these groups might make decisions through the Board's Commodity Sections, Baruch possessed the final right to veto them if they did not conform to the national interest. The members of the WIB had their own reasons for inflating Baruch's image. With the "Zeus of Industry" in the background, they could bring recalcitrant businessmen into line, secure better cooperation from military officials, and gain a cover for their extra-legal activities.

Baruch as symbol also derived strength from the faith of many Americans that public and private power could be united in the common good, an assumption which provided one of the ideological mainsprings of the entire war effort. Even if the WIB was staffed by businessmen, and even if it relied heavily on the cooperation of private businessmen, the dollar-a-year men, for whom Baruch was the symbol, could be depended upon to place the public interest first.

Symbol and myth are important aspects of any governmental process, and never more so than in the highly charged atmosphere of wartime when the self-conscious manipulation of values becomes integrated into a program for national survival. Yet, important as they are, these attributes of mobilization should not divert our attention from the socio-economic realities which they are designed to serve. That the symbolization of Bernard Baruch should become part of the folklore by which participants in industrial mobilization rationalized their endeavors to the public and to themselves strongly suggests the need to be aware of that gap which lay between the ideal and the reality of their collective enterprise.

Notes

1.   Daniel R. Beaver, *Newton D. Baker and the American War Effort, 1917-1918* (Lincoln, 1966), chs. III, IV. . . . Paul A. C. Koistinen's "The Industrial-Military Complex in Historical Perspective: World War I," *Business History Review*, XLI (Winter, 1967), 378-403, is the best single piece available on the relationship between the military services and the WIB.

2.   C. Wright Mills, *White Collar: The American Middle Classes* (New York, 1956), 94.

3.   Anthony Downs, *Inside Bureaucracy* (Boston, 1967), 15. Or, to quote Robert H. Weibe on the wartime mobilization: "Rather than a bureaucratic order, it was actually a number of separate bureaucracies, barely joined in some areas, openly in conflict elsewhere." . . . *Search for Order*, 300.

4.   Victor Thompson challenges the myth of the "boss" in organization in his study of OPA rationing during World War II. He writes: "Rationing executives gave very few orders because they did not know what to order. The complete and technical information on which rationing actions had to be based was processed only by personnel in the rationing branches." . . . *The Regulatory Process in OPA Rationing* (New York, 1950), 429. This comment applies equally well to Baruch, who coincidentally was referred to as "the Boss" by WIB members.

CONCEPT OF THE ORGANIZATION

By Alfred P. Sloan

At the close of the year 1920 the task before General Motors was reorganization. As things stood, the corporation faced simultaneously an economic slump on the outside and a management crisis on the inside.

The automobile market had nearly vanished and with it our income. Most of our plants and those of the industry were shut down for assembling a small number of cars out of semifinished materials in the plants. We were loaded with high-priced inventory and commitments at the old inflated price level. We were short of cash. We had a confused product line. There was a lack of control and of any means of control in operations and finance, and a lack of adequate information about anything. In short, there was just about as much crisis, inside and outside, as you could wish if you liked that sort of thing.

We were not alone among automobile companies. Others were also in trouble. That was no particular comfort, for economic declines have a way of shaking out the weak ones in business, and we have never yielded to economic pessimism and in times of decline have kept in mind the eventual upturn of the business cycle and the long-range dynamics of growth. Confidence and caution formed my attitude in 1920. We could not control the environment, or predict its changes precisely, but we could seek the flexibility to survive fluctuations in business.

The immediate future of the automobile market was, to say the least, uncertain. However, we believed in the future of the product as well as of the economy. I mention this because confidence is an important element in business; it may on occasion make the difference between one man's success and another's failure. It was our settled belief that the automobile was then in the course of creating a new transportation system in the United States, and that the market for it therefore was bound in time to return with strength. We stated this in the annual report for 1920, along with a review of the progress of the automobile industry up to that time; and gave our attention to the problems at hand.

Before anything else, we had to have a new president to take the place of Mr. Durant. I did not have to think twice to decide who I thought should be the new president. I knew Pierre S. du Pont in a personal way only slightly. But it was apparent that he was the one individual in General Motors who had the prestige and respect that could give confidence to the organization, to the public, and to the banks, and whose presence could arrest the demoralization that was taking place. He was chairman of the corporation, and he represented the largest shareholder interest. He had shown his capability for business leadership in the Du Pont Company and in his financial association with General Motors. The only other man in the corporation who might have been considered for president was John J. Raskob, Mr. du Pont's close and influential adviser and chairman of General Motors' Finance Committee.

Mr. Raskob's Alger-boy career has been told many times. I do not personally know his early years, but the story is that he went to work as a typist and secretary to Pierre S. du Pont around the turn of the century. Mr. du Pont was impressed with his lively imagination and financial capabilities. As Mr. du Pont moved up to be treasurer of the Du Pont Company, Mr. Raskob moved with him as his assistant and adviser, succeeding him as treasurer of the Du Pont Company. Mr. du Pont and Mr. Raskob were very close business associates for many years. But they did not at all have the same kind of temperaments.

Mr. Raskob was brilliant and imaginative where Mr. du Pont was steady and conservative. Mr. du Pont was tall, well built, and reticent. He would not put himself forward. Mr. Raskob was short and not reticent. He was very friendly, a fine fellow to talk with, and a man of big ideas. I remember his often coming into my office with an idea and wanting to get it into action by waving a magic wand; he would want the whole organization to come to a meeting right off. His faults, if they should be called that, were those that go with an aggressive, impatient intelligence—the very thing that made him good. Not many men foresaw the future of the automobile industry as well as he did.

Both Mr. Raskob and Mr. du Pont thus had their strong points, but on balance it seemed to all of us who were concerned that Mr. du Pont was the man we needed. No one else at the time could qualify in so many particulars.

There was only one drawback. Mr. du Pont had no intimate knowledge of the automobile business. I happen to be one of the old school who thinks that a knowledge of the business is essential to a successful administration. But in the situation that existed then, the immediate needs for a general constructive leadership in administration and a re-establishment of confidence in the future were more important than intimate knowledge of the business. Other men were available or could be obtained who had that knowledge. Hence I urged in the informal discussions that took place that Mr. du Pont was the logical choice.

Not that my urging had much or anything to do with the decision. Other persons were more influential, and Mr. du Pont had reasons of his own for allowing himself to be persuaded to accept management as well as financial responsibility in General Motors. The Du Pont Company had taken over the Durant stock in the crisis, and by 1921 would increase its ownership to about 36 per cent of the total common stock of the General Motors Corporation. Mr. du Pont had an obvious responsibility in the situation. He later said: "I was very loath to accept the position [of president]. I had recently retired from business, but I said that I would do whatever they thought best, and I was put in as president with the distinct understanding that I was only to stay there until a better posted man could be found to take the job."

When Pierre S. du Pont accepted the presidency, Mr. Raskob continued as chairman of the Finance Committee and for several years served as the public spokesman of the corporation. J. Amory Haskell and I became Mr. du

Pont's right- and left-hand men, so to speak. In a letter distributed at the board meeting of December 30, 1920, Mr. du Pont stated that Mr. Haskell and I were "competent to settle executive questions, acting for the Executive Committee between meetings, and for the President in his absence." The Executive Committee was re-formed and reduced temporarily to four men: Mr. du Pont, Mr. Raskob, Mr. Haskell, and myself. This new committee took charge of operating policy and of a certain amount of administration as well. The old Executive Committee, made up in large part of division managers, was made an advisory operations committee.

These changes, though of an emergency nature, coincided with a sweeping reorganization of General Motors, going to the roots of industrial philosophy. The language of corporation minutes is laconic, but the consequences can be far reaching, as they were in this instance. The first business of the new administration, taken up at the last meeting of the old Executive Committee on December 30, 1920, is recorded as follows:

> The President submitted for the consideration of the Executive Committee a new Organization Chart of our Corporation together with an explanatory letter. and same was discussed at length.

This was unanimously approved and ordered sent to the board of directors, who also approved it. It was made effective on January 3, 1921.

The plan thus adopted was with modifications the one I had drafted about a year earlier under the title "Organization Study" and submitted to Mr. Durant for his consideration. Since this plan has become the foundation of management policy in the modern General Motors—an expression of the basic principles of "decentralization" that govern its organization—and is said thereby to have had some influence on large-scale industrial enterprise in the United States, I shall say something here about its origin and substance.

First as to its origin. It has been supposed by some students that General Motors took its decentralized type of organization from the Du Pont Company, as a result of the relationship of the two companies. Both managements at that time were in fact independently concerned with problems of organization, and both eventually adopted principles of decentralization. But they proceeded from opposite poles. The Du Pont Company then was evolving from a centralized type of organization, common in the early days of American industry, while General Motors was emerging from almost total decentralization. General Motors needed to find a principle of co-ordination without losing the advantages of decentralization. These different backgrounds of the General Motors Corporation and the Du Pont Company, together with the differences in nature and marketing of the products of the two enterprises, made it impractical for the same model of organization to serve properly for both of them.

Du Pont executives had been working on their own reorganization problem for a couple of years; but it was not until nine months after General Motors adopted its plan of organization that the Du Pont Company also adopted a decentralized scheme. The two plans did not share their particulars, but only the management philosophy of decentralization.

The two types of operating problems, one arising from too much centralization (Du Pont) and the other from too much decentralization (General Motors), were soon to be met by many large American manufacturing enterprises. One reason, perhaps, why General Motors and Du Pont met and answered their organization problems early was that in 1920 and 1921 their operating problems were larger and more complex than those of most contemporary American industrial enterprises. I believe it is also true that we recognized the problems and thought more in terms of organizational principles and philosophies than did most businessmen of that time. The principles of organization got more attention among us than they did then in the universities. If what follows seems academic, I assure you that we did not think it so.

I wrote the "Organization Study" for General Motors as a possible solution for the specific problems created by the expansion of the corporation after World War I. I cannot, of course, say for sure how much of my thought on management came from contacts with my associates. Ideas, I imagine, are seldom, if ever, wholly original, but so far as I am aware, this study came out of my experience in Hyatt, United Motors, and General Motors. I had not been much of a book reader, and if I had been, I understand that I would not have found much in that line in those days to help; and I had no military experience. In the course of my twenty years or so at Hyatt I learned to operate a single industrial unit, relatively small in size and with one basic product. This unit contained the elementary functions of a manufacturing business: engineering, production, sales, and finance. But I had only a small board of directors, no executive committee, and no organization problems of the General Motors type.

In United Motors I met for the first time the problems of operating a multiple-unit organization with different products made by separate divisions. All that held United Motors together in its beginning was the concept of automotive parts and accessories. We made horns, radiators, bearings, rims, and the like, and we sold them to both automobile producers and the public. Certain limited areas of possible co-ordination presented themselves; for example, the servicing of the numerous small products made by the different divisions. Separate service agencies for such small items were uneconomic. I therefore set up a single, nationwide organization called United Motors Service, Inc., on October 14, 1916, to represent the divisions, with stations in twenty-odd large cities and several hundred dealers at other points. The divisions naturally resisted this move for a while, but I persuaded them of the need for it, and for the first time learned something about getting decentralized management to yield some of its functions for the common good. The service organization is still operating in General Motors and has grown along with the business as a whole. I considered setting up a common laboratory for research, and most likely would have done so if we had not entered General Motors. I did establish in United Motors a unity of business purpose through the principle of return on investment. By placing each division on its own profit-making basis, I gave the general office a common measure of efficiency with which to judge the contribution of each division to the whole. In this connection I devised a system of standard accounting which Albert Bradley, long-time chief financial officer of General Motors, later was kind enough to say was pretty good for a layman.

In the great expansion in General Motors between 1918 and 1920, I had been struck by the disparity between substance and form: plenty of substance and little form. I became convinced that the corporation could not continue to grow and survive unless it was better organized, and it was apparent that no one was giving the subject the attention it needed.

An example, close to home for me: When the United Motors group was brought into the General Motors Corporation in late 1918, I found that if I followed the prevailing practice of inter-corporate relations I would no longer be able to determine the rate of return on investment for these accessory divisions individually or as a group. This would necessarily mean that I would lose some degree of managerial control over my area of operations. At that time, material within General Motors was passing from one operating division to another at cost, or at cost plus some predetermined percentage. My divisions in the United Motors Corporation had sold both to outside customers and to their allied divisions at the market price. I knew that I operated a profit-making group, and I wished to continue to be able to demonstrate this performance to the general management, rather than to have my operating results on interdivisional business swallowed up in the extra bookkeeping profits of some other division. It was a case of keeping the information clear.

It was not, however, a matter of interest to me only with respect to my divisions, since as a member of the Executive Committee, I was a kind of general executive and so had begun to think from the corporate viewpoint. The important thing was that no one knew how much was being contributed—plus or minus—by each division to the common good of the corporation. And since, therefore, no one knew, or could prove, where the efficiencies and inefficiencies lay, there was no objective basis for the allocation of new investment. This was one of the difficulties with the expansion program of that time. It was natural for the divisions to compete for investment funds, but it was irrational for the general officers of the corporation not to know where to place the money to best advantage. In the absence of objectivity it was not surprising that there was a lack of real agreement among the general officers. Furthermore, some of them had no broad outlook, and used their membership on the Executive Committee mainly to advance the interests of their respective divisions. . . .

At the end of November 1920, when Mr. Durant went out and Mr. du Pont became president, the new administration needed a scheme of organization immediately. Mr. Durant had been able to operate in his own way, as the saying goes, "by the seat of his pants." The new administration was made up of men with very different ideas about business administration. They desired a highly rational and objective mode of operation. The "Organization Study" served the purpose and, as I have related, it was officially adopted, with some revision, as basic corporation policy.

The study was primitive by comparison with present-day knowledge of management. And it was written from the point of view of presenting something that I thought would be acceptable to Mr. Durant. So it was not without constraints. It began as follows:

> The object of this study is to suggest an organization for the General Motors Corporation which will definitely place the line of authority throughout its extensive operations as well as to co-ordinate each branch of its service, at the same time destroying none of the effectiveness with which its work had heretofore been conducted.

The basis upon which this study has been made is founded upon two principles, which are stated as follows:—

1. The responsibility attached to the chief executive of each operation shall in no way be limited. Each such organization headed by its chief executive shall be complete in every necessary function and enable[d] to exercise its full initiative and logical development.

2. Certain central organization functions are absolutely essential to the logical development and proper control of the Corporation's activities.

This does not need much interpretation. It asks first for a line of authority, co-ordination, and the retention of the effectiveness of the then prevailing total decentralization. But looking back on the text of the two basic principles, after all these years, I am amused to see that the language is contradictory, and that its very contradiction is the crux of the matter. In point 1, I maximize decentralization of divisional operations in the words "shall in no way be limited." In point 2, I proceed to limit the responsibility of divisional chief executives in the expression "proper control." The language of organization has always suffered some want of words to express the true facts and circumstances of human interaction. One usually asserts one aspect or another of it at different times, such as the absolute independence of the part, and again the need of co-ordination, and again the concept of the whole with a guiding center. Interaction, however, is the thing, and with some reservation about the language and details, I still stand on the fundamentals of what I wrote in the study. Its basic principles are in touch with the central problem of management as I have known it to this day.

The next point in the study was how to carry this philosophy into action. I wrote:

Having established the above principles as fundamental, and it is believed that all interests within the Corporation agree as to such principles, the definite objects which it is hoped to attain by this study, are enumerated as follows:—

1. To definitely determine the functioning of the various divisions constituting the Corporation's activities, not only in relation to one another, but in relation to the central organization.

That was a big chew, but it is correct. If you can describe the functions of the parts and the whole, you have laid out a complete working organization, for by implication the apportionment of responsibility for decisions at various levels is contained in the description.

I continued with the second objective:

2. To determine the status of the central organization and to co-ordinate the operation of that central organization with the Corporation as a whole to the end that it will perform its necessary and logical place.

This is a restatement of the first point, but in reverse—that is, looking from the top down.

The third objective:

3. To centralize the control of all the executive functions of the Corporation in the President as its chief executive officer.

Decentralization or not, an industrial corporation is not the mildest form of organization in society. I never minimized the administrative power of the chief executive officer in principle when I occupied that position. I simply exercised that power with discretion; I got better results by selling my ideas than by telling people what to do. Yet the power to act must be located in the chief executive officer.

The fourth and fifth points speak for themselves:

4. To limit as far as practical the number of executives reporting directly to the President, the object being to enable the President to better guide the broad policies of the Corporation without coming in contact with problems that may safely be entrusted to executives of less importance.
5. To provide means within each executive branch whereby all other executive branches are represented in an advisory way to the end that the development of each branch will be along lines constructive to the Corporation as a whole.

In brief, the study presented a specific structure for the corporation as it existed at that time. It recognized the form of the divisions, each of which was a self-contained group of functions (engineering, production, sales, and the like). It grouped the divisions, according to like activities, and, as I said in my letter to Mr. du Pont, proposed to place an executive in charge of each group. The plan provided for advisory staffs, which would be without line authority. It provided for a financial staff. It distinguished policy from administration of policy, and specified the location of each in the structure. It expressed in its way the concept that was later to be formulated as decentralized operations with co-ordinated control. *

* See chart on page 130.

The principles of organization in the study thus initiated for the modern General Motors the trend toward a happy medium in industrial organization between the extremes of pure centralization and pure decentralization. The new policy asked that the corporation neither remain as it was, a weak form of organization, nor become a rigid, command form. . . .

GENERAL MOTORS CORPORATION

STOCKHOLDERS

DIRECTORS

PRESIDENT

FINANCE COMMITTEE · EXECUTIVE COMMITTEE

Appropriations Comm.

Secretary & Assistants to V.P.

VICE PRESIDENT (2) IN CHARGE OF OPERATIONS

ADVISORY STAFF COMM.

LEGAL DEPT.

OPERATIONS COMMITTEE

V.P. · V.P.

GENL ADVISORY STAFF

Assistants to V.P. in Charge of Staff

Staff Secretary

- Plant Eng. Pwr. Ho. Constn. & Operation — Real Estate — Organization Line & Staff
- Design & Research Eng. — General Office Bldg. Operations — Inter Division Schedules
- Advisory Purchasing Dept. — Cafeteria & Club Ho. Operations — Durant Bldg. Corp.
- Patent Dept. — Housings Operations — Development Dept.
- Per. Exec. & Clerical Supply — Service Division — Per. Serv., Welfare, Med. & San. Serv.
- Traffic & Tariffs — Mfg. Plant Layout Equipt. — Sales Analysis & Develop.

FINANCIAL STAFF

VICE PRESIDENT CHAIRMAN FINANCE COMMITTEE

VICE PRESIDENT IN CHARGE OF FINANCES

Secretary & Assistants to V.P.

Secretary to V.P.

VICE PRESIDENT GENERAL MOTORS ACCEPTANCE CORP.

AFFILIATED COMPANIES AS TO FINANCES

STOCKHOLDERS SERVICE DIV.

INSURANCE & TAXES

Assistants to V.P.

Treasurer — Asst. Treas. — Asst. Treas.

- Emp. Sav. & Invest. Fund
- Stock Trans. & Dividends
- Employees Bonus
- Auditing Dept.
- Branch Office New York
- Federal Taxes
- Franchise & Excise Taxes
- Statistical Dept.
- Accounting Dept.
  - General Account.
  - Cost Account.
  - Appropriation Account.

OPERATIONS STAFF

Chevrolet Div. — Sheridan Motor Car Div. — Canadian Car Div. — Olds Motor Div. — Gen. Motors Truck Div. — Buick Div. — Gen. Motors Export Co. — Inter Company Parts Div. — Oakland Div. — Cadillac Div. — Accessory Div. — Affiliated Co.'s as to Oper.

Mgr. Production — Mgr. Sales

- Chevrolet Motor & Axle Div.
- Chevrolet Motor Co. of N.Y.
- Chevrolet Motor Co. of St. Louis
- St. Louis Mfg. Corp.
- Chevrolet Motor Co. Bay City
- Chevrolet Motor Co. Calif.
- Chevrolet Motor Co. Texas
- Toledo Chevrolet Co.
- Samson Tractor Div.
- Samson Tractor of Canada Div.
- Olds Motor Wks. of Canada Div.
- McLaughlin Motor Car Div.
- Chevrolet Motor Co. of Can. Div.
- Scripps Booth Corp.
- Muncie Parts Section
- Muncie Products Co.
- Central Parts Section
- Saginaw Parts Section
- Central Gear Div.
- Canadian Products Co.
- Central Foundry Co.
- McLaughlin Crankshaft Div., Lansing
- Michigan Crankshaft Div., Saginaw
- Saginaw Products Co.
- Northway Motor Co.
- Central Forge Div.
- Central Axle Div.
- Lansing Axle Div.
- Saginaw Malleable Co.
- Hyatt Bearings Div.
- Jackson Steel Products Div.
- Harrison Radiator Corp.
- New Departure Mfg. Co.
- Delco Light Co.
- Champion Ignition Co.
- Remy Electric Div.
- Dayton Eng. Lab. Co.
- Lancaster Products Co.
- United Motors Service Corp.
- Klaxon Co.
- Frigidaire Corp.
- Dayton Wright Co.

HERBERT HOOVER,
THE COMMERCE SECRETARIAT,
AND THE VISION OF
AN "ASSOCIATIVE STATE," 1921-1928

By Ellis W. Hawley

In recent years, the traditional image of American governmental activity in the 1920s has been substantially altered. Delving beneath the older stereotypes of "normalcy" and "retrenchment," scholars have found unsuspected survivals of progressivism, a growing federal bureaucracy that tried to use as well as serve business groups, and an incipient form of "indicative planning" based on corporatist rather than classical economics. In many respects, they have concluded, the period should be viewed as the beginning of the "modern era," not as a reversion to past patterns or as a frivolous and wasted interlude between progressivism and the New Deal. And for some, the 1920s has more current relevance than the decades that followed, particularly in efforts to balance technological needs with America's individualistic heritage, build an international community with-

Reprinted with permission from *Journal of American History*, 61 (June 1974). Copyright © 1974 by the Organization of American Historians.

out policing the world, and work out bureaucratic arrangements that would nourish individual, community, and private effort rather than supplant them.

Thus far, however, partly because key collections were long closed, scholars have not examined in detail the most rapidly expanding sector of New Era governmental activity, that connected with Herbert Hoover's transformation and expansion of the commerce secretariat. Nor has there been much study of the goals and ideology involved in his activities, of how he could reconcile his burgeoning bureaucratic domain with his deep distrust of "big government," or of how he hoped, through grafting corporatist and technocratic visions on to a base of nineteenth-century individualism, to build a superior socioeconomic order. Fuller study of such matters seems crucial to an understanding of Hoover and the New Era, and it is now possible with the aid of recently opened materials in the Hoover Papers to shed some further light on them.

Hoover in 1921 saw himself as the protagonist of a new and superior synthesis between the old industrialism and the new, a way whereby America could benefit from scientific rationalization and social engineering without sacrificing the energy and creativity inherent in individual effort, "grassroots" involvement, and private enterprise. Such a synthesis, he argued, would make the "American system" superior to any other, particularly in its ability to raise living standards, humanize industrial relationships, and integrate conflicting social elements into a harmonious community of interests. And the key to its achievement, he had concluded on the basis of his wartime, engineering, and personal experience, lay in the development and proper use of cooperative institutions, particularly trade associations, professional societies, and similar organizations among farmers and laborers. These, Hoover and other associationists believed, would form a type of private government, one that would meet the need for national reform, greater stability, and steady expansion, yet avoid the evils long associated with "capital consolidations," politicized cartels, and governmental bureaucracies. Unlike the earlier trusts, these newer institutions would preserve and work through individual units, committing them voluntarily to service, efficiency, and ethical behavior and developing for them a new and enlightened leadership capable of seeing the larger picture. And unlike governmental bureaus, they would be flexible, responsive, and productive, built on service and efficiency rather than coercion and politics, and staffed by men of expertise and vision, not by self-serving politicians or petty drudges.

To some extent, too, Hoover believed that the components of this associational order were evolving naturally and had been for the past thirty years. Within the womb of the old industrialism there had developed not only the associational structures around which the new system was taking shape but also the moral awakening, the commitment to science and productivity, and the mutuality of interests that would convert such structures into instruments of social progress. As these developments continued, the new private government would take shape on its own and bring with it the superior synthesis that Hoover envisioned. Yet there was no assurance that it would do so, or that it would develop fast enough to meet national needs. There was, so Hoover also believed, a need to manage, speed up, and guide this evolutionary process, both to help realize its full potentialities and to prevent those impatient with persisting social and economic problems from turning to undesirable statist solutions. And to meet this need, he envisioned an "associative state,"[1] tied to, cooperating with, and helping to develop and guide the new associational order. Paradoxically, he saw himself both as an anti-statist and as an ardent champion of one form of positive government and national planning.

For two reasons, however, Hoover did not regard these positions as being inconsistent. In the first place, the structure and methods of the associative state would be different, thus enabling it to escape the torpor and rigidity characteristic of most governmental structures. In so far as possible, it would function through promotional conferences, expert inquiries, and cooperating committees, not through public enterprise, legal coercion, or arbitrary controls, and like the private groupings to which it would be tied, it would be flexible, responsive, and productive, staffed by men of talent, vision, and expertise, and committed to nourishing individualism and local initiative rather than supplanting them. In the second place, the associative state would be needed only during a transitional phase. Like the Marxist state or those posited by some European corporatists, it would theoretically serve as midwife to a new, non-statist commonwealth and, having performed this function, would either wither away or revert to the status of umpire, caretaker, and symbol of unity.

Hoover's New Era activities were in part efforts to implement his vision of an associative state. For him the vision defined the difference between constructive and undesirable activism. Although some of what he did can be attributed to his ambivalent personality, his adjustment of an engineering approach to political realities, his recognition of new technological problems, or his accommodation of business groups desirous of governmental services but reluctant to give up their own autonomy, many of his activities flowed logically from his postwar plans for associative "reconstruction" and particularly from his conviction that the commerce department, if properly expanded and transformed, could become the central agency for implementing such plans. When offered more prestigious positions, he chose and stuck with the secretaryship of commerce, chiefly he implied, because no other department had the same potential for guiding the associational activities that were transforming American society. With Harding's assurance that he could remake the department and have a voice in labor, farm, financial, and foreign policies, he moved into it, as Arthur Schlesinger, Jr., says, much "as he might have into a bankrupt mining company a decade earlier," determined to convert a collection of miscellaneous technical bureaus into the governmental apparatus needed for an assured transition to an American utopia.

Hoover must have realized at the outset that such a task was not likely to be easy. He was beginning with one of the smallest and newest of the federal departments, one whose appropriations for 1920, exclusive of those for the census, had totaled only $17,000,000. He could hardly be encouraged by the inability of his predecessor, William Redfield, to salvage some of the cooperative machinery established during the war. And his plans were bound to collide with the strong sentiment for governmental retrenchment, the popular disdain for overly ambitious bureaucrats, and the entrenched positions of established bureaucratic domains. Yet there was also ground for optimism. Hoover's vision was an attractive and timely one, admirably suited to make him the "old order's candidate for ushering in the new"; and against the obstacles in his path, he could pit his immense prestige and formidable administrative talents, his following of dedicated personal associates, and his extensive ties to like-minded men in the worlds of business, engineering, journalism, scholarship, and social uplift.

Before long, too, by drawing on a variety of recommendations, Hoover was mapping out specific plans for departmental expansion. As visualized, his agency would eventually consist of three great divisions: one for industry, one for trade, and one for transportation and communication. Into the first, in addition to his own bureaus of fisheries and standards, should go the interior department's Bureau of Mines and patent office, plus a new Bureau of Federal Statistics, formed by joining the Census Bureau with the statistical programs of several other departments. Into the trade division, as adjuncts to his Bureau of Foreign and Domestic Commerce, should go the Bureau of Markets from the agriculture department, the foreign trade service and economic consulates from the state department, the Latin-American activities of the treasury department, and the research work of the Federal Trade Commission. And into the transportation and communication division, along with the lighthouse, steamboat, and mapping services, should go a part of the Coast Guard, the navy's Observatory, Hydrographic Office, and Steamboat Movement Service, the army's Lake Survey and Harbor Supervisors, the Panama Canal, the inland waterways, the shipping subsidies, and a new Bureau of Aeronautics. In essence, the commerce department was to become a department of economic development and management; other agencies would still be responsible for special sectors of the economy, but commerce would serve as a general policy coordinator. In effect, as S. Parker Gilbert once put it, Hoover would be "Under-Secretary of all other departments."

Reaching out from this expanded governmental base would be an extensive net of promotional activities, cooperating committees, and other ad hoc structures, all tied to private groupings and associations and all designed to energize private or local collectivities and guide them toward constructive solutions to national problems. From Hoover's standpoint, governmental reorganization was intended not only to reduce wasteful overlap and unwise expenditures, but also to provide the necessary base on which an associative state could be built. Hand in hand with his drive for new jurisdictional boundaries went a series of conferences, negotiations, and "missionary activities," designed to forge cooperative links with the "community at large" and develop the associational apparatus that could speed up and manage socioeconomic progress. Assuming top priority in 1921 were the problems of housing, unemployment, industrial waste, stagnating foreign trade, and inadequate business planning; and in each of these problem areas, Hoover and his deputies were soon moving to resurrect and expand the voluntaristic-cooperationist side of the war government.

Initially, Hoover hoped to secure the necessary jurisdictional base through the general executive reorganization that Wilson had advocated and Harding continued to push. Such action seemed thoroughly consistent with the demands for economy and efficiency, and since Hoover was serving as adviser to Walter F. Brown, chairman of the reorganization committee, he was optimistic about getting the agencies he needed. Once involved, however, he quickly learned that proposals of this sort could generate resistance of the most intense kind. Agricultural leaders were already bitter about Hoover's wartime policies and quickly expressed their determined opposition to his acquiring either the Bureau of Markets or recognized jurisdiction over the marketing of farm goods. State department officials, long irritated about the pretensions of commerce, were determined to expand their jurisdiction over economic activities abroad, not see it whittled away by inexperienced rivals. Labor leaders regarded Harding's proposed department of welfare as a scheme to dismantle the Department of Labor and charged that Hoover's designs on the Bureau of Labor Statistics were part of this broader plot. Governmental statisticians, at least in Hoover's view, reacted emotionally, turning their bureaus into virtual "hornets' nests." Naval leaders, to his surprise and resentment, lobbied against turning anything over to the "politicians." And conservationists, especially those attached to the Forest Service, protested strongly about the proposed transfers to Albert Fall's Department of the Interior. Against the forces of scientific rationality, Hoover came to feel, had gathered an alliance of "vested officials," "paid propagandists," and selfish interest groups, and these enemies of progress had created a "confusing fog of opposition."

Whether right or not, Hoover was unable to get a reorganization measure through, either by going along with interdepartmental bargaining and lowering his own sights or by urging that scientific experts hand a plan "down from on high." In the face of conflicting pressures, Congress simply refused to act. And its failure to do so meant that jurisdictional expansion by the commerce secretariat would come not through some master coup, but through the slower processes of pushing established bureaus into "power vacuums," adding new structures through special laws or administrative innovations, making deals with or raids on other agencies, and carving out "spheres of influence" inhabited by cooperative satellites. By the time he had given up on general reorganization, Hoover was moving along all these lines, and as his operations gained momentum he was expanding slowly both his departmental boundaries and the network of associational activities to which the commerce department was tied.

Under his tutelage, for example, the Bureau of Foreign and Domestic Commerce was reorganized along commodity lines, staffed with men from the export industries themselves, and made the center of an associational system for gathering and disseminating commercial intelligence, dealing with foreign governments and cartels, and organizing trade and investment activities into a rational and integrated set of operations. Tied to and working in conjunction with each commodity division was a cooperating industrial committee, chosen typically by the trade and export associations in the field; and ideally it was these cooperating private groups that would build and develop the steadily expanding market needed for permanent prosperity. The state would act only as a clearing house, inspirational force, and protector of international rights, not as a trader, investor, or detailed regulator. And it was for the former functions that Hoover won larger and larger appropriations, set up one appendage after another, and kept expanding his network of trade commissioners, researchers, and public relations men. By 1925 the bureau's appropriations had risen 140 percent; services rendered, so it claimed, were up 600 percent; and in six months, according to its energetic director, Julius Klein, it had issued "more than enough" press releases "to put 18 columns of type up and down the Washington Monument."

In attempting to expand its jurisdictional boundaries, the Bureau of Foreign and Domestic Commerce was less successful. In the areas of economic diplomacy and international finance, its role remained a limited one, thus hampering Hoover's efforts to guide overseas investment into proper channels. Nor did it ever succeed in taking over the foreign economic services of the Department of State and the Department of Agriculture. Yet its domain did expand. Its new financial division offered advice on foreign loans and investments; its research and public relations arms assumed responsibility for a new program of domestic market analysis, a massive publicity campaign against foreign "monopolies," and a world-wide search for independent sources of raw materials; and its foreign service, to the accompaniment of much friction with the state department, kept expanding and strengthening its intelligence apparatus. In 1922, in return for giving suitable credit to consular officials, it secured the right to request information from them through the diplomatic head of mission. In 1924, it secured an executive order directing all representatives abroad to meet and exchange information at least every two weeks. In 1927, it was given permanent legislative status. And repeatedly, when state department critics struck back by charging it with wasteful duplication and diplomatic bungling, the bureau was able to defend successfully its claim to special expertise.

At the same time, the Bureau of Standards was also doubling its personnel, expanding its jurisdiction, and transforming itself from a "research laboratory for governmental departments" into a sponsor of associational reform, particularly in the areas of research, housing, and industrial efficiency. By the mid-1920s, it was cooperating with some forty private associations to develop new and better products. Its Building and Housing Division, launched in 1921, had become the nucleus of a network of cooperating committees and study groups, each tied to the major trade and professional associations in the housing field and each trying, through organized cooperation and educational campaigns, to overcome the "bottlenecks" that held back "modernization" and "rationalization." The bureau's Division of Simplified Practice, inspired by the war experience and the *Waste in Industry* study of the Federated American Engineering Societies, was directing a similar effort to reduce industrial waste, one that functioned through standardization conferences and implemented its "simplified practice recommendations" through associational cooperation. And attached to the bureau, as further agencies of what its publicists were calling the "new conservation," were such quasipublic organs as the national committees on wood and metals utilization, the one to conserve lumber and find new uses for lumber by-products, the other to reduce wastage of metals. Taken together, so the Hooverites claimed, the new activities had the potentiality for raising living standards 20 to 30 percent.

Similar growth and transformation also occurred in the Census Bureau, which, in spite of Hoover's inability to carry out his original plans, added new services to facilitate business planning and tied these to private associational activities. In July, 1921, acting in consultation with business leaders and statistical experts, the bureau launched the *Survey of Current Business*, designed to publish data on current production, prices, and inventories, most of it supplied by cooperating trade associations. In 1922, when antitrust action threatened private statistical exchanges, it spouted a special appendage, which, for a time, mailed out data submitted by private groups. Simultaneously, it added more and more data-gathering programs for particular industries, and after 1925, when new court rulings again sanctioned private exchanges, it remained the focal point for promoting them. From a bureau expected to lapse into inactivity during intercensal periods, it had transformed itself into a dynamic sponsor of the "new competition," which, by encouraging cooperative data gathering and educating business decision makers to respond properly, was supposed to stabilize the economy without sacrificing competitive incentives and safeguards.

Building on existing bureaus, Hoover was moving to implement his original designs, both of an expanded departmental jurisdiction and of an associational bureaucratic structure. And while a few critics charged that he was fostering either "big government" or "monopoly," he and his publicists were highly successful in bucking the sentiment for "economy in government" and selling their programs to the President, the budget bureau, the appropriations committees, the business community, and the general public. Their bureaucracy, they kept saying, was "different." Unlike the typical variety, with its tax eating propensities, red tape, and rigid controls, this new species paid returns on the money "invested" by generating new expansion and new revenue, delivered efficient and business-like service, and functioned under "responsive" and competent men, who understood national needs and "cooperated" instead of "meddling." Besides, its whole purpose differed. By building industrial self-government and thus reducing the need for governmental controls, it was actually checking the whole movement toward big government; and by fostering and nourishing the grassroots activities of private groups and local communities, it was promoting democratic decentralization rather than bureaucratic centralism.

The same rationale also helped Hoover to become the administrative beneficiary of new laws. In 1924, for example, when he finally secured a measure to regulate the Alaskan salmon industry, few questioned his assumption that the Bureau of Fisheries should administer it or that cooperative arrangements with the canners' association should remain a central feature of regulatory practice. In 1926, when his long campaign for aviation aids and controls led to the Air Commerce Act, he was able to add an Aeronautics Branch with its own outcropping of cooperative committees and associations. And in 1927, after the courts had upset his informal controls in the radio industry, a new law was passed, creating a commission to allocate frequencies but entrusting all administration to his Radio Division and permitting private associations to implement large areas of "self-regulation." In these special areas, special because of the public nature of the industries involved and the unquestioned federal jurisdiction, Hoover was ready to establish some measure of legal coercion, at least temporarily. But still, he argued, these governmental ground rules should provide the base for a developing associationalism, not a substitute for it. And this was the approach adopted by his new and rapidly expanding regulatory arms.

In addition, through a process of bargaining with and pressuring other departments, Hoover was able to capture some of the agencies that he had tried but failed to capture through a general governmental reorganization. Negotiations with the treasury department brought him the Bureau of Customs Statistics, transferred in 1923, plus effective control of the Inter-

American High Commission, designed to promote trade in Latin-America. Negotiations with the agriculture department garnered the seismology section of the Weather Bureau, plus the statistical programs for the wool, naval stores, meat packing, and farm machinery industries. And in his greatest coup, negotiations with the interior department produced executive orders in 1925 giving him the Patent Office, the Geological Survey's work in mineral statistics, and the Bureau of Mines.

Most of these new accessions were tied to Hoover's associational reform efforts. Those from the treasury department became part of the Bureau of Foreign and Domestic Commerce's program of trade expansion through associational activities. The statistical programs from the agriculture department became part of the broader effort to stabilize the economy through decentralized business planning. And the mineral agencies from the interior department finally provided a departmental base for Hoover's efforts to stabilize the coal and oil industries, areas in which he had early staked a claim of special competence and received special grants of authority from Harding and Coolidge. By 1925 he and his lieutenants had been largely responsible for an associational program intended to reduce intermittent production in the coal industry, for setting up and administering an emergency distribution program during the coal strike of 1922, for directing the subsequent studies of the United States Coal Commission, and for guiding the work of the Federal Oil Conservation Board. Through extra-departmental and ad hoc bodies, they had largely taken over the whole field of mineral conservation and management, relegating the established interior agencies to a secondary role; the annexations of 1925 were in part merely a recognition of this *fait accompli*.

At the same time, in further efforts to implement his original plans, Hoover was trying either to convert other departments into cooperative satellites, preempt their domains through the sponsorship of new associational bureaucracies, or fill "power vacuums" into which they had been slow to move. In his relations with the interior department, he pursued all three approaches; and once Albert Fall had been replaced by the cooperative and colorless Hubert Work, the efforts of the secretary of commerce to set up associational machinery in such areas as power and waterway development, transportation improvement, and construction planning met with little resistance. In each of these areas, Hoover soon established networks of cooperating committees and allied associations, and in each of them the commerce secretariat assumed new responsibilities for making policy, stimulating "grass-roots" activity, and fostering "industrial self-government."

In the power field, Hoover tried to devise a "middle way" by seizing on the idea of "superpower," the notion of regionally coordinated and technically advanced power networks developed by a cooperative alliance of state agencies, private groups, and public-minded engineers. First set forth in "superpower surveys" sponsored by the interior and war departments, this vision received wide publicity in the early 1920s. Beginning as a member of the interior department's Superpower Advisory Committee, Hoover quickly assumed leadership, worked with the surveyors, especially with engineer William S. Murray, to promote the idea, and began organizing the necessary cooperative alliance. The practical results of his efforts were minimal, partly because of the increasingly acrimonious polarization of power politics. But by 1924 he had set up a Northeastern Super Power Committee with himself as chairman and assistant Paul Clapp as secretary, surrounded this with an apparatus of study groups and publicity campaigns, and tied the governmental activities to interlocking private committees representing the power producers and consumers, the Chamber of Commerce, and the utility engineers.

Pushing the same type of cooperative machinery, the commerce department also took the initiative in promoting waterway development and transportation reform. Around such Hoover-chaired commissions as those for the Colorado and St. Lawrence rivers, there developed an "educational campaign" to promote a national waterway plan, plus extensive ties to a web of waterway associations and reclamation groups. In conjunction with Hoover-dominated presidential committees or special presidential assignments, there developed a largely unimplemented vision of how industry and government could cooperate to modernize and rationalize the railroad and shipping industries. And tied to the Transportation Division of the Bureau of Foreign and Domestic Commerce was the cooperative machinery generated by a series of conferences with interested associations. From those in 1923, for instance, had come the establishment of regional shipping boards, designed to work with the railroads for purposes of eliminating periodic car shortages; and from the National Conference on Street and Highway Safety, held in 1924, had come agencies for safety education and the promotion of uniform traffic control laws.

Still another line of activity in which the commerce department took the initiative was that of construction planning. To Hoover and a number of his associates, the development of a "balance wheel" through the proper timing of public works and new construction had long seemed highly desirable; once in office he took the lead in organizing and directing the Unemployment Conference of September 1921, using the conference machinery to push construction activities during the recession, calling for a cutback during the subsequent boom, and urging, through such conference offshoots as the Business Cycle Committee and the Committee on Seasonal Operations, that private groups adopt regularization programs and governments set up public works reserves. In this field, as in those previously noted, a commerce-dominated "adhocracy" took shape, most of it directed by Edward Eyre Hunt, the Hoover aide who served as secretary to the Unemployment Conference and its offshoots. Working in conjunction with Hunt and his associates was the American Construction Council, a private stabilizing agency that Hoover helped to set up in 1922. And trying to mold public opinion into a force capable of securing the desired public and private actions were such attached "missionaries" as Otto T. Mallery of Pennsylvania and John B. Andrews of the American Association of Labor Legislation.

In many respects, too, Hoover functioned as the real secretary of labor and proceeded to organize association reform efforts in that field. It was Hoover, not "Puddler Jim" Davis, who sponsored the Unemployment Conference and tried to meet the unemployment crisis through expanded construction activities. Even more indicative of his role, it was Hoover rather than Davis who took the lead in pressuring the steel industry into giving up its twelve-hour day, urging business and labor groups to develop programs of unemployment insurance, and trying to substitute cooperation for conflict in the railroad and coal industries. Davis thought it more important to be at a meeting of the Loyal Order of Moose than at the Unemployment Conference. And while he sometimes complained about Hoover's expanding machinery and activities, he was usually content to echo Hoover's policies and allow what remained of the labor department to atrophy.

Although the labor department retained its welfare agencies and efforts to create a new department in the welfare field had been blocked, a new welfare "adhocracy" was taking shape, attached, appropriately enough in an era of welfare capitalism, to the Department of Commerce. To deal with problems of housing, child welfare, and emergency relief, Hoover put together associational structures similar to those used to tackle economic problems. At the centers of these structures, stimulating and guiding them toward "constructive action," were men who were also serving as officials or associates of the commerce secretariat.

In the housing field, for instance, Hoover was concerned not only with stabilizing the construction industries and breaking the "blockade" against mass production but also with relieving a national housing shortage, fostering urban zoning and planning, and securing the social stability and "spiritual values" inherent in widespread home ownership. John Gries, who headed the Building and Housing Division, came to think of his organization not only as a "division of construction" but also as a housing expediter, "bureau of municipalities," and social stabilizer. And to fulfill these added responsibilities, new campaigns of associational reform were constantly launched. The division was soon working with the Chamber of Commerce to devise community housing plans, with the American Institute of Architects to set up small house service bureaus, with a network of expert committees and cooperating interest groups to develop model building codes and model zoning and planning laws, and with realtors, loan associations, and interested philanthropists to educate prospective home owners and develop better methods of mortgage and construction financing.

In addition, Hoover utilized an organization known as Better Homes in America to carry on a massive educational campaign, one that reached out through some 3,600 local committees and a host of affiliated groups to provide exhibits of model homes, foster better "household management," promote research in the housing field, and generate a "greater, steadier, and more discriminating demand for improved dwellings," especially for families with "small incomes." Originally founded by Marie Meloney of the *Delineator*, Better Homes had first operated independently. But in late 1923, seeing the potentialities in the organization and taking advantage of Meloney's desire to reduce her own role and to keep what she had started from being "commercialized," Hoover reorganized it as a public service corporation with himself as president, thus converting it, in his words, into a "collateral arm" of the commerce department. He then secured operating funds from private foundations, persuaded James Ford, a professor of social ethics at Harvard, to serve as executive director, and tied the whole apparatus to his Housing Division by having the directors of that agency serve as officers in the new corporation. Again, by building another dependent "adhocracy" that could stimulate and work through private groups, he was able to reconcile his conflicting roles as a bureaucratic expansionist who was also a declared foe of "big government."

Similar, too, were the secretary's operations along a second welfare front, that of improving child health and well being. Here the major vehicle, analogous to Better Homes, was the American Child Health Association, formed in 1922 when Hoover arranged a merger between the American Child Hygiene Association and the Child Health Organization of America, installed himself as president of the new body, and brought in his lieutenants from the American Relief Administration to direct it. After a fund-raising campaign failed, financing was also arranged through the A.R.A. Children's Fund. And since Hoover and his lieutenants, at the expense of some internal friction and several reorganizations, managed to impose their program and priorities on the association, it too became a "collateral arm" of the commerce secretariat, filling another "vacuum" and in the process colliding at times with the Children's Bureau of the labor department and the treasury department's Public Health Service. By 1927 the American Child Health Association was working to survey, rate, and upgrade municipal health services, to assist and coordinate local health programs, to promote health education, both in the schools and through demonstration and publication projects, and to secure comprehensive birth registration, cleaner milk, improved prenatal care, and better control of communicable diseases.

Given Hoover's previous experience, it seemed logical for him and his department to handle federal relief activities and thus to broaden still further their responsibilities in the welfare field. The Unemployment Conference was largely a Hoover production, and its subsequent Committee on Civil and Emergency Measures, which tried to provide unemployment relief during the winter of 1921 and 1922, functioned essentially as a departmental appendage and model of how an associative state should function. Its approach was not to provide jobs or funds but to organize, coordinate, and inform a "cooperative" effort, thus enabling a grassroots network of mayors' emergency committees, public-minded business groups, concerned social organizations, and ad hoc employment bureaus to meet the needs of the jobless. And similarly in 1927, during the decade's greatest natural disaster, it was the secretary of commerce who took charge of a special Mississippi Flood Committee and drew on both personal and departmental resources to construct another special bureaucratic apparatus, one that worked with and through a network of local citizens' committees, Red Cross chapters, and cooperating private organizations and public agencies to provide systematic coordination, make available the needed refugee centers and rehabilitation credits, and consider future flood prevention and social "reconstruction."

While constructing new bureaucracies in areas that might more logically have been left to the secretaries of labor or interior, Hoover was also trying, with somewhat greater difficulty, to convert other departments into cooperative satellites or friendly allies. In the antitrust realm, for example, where "outmoded" interpretations of the law threatened to wreck Hoover's cooperative machinery and undermine his vision of an associational order, the commerce department appeared at first to be losing the battle but by the mid-1920s had emerged victorious. Initially, efforts to secure a new interpretation of antitrust regulations through proposed amendments, expanded governmental cooperation, clarifying letters, and "friendly criticism" from sympathetic Federal Trade Commissioners all seemed ineffective. But after Harry Daugherty's resignation in 1924, the picture changed rapidly. The new attorneys general, first Harlan Stone and later John Sargent, were more sympathetic. The Supreme Court in June, 1925, sanctioned the associational activities of the maple flooring and cement industries. And following the reorganization of the Federal Trade Commission and the appointment of William Donovan to head the Antitrust Division, these agencies became friendly allies. The former, through its trade practice conferences, was soon promoting numerous codes of ethical behavior, devices that Hoover regarded as highly "constructive," and Donovan was ready to give friendly advice to business cooperators on how to stay within the law.

By the mid-1920s, too, another Hoover protégé, William Jardine, had succeeded Henry C. Wallace as secretary of agriculture and was trying, although only with limited success, to win support for Hoover's associational approach to the farm problem. Initially, attempts to expand in this direction met with stiff resistance, resulting in bitter jurisdictional conflicts over export promotion, lumber standards, and farm processing statistics, and in heated policy debates, with each side impugning the motives of the other. As Hoover saw it, he was fighting socialists and petty bureaucrats, men who could see nothing but the pernicious McNary-Haugen bill and the preservation of their own domains and men who were ready to use "smear tactics" to achieve their ends. To Wallace, the struggle was a defensive battle against business aggression, particularly against a cooperative mar-

keting plan intended to cripple genuine cooperatives, divert attention from
real relief measures, and shift marketing activities to a farm board dominated
by the commerce department. For a time, Hoover's offensive scored few
gains, but with the death of Wallace in 1924 he was able to select the new
secretary, shape the recommendations of Coolidge's Agricultural Conference, secure a "purge" of the "petty bureaucrats," and bring the Department of Agriculture into alignment with his vision of agricultural self-
government through cooperative marketing associations. Given the new
relationship, he was even ready to establish sharp boundaries between
forestry activities and his own wood utilization program, conceding while
doing so that his Lumber Standards Committee had "embarrassed" him by
trying to move into areas which did not "rightfully belong in the Department
of Commerce."

Hoover had less success in his efforts to influence the state department,
the treasury department, and the Federal Reserve Board, partly because in
these areas he came into conflict with powerful men. He was forced to accept
a continued division of foreign economic activities, and in the face of strong
opposition from the treasury department, state department, and banking
leaders, he was unable to establish the qualitative standards and purposeful
controls that he hoped to use in guiding American investment abroad. He
was also reluctant to challenge Andrew Mellon's dismantling of the progressive tax system. He was unable to do much about the "pro-British," "easy
money" policy of the Federal Reserve Board. And although his role in the
making of foreign policy was far from insignificant, he was frequently
unable to move the diplomatic establishment in directions he felt desirable.

In later years, Hoover would attribute some of the difficulties after 1929 to
the resistance that he had encountered from financial and foreign policy
makers. But at the time he did not seem to regard his failures in these fields as
constituting major threats to the continued development of a superior
socioeconomic order. Although some of his initial plans had miscarried, he
had succeeded in raising the commerce department to the "first rank" and
transforming a collection of technical bureaus into a unified, purposeful, and
rapidly expanding organization, with a strong sense of esprit de corps and
with a far-flung apparatus that was attempting to guide socioeconomic
development as well as serve business groups. Essentially, he believed, he
had created the type of governmental tool that he had envisioned in 1921,
one that functioned as an economic "general staff," business "correspondence school," and national coordinator, all rolled into one, yet preserved

the essentials of American individualism by avoiding bureaucratic dictation and legal coercion, implementing its plans through nearly 400 cooperating committees and scores of private associations, and relying upon appeals to science, community, and morality to bridge the gap between the public interest and private ones. It was a tool, moreover, whose use was hastening the day when "functional self-government" through a "cooperative system" of self-regulating "organisms" would meet the needs of industrial democracy without statist interference. Like the war to end all wars, it was the bureaucratic empire to end future bureaucratic empires; and in theory at least it was supposed to wither away once the new order was built.

As Hoover surveyed the state of associational development in the late 1920s, he was also optimistic about the progress that had been made toward his ultimate goal. The number of national associations had multiplied from approximately 700 in 1919 to over 2,000 by 1929. Inspired and coordinated by the right kind of governmental structures—those fostering "associational activities" imbued with "high public purposes"—these associations had in Hoover's eyes become "legitimate" and "constructive" instruments for advancing the "public interest" and ushering in a "fundamentally new" phase in the nation's economic evolution. The dream of an associational order, it seemed, was on the way to realization; and as if to symbolize the role of the commerce secretariat in making such a superior system possible, a new "temple of commerce" was under construction, which, except for the Capitol, would be the largest building in Washington.

The next few years, of course, would demonstrate that Hoover's utopia was not to be. Viewed from the altered perspective that took shape after 1929, his emerging private government seemed increasingly undemocratic, oppressive, and unresponsive. Associationalism, once widely accepted as a new and superior formulation of the "American way," became for many a mere facade behind which "selfish monopolists" had abused their power and plunged the nation into depression. And the leaders of his new order, revealed now to be far less altruistic and far less prescient than Hoover had hoped they would be, seemed unable either to sustain expansion, solve festering social problems, or check the greatest economic contraction in the nation's history. As conflict mounted, moreover, demands for more effective "coordination" were soon transforming Hoover's efforts at associational direction and reform into programs and agencies he had never intended. Ironically, by demonstrating that they could not achieve the sustained expansion, rising living standards, and decentralized, noncoercive planning that they were supposed to achieve, he helped open the way for "big government" and state-enforced market controls in the 1930s.

Viewed in terms of its utopian goals and assumptions, Hoover's approach can only be adjudged a tragic failure. Yet this should not obscure the fact that he and his New Era associates, far from being mere tools of rapacious business interests or unimaginative proponents of laissez-faire, drift, and governmental inaction, were groping their way toward a form of American corporatism and indicative planning, were engaged in imaginative processes of state building and bureaucratic expansion, and were wrestling actively with the still unsolved problem of reconciling techno-corporate organization with America's liberal-democratic heritage. If historians are to understand either the men involved or the era in which they operated, it seems imperative that their associational structures and activities be explored in greater depth. And viewed from the perspective of the 1970s, from a time of disenchantment with the solutions flowing from the 1930s and of a search by "neo-federalists," "new radicals," and "post-liberals" for new organizational arrangements that will liberate and humanize rather than mechanize and oppress, such explorations may be more relevant and more instructive than most historians have previously assumed.

Notes

1.   The term is the author's not Hoover's. He and his associates usually employed such labels as the "Cooperative Committee and Conference System," the "American system," or "progressive democracy."

EISENHOWER AND THE CREATION OF
A COMMAND STRUCTURE, 1942-1945

By Alfred D. Chandler, Jr.

The selected documents show clearly that as theater commander in North Africa, the Mediterranean, and Europe, Eisenhower concentrated his personal attention on two basic concerns. One was the creation of a command organization or structure. The other was the planning and carrying out of broad strategies to defeat the Axis forces in Europe. The first was essential to the second. Eisenhower wanted to have not only the best possible staff and set of commanders but also a clear definition of the lines of authority, responsibility, and communication within this organization. Such a structure was essential if he was to have the data he needed to formulate strategic plans and the power to carry them out.

The building of a command structure and the planning and carrying out of broad strategy are, of course, basic functions of leadership in any large twentieth-century organization. As a military officer Eisenhower had been trained to handle both activities, but in carrying out these functions in World War II his tasks were unprecedented. The great size and complex composition of his forces made a clear-cut structure particularly imperative. And never before were the strategic decisions of any American field officer carried out on a continental scope. A brief review of Eisenhower's novel and complicated challenges and his response to them can help to place these documents in their broader setting and so assist the reader in evaluating their contents.

Of all the field commanders—Allied or Axis—Eisenhower had the most complex unified and allied command. Until World War II no American had ever headed a large unified command of armies, navies, and air forces; none had ever directed the forces of allied nations. Unified operations were less complex in the Central Pacific because the forces were largely naval and in the Southwest Pacific, the Middle East, and Southwest Asia because the forces there were much smaller. The German, Italian, and Russian forces in Europe and Africa consisted largely of ground soldiers and were not placed into a unified command. Of the Axis powers, only the Japanese attempted to unite land, sea, and air forces under a single officer.

During the early part of the war Eisenhower's command was the only one that was truly allied as well as unified. Recognizing the nature of the complex operations involved, the Combined Chiefs of Staff in the spring of 1942 divided the world into several spheres of operation, which Marshall then called theaters. The Pacific theaters were so predominantly American that their commanders reported to the Combined Chiefs [of the United States and Great Britain] through the American Chiefs of Staff. The forces of those in Southeast Asia and the Middle East were so predominantly British that they reported through the British Chiefs of Staff. Only in the European theater did the senior officer report directly to the Combined Chiefs of Staff.

To be called on to combine units of the army and navy was challenge enough for any military commander. Since they employed different instruments of war and different technologies, the two services had developed their own tactics and strategic concepts. Except for small sporadic raids, a twentieth-century army and navy had joined in a unified operation only once before World War II. That campaign, the British attempt to seize the Dardanelles, ended in disaster. Furthermore, in World War II the theater commander had to unite still a third military service with the army and navy. From their small beginnings during World War I, the British, French, and

American Air Forces, as well as those of other nations, had by 1939 fashioned their own tactics and strategies and had developed their own special *esprit de corps* and traditions. To blend three disparate elements of more than one nation into a single operating unit was, indeed, a formidable task demanding innovation and imagination.

In building a unified command from three services of two nations Eisenhower had the strong support of Army Chief of Staff General George C. Marshall. Well before World War II, Marshall and a few American Army officers had become advocates of unified command in field operations. They argued that complex military movements could not be efficiently planned and carried out and that vast amounts of men, equipment, and supplies could not be quickly allocated unless one single commander had the final say. It was not safe, they insisted, to assume that the commanders of land, sea, and air forces could agree promptly on a course of action, especially under battle conditions. But the American armed services had not had a chance to try out their ideas in practice. Consequently, the concept of unified command was still largely theoretical in December, 1941. Even the theory dealt only with unified command for a "task force," a force organized to carry out a specific objective, not with the formation of a permanent command organization for a continental area.

Unlike the Americans, the British had no commitment to the idea of unified command. They managed their campaigns through a committee of commanders from the three services with no one officer having full authority or responsibility for the total operation. Since in 1942 the British had had more than two years of practical fighting experience against the Axis powers, they felt little need to try an untested mode of organization.

Eisenhower first encountered these organizational problems when he arrived in Washington in December, 1941, to take over the Pacific and Far East Section of the War Department's War Plans Division. On Christmas day he attended a meeting of the British and American Chiefs of Staff, the first of the purely military meetings in the series of Anglo-American conferences held in Washington and identified by the code name *Arcadia*. Eisenhower listened to Marshall agree to a British proposal to form a committee—the Combined Chiefs of Staff (CCS)—to manage the war as a whole and then heard his chief argue passionately and persuasively for a single unified command in the areas of actual fighting. At the end of the meeting Marshall asked Eisenhower to draft a directive for a "supreme commander," yet to be appointed, for the new American, British, Dutch, and Australian (ABDA) Command in the Western Pacific. In writing his directive Eisenhower had to meet the difficulties involved in getting the senior officers of one military service to serve under those of another and in convincing one sovereign nation to place its forces under the command of another. In an effort to persuade the several nations and their services to approve the directive, Eisenhower felt it necessary to include a number of specific restrictions on the authority of the supreme commander.

A few weeks later, after Marshall had promoted him to head the War Plans Division, Eisenhower again faced these problems, this time within the American forces. He helped to set up the American-dominated theaters in the Pacific. One reason for the formation of more than one Pacific theater was that General MacArthur would not serve under a naval officer and the Navy did not want its ships controlled by General MacArthur. Later, when Marshall decided to transfer MacArthur from the Philippines to Australia and to form a new organization to replace the short-lived ABDA Command, Eisenhower again observed the problems involved in setting up a unified allied command. Therefore, when early in May, 1942, Marshall asked Eisenhower to draw up a directive for the future American commander of a European Theater of Operations, Eisenhower insisted that the officer must have absolute control over the planning and carrying out of operations. He would not permit restrictions on the commander's authority similar to those he had included in his earlier proposal for the ABDA commander.

Shortly after Eisenhower drafted the directive for the European theater, Marshall informed him that he was to be the commander to carry it out. Even before he left for Europe, Eisenhower knew that the British would resist his views on forming a unified command for any operation involving Allied actions. On a trip to England late in May, he had found the British Chiefs opposed to the appointment of a single commander to head even the assault forces in a proposed emergency cross-Channel attack.

During his first weeks in Great Britain, Eisenhower was more involved in the planning of grand strategy than in the building of a command structure; but once the decision was made for Allied landings in North Africa, the landing sites agreed upon, and his appointment as commander of the Allied expedition decided, he turned his full attention to the problem of organization. This involved three separate matters: first, he had to make certain that the lines of authority and communication assured him of complete control of all three services of the two nations; second, he had to build his own completely integrated staff; and third, he had to select the subordinate American commanders.

Eisenhower began the last of these three tasks by convincing Marshall that he must have for his Chief of Staff Brigadier General Walter Bedell Smith, then Secretary of Marshall's own General Staff. Next, through an exchange of cables and letters, Marshall and Eisenhower agreed on the American commanders for the landings and follow-up operations. By then Eisenhower had already begun work on the first of the tasks by asking the British to have the Allied naval and air commanders placed directly under him. He emphasized the importance of direct control of the air forces. The ground forces for the landing and those to be used for the follow-up advance into Tunis must also be under his direct command. He further requested the British Chiefs to assign two army, two navy, and two air officers to his staff, one from each force qualified for planning operations (G-3) and the other for intelligence (G-2). In addition, he asked for a signal officer from each of the British services, two administrative officers, and a unit of political warfare and special intelligence officers.

Eisenhower was pleased when the British provided him with the staff he wanted, but he was less happy about the instructions given to his British army commander Major General Kenneth A. N. Anderson, who was to head the postinvasion drive into Tunis. Anderson's directive was worded in almost precisely the same way as the one the British War Office had given General Douglas Haig, who had served under Marshal Ferdinand Foch in World War I. On reading Anderson's directive, Eisenhower immediately protested that it violated the principles of the unity of command. He was particularly disturbed by the statement that Anderson could report to the British War Office any time he thought the British forces might be "imperilled." Instead, Eisenhower urged that the order "be deliberately written so as to emphasize the purpose of the U.K. and the U.S. to unify the Allied Force and to centralize responsibility for its operation, and that any authorization for departing from normal channels of command and communication should be made specifically dependent upon the rise of extraordinary and grave circumstances." The British complied handsomely. The revised and final directive stated firmly that Anderson was to "carry out any orders issued" by his commanding general. "In the unlikely event" that Anderson received an order that he believed would "give rise to a grave and exceptional situation," he could appeal to the War Office, but only if he lost no opportunity and did not endanger any part of the Allied forces by so doing. Even then, he was first to inform General Eisenhower. During the weeks after the successful landings Eisenhower continued to build up his command organization. His staff now had its first real test. Because of the cramped quarters in Gibraltar, most of the staff remained in London during the first three weeks of the campaign. During that time Eisenhower had to run the high command with only a handful of assistants. Early in December the General's staff joined him at headquarters in the St. Georges Hotel in Algiers. The documents of this period indicate how quickly the staff took over many of the activities that Eisenhower had handled personally at Gibraltar, but it was some time before they became a smooth, well-co-ordinated organization. Eventually, they worked together so well that Eisenhower came to view his own staff as the best example of how allied unity could be operationally achieved.

After the Germans and bad weather had halted the dash for Tunis, Eisenhower began to restructure his larger organization for a hard winter campaign. He was much taken aback when he learned that his superiors had made some basic organizational decisions for him. At the conference in Casablanca in January, 1943, the President, Prime Minister, and their Chiefs of Staff determined both grand strategy and command structure. Eisenhower fully accepted the broad strategic decision to invade Sicily once the Axis forces were driven out of North Africa—this was the type of decision that should be made by his superiors—but he was angered by the command arrangements that were to go into effect after the British forces under General Harold Alexander, driving west from Egypt, reached Tunis. Such arrangements interfered with and indeed threatened the authority he needed to achieve the objectives the CCS had just given him.

At Casablanca the British argued successfully for the continuation of the committee system of command that they had been using in the Middle East since the beginning of the war. Eisenhower would become, for all intents, the chairman of a committee of the ground, sea, and air commanders in the new Mediterranean theater. These commanders were directed "to cooperate" with one another. The air commander, however, was given the authority to organize his own subordinate organization. Moreover, Alexander, as deputy commander, was put in charge of planning the invasion of Sicily. On learning of these decisions Eisenhower reacted sharply. He was prepared to send a message to the Combined Chiefs insisting that they adhere to the principles of unified command. General Smith persuaded him not to send this message, but in a strong letter written on February 8, 1943, Eisenhower made his position perfectly clear to Marshall.

As that letter indicated, Eisenhower was determined to manage his theater in his own way. Through his own efforts—by force of his own personality and by the internal administrative arrangements he perfected—he created the unified command organization that the CCS had denied him in a formal directive. He kept close personal contacts with Admiral Andrew Cunningham and Air Chief Marshal Arthur Tedder, whose headquarters he placed next to his own in the St. Georges Hotel in Algiers. Every morning their Chiefs of Staff and their G-2 and G-3 officers met with Smith and with Eisenhower's intelligence and operations officers. The Commander in Chief also maintained a close liaison with Alexander's headquarters at Constantine by wire, phone, and personal visits and by exchanging staff officers and other personal representatives. He permitted Alexander to command only those forces in actual combat. Cunningham, Tedder, and Alexander, captured by Eisenhower's honesty, fairness, and decisiveness, quickly began to work closely with each other and with their Commander in Chief.

The Commander in Chief also made it clear that he would take the responsibility for planning the Sicilian campaign. Here he was helped by the inability of the British commanders to agree on strategy. Eisenhower decided in favor of Montgomery and Alexander's plan to concentrate on landings in the southern part of the island, and from that point on he determined the key strategic moves. With the backing of all his commanders he turned down the CCS proposal for a quick impromptu invasion of Sicily and then, against the advice of his land and naval commanders, he decided to seize the small island of Pantelleria. He approved the use of paratroopers in the main landings and determined the allocation of shipping and other resources. After the Sicilian campaign began he met weekly and often daily with his commanders and so strengthened his control over the forces in his theater.

By the end of the Sicilian campaign Eisenhower's position was stronger than it had been before Casablanca. His command structure had become remarkably similar to the ideal one that he had outlined to the British Chiefs in the summer of 1942. Alexander (like Anderson before him) had charge only of ground forces in actual operations. Eisenhower remained the over-all ground commander. Tedder had complete direction of the air forces, and Cunningham of the navy. The Combined Chiefs of Staff were impressed enough by Eisenhower's control of his forces and his ability to use them to let him have full discretion as to where and when to make the future landings in his Mediterranean theater.

In September, just as the battle for Italy was beginning, Eisenhower had an opportunity to summarize his views and experience on the role of a modern theater commander. Lord Louis Mountbatten, whom the CCS had just appointed the Supreme Commander of the Southeast Asia Theater of Operations, had asked him for advice. In his detailed reply Eisenhower stressed that personal relationships were of more importance in creating a unified allied command than any written orders. Ideally, an allied commander in chief, he continued, should be permitted "to set up his own organization and submit a list of commanders to the Combined Chiefs of Staff that he desired as his principal subordinates." He doubted, however, that the CCS would ever permit this. "Fundamentally this is an error since it tends to weaken an authority that has no legal basis, such as exists in a single national fleet, army, or air force." And so, he added, pointing to the basic difficulty of any allied operation, "it can be wrecked at any moment not only by dissatisfaction on the part of either Government, but by internal bickering."

In a well-ordered command the three service commanders in chief "must each have a great degree of independence in his own field. Without a great degree of decentralization no allied command can be made to work." On the other hand, the commanders and their staffs must be physically near the supreme commander so that there can be constant close personal contact. "As Allied Commander-in-Chief there is an enormous amount of logistic, civil, political and economic work to do, to say nothing of forming the connecting link with the Combined Chiefs of Staff and in planning over-all grand strategy." In his theater, Eisenhower pointed out, he was in actual fact Commander in Chief of all the ground forces, and so "both the navy and air Commanders-in-Chief must, therefore, have their headquarters and their staffs with me and my staff. The three staffs made up the *true Allied Headquarters.*" He was willing to have his British Commanders in Chief remain in correspondence with their service chiefs in London, since this had long been their custom, and he thought Mountbatten should do the same, but they reported all actions and plans to and took their orders from the Supreme Commander. He emphasized, "All communications to the Combined Chiefs of Staff must pass through you and no one else must be allowed to send communications to that Body. This means that final recommendations as to operations to be undertaken and requests for needed resources must likewise pass through you.'' The memorandum ended as it had started: *''The thing you must strive for is the utmost in mutual respect and confidence among the group of seniors making up the allied command.''* Suspecting that the CCS would not give Mountbatten complete control, Eisenhower added, ''While the set-up may be somewhat artificial, and not always so clean-cut as you might desire, your personality and good sense *must* make it work. Otherwise *Allied* action in any theater will be impossible.''

Four months after writing to Mountbatten, Eisenhower was himself once again building a new unified command—this time for the invasion of France. His immediate response upon learning of his appointment to head *Overlord* was to begin to plan his command organization, drawing heavily upon his Mediterranean experience and personnel. Despite the protests of Marshall and others of the CCS, he brought with him Smith and many of his combined staff from the Mediterranean. He also persuaded the British to make Tedder his deputy, and he was able to obtain the American commanders he had come to know well, Generals Omar Bradley and George Patton. The over-all structure remained much the same. General Bernard Montgomery had a status similar to Alexander's—he was to command only those ground forces committed to the assault. Once the breakout from the landing areas was achieved, Eisenhower planned to place the American forces under Bradley, as commander of one army group, while Montgomery commanded the other group made up of the British and Canadian Armies.

In defining the command organization of *Overlord*, no one—British or American—challenged the validity of Eisenhower's views on unity of command. Nevertheless, he was not given authority over all the forces in his theater. Although he commanded all land, sea, and air forces to be used in the cross-Channel invasion, he did not directly control the British and American strategic (or long-range) bombing forces. Recalling the lessons of Salerno, Eisenhower wanted to have the authority to set the targets for these bombers, at least during the several months before and after the landings. Specifically, he wanted to be certain he could use them to destroy the railroad system in France and the Low Countries so that the Germans would be unable to move men and supplies quickly after they knew the location of the attack.

The commanders of the two bombing forces—Air Chief Marshal Arthur Harris and General Carl Spaatz—vigorously resisted any change in command structure. They did not want to be diverted, even temporarily, from their basic plan to knock Germany out of the war by strategic bombing of industrial targets. However, they promised to co-operate with Eisenhower to the fullest and give him aid in any crisis. At the same time they mustered strong support for maintaining their autonomy, including obtaining the backing of Winston Churchill. Eisenhower insisted on firmly securing control. After several weeks of discussions the Supreme Commander was finally able to get the British Air Chief of Staff, Air Chief Marshal Charles Portal, to accept an arrangement that gave Eisenhower the power he wanted. Under this new setup, the bomber commanders reported to Eisenhower's deputy, Air Chief Marshal Tedder, as did the commander of the tactical air force already assigned to his command. Thus Tedder became, as he had been in the Mediterranean, Eisenhower's senior officer for both the tactical and strategic air forces. With this change in structure came a change in strategy. The destruction of the railroad network now had priority over industrial targets in Germany.

Differences in strategy led to one final debate over structure. After his armies had successfully broken out of the Normandy beachhead and swept across France in the summer of 1944, Eisenhower began to formulate a strategy for the invasion of Germany. Here, as in Sicily and Italy, he had to decide against the competing claims of his commanders for the limited available supplies. He rejected Field Marshal Montgomery's plan to place under British command all available material for a single thrust to Berlin because, he told his British commander, "no allocation of our present resources would be adequate to sustain a thrust." Instead, Eisenhower decided to move on the Rhine and the industrial heartland of Germany on a broad, rather than a narrow, front. Montgomery still obtained the lion's share of available men and materials, including the new First Allied Air-borne Army, to mount a drive to open Antwerp, to capture the V-1 buzz-bomb sites, and to reach and cross the Rhine by an air drop at Arnhem and Nijmegen. Patton also received enough fuel and personnel to move toward the Saar and Frankfort. Further planning for the advance into Germany was postponed until 1945 because of logistical difficulties, the failure of the effort to get the Allies across the Rhine, and then the sharp and sudden German counterattack in late 1944. Then Eisenhower again outlined a strategy that ran counter to British views. Instead of giving Montgomery's armies existing resources for a drive to Berlin, he continued to follow the broad-front plan by insisting that the Rhine should not be crossed until all the territories west of it were in Allied hands and by allocating enough resources to the Americans to close up to the river.

When the British were unable to persuade Eisenhower to alter his strategy, they tried to achieve their objectives by changing his command structure. Montgomery first suggested to Eisenhower, and the British Chiefs later proposed to their American counterparts, that the task of planning and carrying out the war in Europe was too immense a job for any one man. To lessen the load on Eisenhower, they argued, a single ground commander (first Montgomery, later Alexander) should be appointed to command the army groups. As Supreme Commander Eisenhower would co-ordinate land, sea, and air forces, as well as handle logistical and governmental affairs. The Britisher at the head of the land forces could then set the strategic objectives. Despite a long and arduous debate and a personal visit from the Prime Minister, Eisenhower refused to agree to any basic change in the structure of command. He was willing to substitute Alexander for Tedder as his deputy, but only as long as it was absolutely clear that he—and not Alexander—was the over-all ground commander. Marshall would not entertain even this suggestion. Neither would the American Chiefs, so Churchill and his military advisors were forced to drop the proposal.

As his debate with the British testifies, Eisenhower was always sensitive to the need for a careful definition of the channels of authority, responsibility, and communication. But a clear-cut structure was in itself hardly enough. Obviously, no command organization could be better than the officers who manned it, and Eisenhower paid close personal attention to the selection of his staff and of his subordinate commanders. Until the summer of 1944 he personally reviewed and made recommendations for promotions to general officer rank of all American officers in his theater. He wanted men whom he trusted because, as he pointed out to Mountbatten, he firmly believed in the decentralization of decision-making in the field. His subordinates must be responsible for tactical moves. Given the size of the forces in this theater, these military decisions were actually of the same scope and complexity as those made by Lee, Grant, or even Pershing in earlier wars. Yet they were carried out within larger strategic plans on which Eisenhower had the final say.

Eisenhower conceived of strategy-formulation as the setting of basic objectives for his commanders and the allocating of necessary resources to achieve them. He realized clearly that activities involving vast numbers of men, huge volumes of materials, and a wide variety of tasks required the delegation to others of authority for developing detailed plans and for directing operations. Thus, when the Germans thwarted the initial plans for the breakout from the beachhead in Normandy, he let Generals Montgomery and Bradley work out the new tactical movements that became Operations *Goodwood* and *Cobra*. But once the breakout was achieved, it was Eisenhower, not Montgomery or Bradley, who determined the next set of objectives and the broad plans for the next major campaign—the crossing of the Rhine and the attack on the West Wall. Eisenhower also decided how his forces should respond to the sharp German counterattack in December, 1944, and he determined the shape of the final campaigns in Germany in 1945.

In formulating his broad plans Eisenhower conferred constantly with his commanders and relied heavily on his staff. In modern war, as in modern business, strategic planning has become a staff activity. Eisenhower's staff had to work out the broad over-all plans and co-ordinate the more specific proposals of subordinate commands concerning loading schedules, air cover, naval support, a continued and assured flow of supplies, the location of reserves, the moving in of replacements, and the care, feeding, and even government of civilians. Such planning required weeks and months of concentrated effort.

Because Eisenhower worked so closely with his staff and commanders, [his published papers] do not fully reveal the ways in which the details of strategy for his theater were formulated. Little correspondence passed between Eisenhower and senior members of his staff, whom he saw almost daily. When the commanders were close by and when there was little controversy over the plans and the resulting allocation of resources, Eisenhower dictated few letters or messages about strategy. Often he did little more than sign the directive that he, his staff, and his commanders had spent so much time reviewing and discussing. On the other hand, when his commanders were at a distance or when he and they differed over objectives and the allocation of resources and other fundamental matters, then the flow of memorandums letters, and messages on strategy was ample. However, . . . the final decisions on broad strategy within his theater were his. From North Africa to the Elbe, Eisenhower—not his staff or his commanders—defined the basic strategy for the approval of the CCS and made the key decisions required to carry it out.

Strategy-making and execution involved, of course, working with superiors as well as subordinates. . . . Much of Eisenhower's correspondence with the American Chiefs of Staff involved obtaining scarce men and materials that he needed to realize the objectives they and the British Chiefs had given him. He also frequently reported to them on the progress of the current campaign. . . . But even more significant than requests and reports were letters and messages to his superiors on the formulation of strategy for his theater.

In theory, the CCS and the heads of state—Churchill and Roosevelt—defined the goals and allocated the resources with which Eisenhower had to work. In practice, however, the Chiefs of Staff and the heads of state at times themselves failed to agree. When such divisions occurred, Eisenhower, as senior American military officer in Europe, was often forced to take part in working out solutions to critical issues involving political as well as military matters. There were two basic disagreements that brought Eisenhower into the process of resolving larger issues. One was the genuine difference between British and American opinions over the grand strategy for defeating Hitler. The other arose when Roosevelt and De Gaulle, who was normally supported by the British, disagreed over the present and future status of the French government.

Thrust between Churchill and the American Chiefs on the one hand, and De Gaulle and Roosevelt on the other, Eisenhower was forced to become a master diplomat. When he became involved in these controversial issues, his method was first to determine what he considered the most satisfactory position concerning the strategic objectives for his current campaign. He would then define his position on these matters in terms of the most satisfactory military solution. Next he would point out that he was ready to be overruled by his political superiors on political, but not on military, grounds. Precisely because there were differences at the top and because the winning of the war was normally defined in military terms, these tactics proved to be very successful. Eisenhower almost always had his way.

With the British, the controversies centered around grand strategy. As every student of World War II knows, the British, particularly Churchill, preferred a peripheral strategy of tightening the ring around the German homeland until the exhausted enemy was on the verge of collapse; the Americans, particularly Marshall, wanted to concentrate the Allied resources in a massive thrust to the Ruhr, the heart of German industrial and military power. The British strategy reflected their fear of repeating the disastrous World War I trench warfare that had decimated a generation of young men; they were also simply adhering to a strategy that they had traditionally used in continental war. By contrast, American plans focused on the exploitation of America's vast industrial resources to defeat the enemy as quickly as possible and to do so by eliminating the industrial base of its military power.

Eisenhower was fully aware of the differences between the American and British concepts of grand strategy when in June, 1942, he took command of the European Theater of Operations. He had been one of the authors of the American strategy. In February, 1942, as Chief of the War Plans Division, he had presented to Marshall the first specific plan for a cross-Channel invasion. Since it was fully in line with Marshall's views, the Chief of Staff asked Eisenhower and his assistants to work out the details of such an operation. The result was a three-phased proposal: a buildup in England that was given the code name *Bolero*; an emergency cross-Channel attack to take place in the fall of 1942, if either a Russian or a German collapse seemed imminent (code name *Sledgehammer)*; and *Roundup*, the full-scale invasion of the Continent in the spring of 1943. Roosevelt liked the plan and sent Marshall and Hopkins to obtain approval. Surprisingly, the British agreed to it, prompted by fear that the Americans might turn to the Pacific and by a desire to get American reinforcements (particularly air forces) to England as quickly as possible. Once Churchill and the British Chiefs gave their assent, Eisenhower's War Plans Division began to concentrate on putting the proposal into action. It was to carry out this strategy that Marshall sent Eisenhower to England in June, 1942.

Just as Eisenhower was leaving for his new command, Churchill arrived in the United States to inform the Americans that the British had changed their minds. He and his Chiefs now opposed *Sledgehammer*, and he, but not his Chiefs, hoped to talk Roosevelt into undertaking instead an invasion of French North Africa. The meetings at the end of June proved indecisive, so in mid-July Roosevelt sent Marshall, Chief of Naval Operations Admiral Ernest J. King, and his most trusted advisor, Harry Hopkins, to London to come to a final decision on grand strategy for 1942 and 1943. If the British rejected *Sledgehammer*, Roosevelt instructed his representatives to accept a plan that would bring American troops into combat with the Germans before the end of 1942. During these London conferences Eisenhower and his staff drafted the proposals and counterproposals that Marshall and others presented. The British, however, remained adamant. Finally, to comply with the President's instructions, Marshall decided that if the Americans must fight in 1942, they would gain the most by fighting in North Africa rather than in Norway, the Middle East, or any other possible alternative.

In this debate and in the one that followed over the number and location of the landings in North Africa, Eisenhower's role was more that of a staff man—a planner—than that of a negotiator and decision-maker. The Combined Chiefs of Staff and the heads of state made the final decisions. Eisenhower had little to say about grand or inter-theater strategy after the North African landings. He made only one short visit to Casablanca, where his superiors agreed to follow up a victory in Tunis with the invasion of Sicily. Nor did he have a place in the *Trident* conference in Washington that set Italy as the next objective. He was, of course, pleased and reassured when the CCS and heads of state left the theater strategy for realizing this objective entirely in his hands.

Eisenhower was not involved in the formulation of grand strategy after the summer of 1942 primarily because the British had their own way. North Africa, Sicily, and Italy fitted Churchill's peripheral strategy. American troops were sent to Britain, but the campaigns to the south forced a postponement of cross-Channel landings to at least 1944. Even at the end of 1943, only strong pressure from Stalin persuaded Churchill to commit the British to a definite date for the cross-Channel attack.

Once the planning for that attack began, however, Eisenhower became fully involved in determining grand strategy. The American Chiefs proposed *Anvil*, a landing in southern France, to support the Normandy invasion. The British strongly opposed diverting any forces from Italy, wanting instead to continue the drive up the peninsula toward the Balkans and Vienna. When he arrived in London in January, 1944, Eisenhower was firmly committed to *Anvil*. Besides pinning down German troops in France, the operation would assure full use of Allied troops in the Mediterranean and so keep up the continuing momentum of the campaign there. It would be particularly valuable in employing the French by landing where the Resistance was strongest and by permitting tne French forces then in the Mediterranean to take a major part in the liberation of their homeland. However, Eisenhower fully appreciated that no further operation in the Mediterranean was feasible until the Allied forces in Italy had linked up with the beachhead at Anzio and had captured Rome. The determined German resistance in Italy continuing, he reluctantly agreed to have *Anvil* come after the Normandy landings and even to postpone until after the June 6 D-day the decision on where and when to have the operation.

Once the landings had taken place, Eisenhower developed a new perspective on *Anvil*. By then Rome had finally been taken. Of more importance, the great storm of June 19-22 had dramatized the difficulties of reinforcing his huge armies over the beachhead. Eisenhower now wanted Marseilles, an undamaged deep-water port, to land and deploy fresh diversions and to bring in vast amounts of munitions and other supplies directly from the United States to France. Churchill was still determined not to divert Allied forces from Italy. He met with Eisenhower, begged, cajoled, threatened, and wept. At one session that lasted for six hours the Prime Minister said that if he did not have his way, he would "have to put down the mantle of his high office." Eisenhower insisted that his was a military decision that could be changed only on political grounds. Churchill then turned to Roosevelt and Hopkins, advancing what he still defined as military rather than political arguments for his position. At the last minute, the Prime Minister even proposed an alternative attack on the Bay of Biscay. All to no avail. The *Anvil* landings followed the schedule set by Eisenhower. Marseilles became and remained during 1944 and 1945 a critically important supply port for the Allied armies in France.

Churchill and Eisenhower became involved in another dispute over plans for *Overlord*. The Prime Minister had supported the American and British strategic bombing commanders when they opposed Eisenhower's plans to use their planes to knock out the rail transportation network in the Low Countries and France, fearing that the bombing of railroad yards and terminals would kill many civilians and so leave in France, Holland, and Belgium a lasting hatred of the Anglo-American forces. A lengthy debate over the military value of Eisenhower's "Transportation Plan" and the support of De Gaulle's military commander in Britain, General Pierre Koenig, were required before Churchill and the British War Cabinet finally accepted Eisenhower's proposal.

After the successful landings in Normandy and the sweep across France, British and American differences once again surfaced. To Churchill and Montgomery the proper objective became Berlin. The capture of the German capital would be a magnificent symbol of victory to a British nation that had endured five years of sacrifice. It would also be a trump card in postwar negotiations with the Russians. To Eisenhower the defeat of the German armies had priority. Before crossing the Rhine, Eisenhower and Montgomery had argued about these strategic differences, leading the British to try unsuccessfully to alter SHAEF's command organization. In March, 1945,

Churchill again took up the issue. The Prime Minister was most disturbed when he learned that after capturing the Ruhr, Eisenhower planned to move his forces directly east to Leipzig and Dresden and to meet the Russians on the Elbe. Churchill begged Eisenhower to shift his thrust northeast to Berlin. His argument was explicitly political. If Berlin were deliberately left to the Russians, they would be more convinced than ever that they—not the Allies—had defeated Germany. Eisenhower admitted the validity of the Prime Minister's political arguments but insisted that military objectives came first. A drive directly east was the shortest route to link up with the Russians and so divide Germany in two. The Elbe was the most obvious geographical landmark suited to the difficult and dangerous maneuver of bringing together two great armies. Moreover, the Leipzig-Dresden area was the one remaining industrial center under German control.

Once the objectives in the center were reached, Eisenhower promised to give the British the forces needed to reach the Baltic as well as Berlin; he would also give the Americans what they required to move south to forestall a possible last-ditch stand in the mountains of southern Germany. If his superiors overruled him and put political ahead of military goals, Eisenhower told the Prime Minister, he would, of course, give Berlin first priority. Eisenhower's definition of the situation had the complete support of Marshall and Roosevelt, so Churchill acquiesced in good grace.

In his dealings with the French—from his first campaign until the last— Eisenhower also defined his position in terms of current military needs. At the landings in North Africa his goal was to stop the resistance of the Vichy French forces as quickly as possible, and, on his own initiative, he made a deal with Admiral Jean Darlan to end the fighting. In the subsequent campaigns in Tunis, Sicily, and Italy, Eisenhower counted heavily on friendly French forces to protect rear areas by guarding supply lines, ammunition dumps, and prisoners of war. He also used the French civil government to maintain order throughout North Africa. As he so often stressed to Marshall and the CCS, his military problems would be increased enormously if the local French forces became hostile or even remained neutral. At the same time, Eisenhower had no desire to let the French become involved in the councils of war, particularly not in strategic planning.

Eisenhower's difficulties in dealing with the French were intensified in June, 1943, when Charles de Gaulle achieved control of the French Committee of National Liberation and became the *de facto* head of the French government-in-exile. Franklin Roosevelt and his Secretary of State, Cordell Hull, distrusted De Gaulle. Neither would accept him as the spokesman for free France. The American President repeatedly insisted that the Allies should not give De Gaulle or any other French leader the advantage of formal recognition until free elections had been held in liberated France.

The President's policy ran directly counter to Eisenhower's need for a legitimate political body that could control the rear areas first in North Africa and then in continental France. This fact De Gaulle fully appreciated, and he timed his demands for *de facto* recognition so that they came just before a major campaign. Eisenhower walked a tightrope for more than a year, encouraged in this difficult task by the knowledge that he had the support of Marshall and the British Foreign Office, and managed to maintain a working relationship with De Gaulle without disobeying his Commander in Chief. It was not until August, 1944, that the President finally modified his position by permitting Eisenhower to formalize his relations with the French.

After the signing of agreements between the French and Americans— agreements that in fact recognized the De Gaulle regime—Eisenhower continued to deal directly with the French leader. He conferred with him on the liberation of Paris, the use of French troops in the Allied command to maintain order in the capital, and the holding of Strasbourg during the German counterattack at the end of 1944. In all cases Eisenhower based his position on the same military considerations he had defined earlier, that is, the need to assure stability behind the front. De Gaulle respected Eisenhower's abilities at negotiation and the position he took: "By choosing reasonable plans, by sticking firmly to them, by respecting logistics," he noted in his memoirs, "General Eisenhower led to victory the complicated and prejudicial machinery of the armies of the free world."

In addition to dealing regularly with the heads of two leading European powers, Eisenhower and his staff also worked closely with those of the smaller governments. This was especially true during and after the liberation of these countries from German control. As the senior American military officer he was also the first to negotiate with the enemy. He had to work out the arrangements to end hostilities, first with the Vichy French in North Africa and later in the complex and tortuous negotiations that led to the Italian surrender. Finally, he had to handle the German capitulation. Indeed, it is hard to think of another American who for so long and continuously played such a critical role in negotiations that so affected the destiny of Europe and the United States.

As the senior commander of the American forces in Europe, Eisenhower obviously had other duties besides those involved in diplomacy, in defining strategy, and in creating a command organization. He was concerned with the morale of his officers and men. He paid close attention to training and discipline, especially in the early months of the war. He kept an eye on the recreational facilities provided for his troops, arranged for rest and rotation of battle-worn officers, and checked to see that those who deserved it were rewarded by decorations, promotions, and larger commands. He realized the importance of the press and public relations officers in maintaining troop morale. Most important of all, he kept in touch with his officers and troops by constant visits to the field on which he tried to see and talk to as many men as possible. He understood that he was the symbol, as well as the reality of command.

The command abilities and organizational skills that Eisenhower demonstrated in World War II reflected his whole army experience. His close association with Major General Fox Conner, who had been General Pershing's operations officer in World War I, his studies at the Army's Command and General Staff School and its War College, his years with General MacArthur in Washington and then in the Philippines, and his tour of duty after returning to the United States from the Philippines (first with the 3d Infantry Division and then as the Chief of Staff for General Walter Krueger's Third Army) all helped to give Eisenhower an understanding of modern organization and command.

THE TRUMAN ADMINISTRATION AND THE ENLISTMENT OF THE AVIATION INDUSTRY IN POSTWAR DEFENSE

By Donald J. Mrozek

In the years since it became fashionable to speak disparagingly of the "military-industrial complex" as a threat to world peace and a challenge to domestic liberties in the United States, the move to integrate industry into national defense planning after World War II has often been misinterpreted. Many recent analysts have identified either business or military leaders as the primary source of pressure and rationales for a "merger" of military and government interests on the one hand with business and civilian society on the other. Customarily, the role of civilian administrators in that period has been portrayed as one of subservience to the industrial community or as dereliction of responsibility.[1]

That view, however, does not give sufficient weight to the key role of presidential planning at the end of the war. Harry S. Truman and particularly his close advisers such as Clark Clifford and George Elsey were anxious to link business to the military establishment.[2] The President, however, sometimes confronted what a Marxist might call a problem of false consciousness. Those who might most profit from his program were slow to identify their true interests. Businessmen disagreed sharply among themselves on the extent to which government support of industry was beneficial. Late in World War II and soon after, it was not business but the President and his advisers who saw the most merit in linking industry to postwar defense. After a wartime collaboration checkered with quarrelsome incidents and ill-feeling, both business and military leaders zealously sought to guard their independence of action and therefore failed to unite behind the presidential policy of closer military-industrial integration in the postwar era.

The case of the aircraft industries illustrates this reticence among many businessmen. Aircraft firms had expanded well beyond all predictable peacetime demands under the pressure of production requirements during the war. After the conclusion of hostilities, however, leaders of the large aviation companies hoped to minimize continuing government intervention, even though they might face risks in the marketplace. In some respects, this obsession with independence represented something of a reversal of earlier form. The leaders of aircraft companies and of airlines had, for example, pressed steadily for government aid in the 1930s. After their wartime experiences and in the much improved economic environment of the postwar years, however, businessmen from those industries initially resisted absorption into a complex which might significantly erode their ability to direct their own futures.

The process of the evolution of postwar ties between the military and the aviation industry, like the restructuring of any institutional relationship, can be interpreted as a competition for power by various interest groups. In such an interpretation, the role of conflicting ideologies or differing defense strategies is held to be subordinate to (or determined by) the interest groups' basic instincts for self-preservation and self-aggrandizement. There are, however, some difficulties in applying such an analysis to the origins of the American defense system in the years following World War II. While different interest groups, including persons in government, the military, and the leadership of the aviation industries, all played roles in the early evolution of what has come to be called the military-industrial complex, by far the most significant part was played by the Truman administration. Change seemed almost inevitable, and the unique influence of the President and his major defense policy advisers (who will hereafter be referred to collectively as "the administration") made them the leading force. In explaining the immediate postwar changes, moreover, ideology cannot be made wholly subordinate to the search for power by interest groups, for the Truman administration was motivated primarily by its pursuit of a conscious and well articulated set of ideas about national defense and national interests.

The importance which leading administration figures attached to the aircraft industries depended directly upon their defense strategies for the postwar world, strategies which were of far less interest to industrialists than to top officers from the various branches of military service. The atomic bomb had breathed new life into the theory of strategic bombing and had made defense planning more urgent. Although it had long been common-place to regard American industrial capacity as the most reliable and ulti-mately decisive weapon that the nation possessed, the time period available to mobilize that capacity and bring it into play in wartime had been drasti-cally reduced because of the increasing range of manned bomber aircraft. The United States could no longer risk taking months or years to achieve mil-itary production. A defense which was not already in being was illusory. Thus industrial mobilization and a close working relationship between in-dustry and its military customers had become essential, not merely as meas-ures to meet future crises, but as permanent aspects of current national defense.

ADMINISTRATION PRESSURES, 1944-1948

The Truman administration[3] consistently sought business participation in the defense effort during the postwar period in the conduct of basic research, in the development of military hardware, and ultimately in assuring victory through the full mobilization of industrial production if national policy failed to prevent a protracted war. By 1944, leading defense officials had already sought to win that participation. For example, Secretary of the Navy James Forrestal told a meeting of the Navy Industrial Association in New York City in September of that year that "the question of research for military pur-poses" was a matter of "paramount importance to you men in industry, as well as to the whole country." Such work could no longer be deferred, due to the "telescoping of time and space which has occurred as a result of expanded uses of the airplane, of the development of long-range missiles, and of radio and radar." In the coming days of peace they must prepare for future war. For "this war has established the fact that research in new weapons must, broadly speaking, take place before the beginning of a war."

The achievement of scientific and technological breakthroughs, while necessary, was insufficient. The administration wished to improve the organization of industry for war, to integrate business planning and practices with government defense requirements. In January, 1946, Army Air Force General Ira C. Eaker circulated a letter among the commanding officers of his service aimed at guiding industrial mobilization efforts. "The development of outstanding weapons," he argued, "and the training of skilled personnel to use them will be of little value in a future emergency if the weapons cannot be produced in accordance with mobilization requirements." Therefore planning for mobilization "provides the only possible assurance that a maximum industrial effort can be achieved in a minimum of time." Eaker considered this especially true of the aircraft industry. It followed that the Air Force, as it became pre-eminent in national defense, had to "accord industrial mobilization planning a position of equal importance with research and development and military training as a vital element in preparedness." In other words, the military and business sectors were to adopt patterns of mobilization that were coordinated and compatible.

One barrier to reaching this goal, according to a Budget Bureau staff memorandum, was the "misconception that the terms 'war effort' and 'military effort' are synonymous." The danger in associating military preparations with a war effort was that this identification could give rise to the belief that military preparations were no longer critical in a time of formal peace. The same memorandum criticized as an illusion that persistent notion that "apart from military requirements there remains only something called the 'civilian economy.' " The staff even objected to the use of the term "industrial mobilization," fearing that it would fail to indicate the broad character of the government's program. They called for an even greater integration of the military and civilian sectors. Without recommending a specific master plan, they urged comprehensive development of all resources that might be needed to fill the requirements of any plan likely to be advanced.

Consistent with this thinking, the National Security Resources Board (NSRB), which was responsible for creating plans for mobilization in a war, became more important in peace in order to maintain "readiness both of plans and of the resources—physical, human, governmental, financial, economic, political, and other—essential to the national security." If the resources were ready, the plan could be modified without any serious difficulty. As the Budget staff also recognized, the NSRB would work toward organizing total national production to meet any emergency, not merely toward organizing a limited, selected list of those industries deemed particularly critical. The NSRB was to "cover the broadest front" and plan a mobilization for the nation as a whole.

The thoroughness of this planning and the desire for constant readiness followed largely from theories of atomic warfare. As one proposal for the National Security Resources Board noted, "atomic and other types of modern warfare have shortened the time in which it is possible to prepare for defense once hostilities have begun." Therefore "to permit neglect to prolong the period required to get industrial mobilization to full strength is to heighten needlessly the peril of our national security." Early and steady efforts might reduce disruption of the American democratic process and the business system. "Preparation in advance of an emergency," the same proposal argued, "will lessen the strain, particularly when it is consciously directed to mobilization measures consonant with the American system of free enterprise." While businessmen feared that permanent links with the military might lead to government control of the industrial system, planners within the administration regarded such ties as a means of preventing gross distortion of the economy in times of crisis. Clark Clifford and other proponents of the NSRB hoped that, even in an atomic emergency, careful planning would allow industrial and military activities to continue relatively smoothly.

Contemporary critics of the military's role in industrial preparedness generally accused the services of *underestimating* the need to integrate the military and civilian sectors. In testimony delivered to the President's Air Policy Commission in 1947, George P. Saunders, formerly of the Industrial Preparedness Staff of the Air Force, warned that private business control in defense preparedness was waning precisely because of the low dollar volume of defense contracts. He attacked the military for not persuading the American public to support enormous outlays for aircraft procurement and so blamed them for the weakness of the aircraft industries. Saunders assumed that the officers had a mistaken and hostile view of businessmen, "as though the problem were primarily one of industrial self-interest rather than one of national defense." He concluded that, although industrial mobilization was important to the government, to the Air Force it was "an unpopular orphan, subject to neglect, non-support, and hostility from many different directions.''

The lack of enthusiasm within the Air Force for the new planning program stemmed, Saunders reported, from the service's conviction that war would not come for at least seven years. Since their planning was premised upon that assumption, he argued, they tended to feel that ''the militarization of the industrial planning program has not been completed.'' Ironically, this charge of ''militarization'' grew from the reluctance of the Air Force to branch out into a collaborative program with sectors of the civilian society. What Saunders called ''militarization'' was apparently an armed service's effort to avert a thorough integration with industry.

Saunders' criticisms exemplified some civilians' concern over the state of the aviation industry. The reluctance of industrialists to tie their companies to defense policy, as well as the desire for comprehensive preparedness in defense production and the need to study the implications of overall defense strategy, persuaded President Truman to establish his Air Policy Commission. In his letter of July 18, 1947, appointing Thomas K. Finletter as commission chairman, he called for ''an integrated national aviation policy.'' The President implied that he expected proposals to make the civilian and military aviation programs support one another, since he directed the commission to explore the use of commercial aircraft by the military, the size of the industrial plant required for national defense, and methods for encouraging research and development for ordnance. Whatever the reasons for the unsettled state of affairs in the aircraft industries, Truman wished things set right.

The President's Air Policy Commission—manned by government and business leaders such as the future Secretary of the Air Force Finletter, Arthur Whiteside of Dun & Bradstreet, publisher Palmer Hoyt, John McCone, and, for a time, Henry Ford II—offered little in the way of new strategic thinking. The commission did collect many previously scattered opinions about the impact of air power and atomic weapons on American society. In hearings held during 1947 and 1948, among the most recurrent themes raised by witnesses was concern over the relationship of a stable rate of industrial production to defense. Representatives from business and government were practically unanimous in arguing that government subsidies had become essential to save the private aircraft companies from financial ruin and that these industries were essential to the nation's security. This unanimity was neither customary nor automatic.

AIRCRAFT INDUSTRY VIEWS, 1941-1948

As indicated earlier, the industry itself had opposed the continuation of government influences after World War II. As the war neared an end, it hoped for a peace in which civilian orders would pick up much of the slack from diminishing military procurement and in which military orders were supplementary rather than basic to the prosperity of the aircraft companies. Not all aviation executives were sanguine about the industry's future or loath to accept government contracts. But there were many ways to meet the anticipated problems. John P. Gaty, vice-president and general manager of the Beech Aircraft Corporation, had warned then Senator Harry Truman as early as October of 1941 that the industry needed a broad tax shelter since the companies "will have to depend largely on their own resources to carry them through a difficult period of readjustment" after the war. Gaty had further suggested that the preservation of the aviation industry would serve both financial and defense purposes. With humor and prophecy, he concluded that "it may be your decision which will determine whether the new-born aircraft industry can be an asset of great value for commerce as well as for future National Defense or whether it shall be 'given back to the Indians' and its facilities allowed to deteriorate to a condition where they will be useful only for the propagation of owls."

During the war, the National Aircraft War Production Council (NAWPC), a significant lobby and public relations group for the industry, attempted to plot a course for the postwar years. NAWPC officials wanted government contracts without government controls. For example, on December 31, 1943, Clyde Vandeburg told the board of directors of the group's east coast council that they should engage in a skillful public relations effort to ensure popular support for the industry's objectives. They must argue that, "under the whip of urgency, our segment of industry quietly put aside the luxury of individual competition in favor of a seasoned brand of cooperative competition remembered from the Argonauts in wagon trains and settlers in log forts of Indian country." Such a supposed sacrifice must surely justify special concessions to the industry, particularly in the realm of economic adjustments.

The industrialists, however, were equally determined not to win these advantages at the cost of accepting government, especially military, control. This became clear when Richard Palmer, head of the NAWPC's Washington office, reported with transparent joy General Lucius Clay's departure from his post as production consultant to James Byrnes, charged by Franklin Roosevelt with handling mobilization and reconversion problems. According to Palmer, Clay had been appointed to "see that [Julius] Krug did not become too civilian production minded and also to make certain that the Army and Navy not only came first but maintained an iron grasp on the country's economy." With obvious disapproval, Palmer reported: "This Clay has done exceedingly well." The aircraft manufacturers wanted that iron grasp broken. Nor did they anticipate comparable danger from over-emphasis on civilian sales. Thus, at the end of the war, the industry was unwilling to sell its freedom or mortgage its future for the sake of a government-guaranteed but government-controlled prosperity.

By the time of the Air Policy Commission hearings, the situation had changed dramatically. The hopes of the aircraft industry for pursuing an independent course had faded. During the two years following the end of the war, representatives of the larger companies gradually realized that they had seriously overestimated the size of the civilian market in the postwar period. Oliver Echols, a retired general heading the Aircraft Industries Association, told Palmer Hoyt in October, 1947, that some manufacturers were near bankruptcy. "Maybe some of them should go broke and some new ones come along," he said. But the important thing was for the government to establish a complete and coordinated program, a matter of "knowing what size industry you want, getting the business, giving it to Government agencies, giving them a policy and telling them to set up a system to execute it." In a face-saving manner, Echols was trying to tell the commission to rescue the aviation industry, which could not raise enough orders on its own to remain solvent. Nevertheless Hoyt explored the administration's hope of using commercial civilian orders as a kind of subsidy for the military program:

Mr. Hoyt: Is the ratio of commercial business to military business improving or is it getting worse?
General Echols: It is definitely getting worse.
The Chairman [Finletter]: You mean that there are fewer commercial aircraft being purchased?
General Echols: That is right. There is almost none.

The ratio of commercial to military orders was getting worse even while defense spending was being restrained. Obviously, the prospects for much help from the commercial sector in reducing defense costs were not very bright.

Surely Echols was more interested in saving the industry and improving its profit picture than in revitalizing commercial aviation for defense purposes. His support for competitive contracting—the prewar practice of letting out at least two development contracts for aircraft of approximately equal performance specifications—illustrated this bias. Although competitive contracting had been a common procedure before the war, the urgency of calls for its restoration stemmed from the financial condition of the aircraft companies. Echols claimed that it would ensure the swiftest progress and would restore the industry to what he considered the traditional pattern of inter-corporation competition. It would also mean more work for more aircraft companies. Fascinated by these intimations of weakness in the aircraft industry, Palmer Hoyt asked how big the industry would be "if the millenium arrived and there were no more military planes." "I do not want to exaggerate," Echols answered, "but I just think it would collapse." One could seek no clearer admission than this that the industry's earlier hopes for independence from the military had been dashed by economic realities. The alternative to military involvement in the aviation industry, which the NAWPC had attempted to challenge immediately after World War II, was economic collapse.

GOVERNMENT INITIATIVES, 1947-1948

Even those who believed that commercial aviation had a strong future agreed with Echols that the commercial aircraft program would lend little assistance to the nation's defense posture, except perhaps in the long run. Under Secretary of Commerce William C. Foster told the Air Policy Commission in September 1947 that "aviation's economic and cultural contribution to civilization will ultimately far outweigh in value the war-making potential." But for the present "if we do not concentrate upon the war-making potential, we may never have an opportunity to develop the basic qualities inherent in aviation as an economic and cultural asset." Peaceful uses of aviation would take second place to military applications "if we are to survive until better times." For the short run, Foster thought, government subsidy must "maintain an aviation potential of the size and quality needed for our welfare and security." Still the long-range objective was to establish a commercial aviation industry that would not only support itself but would also "provide unsubsidized support for necessary military potential."

In theory, the civil aviation program could underwrite a military potential much greater than that reflected in the annual defense budget. Secretary of Commerce Averell Harriman explained the urgency of this relationship by noting that, although a military air force was "essential regardless of cost. . . , there is of course a limit to which it would be possible to obtain appropriations." Therefore he emphasized the "need for the expansion of civil aviation as a means of maintenance of our manufacturing facilities." Civil aircraft types might be designed to serve military as well as commercial purposes. This would provide additional support for defense, Harriman suggested; new planes might be "constructed [so] that they will be readily made available to the air force."

Secretary of the Air Force Stuart Symington suggested that the creation of a large civil air transport fleet would expand the industry's base of production and provide a back-up fleet for the Air Force. It would also preserve the promise of controlling budget problems. "Since it would be extremely expensive to maintain in peacetime all the military air transport required to meet initial wartime requirements," Symington argued in October, 1947, "a means must be found of bridging this gap. We believe that rapid development of the commercial air cargo industry is a practicable way of bridging this gap." The coupling of military and civilian programs in aviation development would thus enlarge the nation's preparedness, even if it deviated from optimum commercial development.

In a like manner, Symington suggested a way to break old limits in foreign relations. The United States might reap auxiliary military advantages from the activities of the International Civil Aviation Organization (ICAO), including "worldwide standardization of civil operating procedures and establishment of facilities which can be utilized by the immediately available air contingents of various nations operating under the direction of the Security Council of the United Nations." But the promulgation of international air rules opening airports around the world to carriers from all nations could also directly serve the unilateral interests of the United States since "some of these facilities would also be available to the United States in the event of a total war." The ICAO could thus serve as a substitute for what "cannot be accomplished by other means, that is, by treaty." In this way, Symington suggested that the benefits of civil-military integration could come from international as well as domestic measures.

One way or another, government leaders were intent on fusing civilian and military aviation into a single program. Whether the civilian sector would finally support the military, or whether the reverse would occur, the national leadership group who appeared .before the Finletter Commission (the President's Air Policy Commission) seemed satisfied that the futures of civil and military sectors were inseparable. "With the new national defense set-up [through the National Security Act of 1947]," Arthur Whiteside said, "it seems that foreign and domestic commerce should be built up comparable to something else. That is it should be comparable, to the mobilization of the military to some extent. It never performed that function, but it is the logical place to perform it. It is to get a balance there between the civil and military, under any circumstances."

Representatives from the Bureau of the Budget, particularly J. Weldon Jones and Ralph J. Burton, agreed. "Heretofore, you have had this whole business of industrial mobilization and preparedness treated at the military level in terms of the Munitions Board," Burton noted in October 1947. "You have had it built up now in terms of an over-all, total governmental participation." That, among other things, was the point of the National Security Resources Board. Burton suggested that the relevant political and practical issue was not a conflict between civil and military sectors. It was the total participation of the government in industrial concerns for the sake of military preparedness. Frederick B. Rentschler, the chairman of the United Aircraft Corporation, suggested the alternative. If commercial aircraft were not regarded as a "going military type" and if the government declined "to substantially assist in the development and first production of new and improved types," then there "will be no way of radically improving or eventually replacing our present transport types."

This linking of government plans to aircraft production demands was more than a matter of industrial security and prosperity to the high officials of the government. It was considered a requirement of strategy and defense. Secretary of Commerce Harriman had suggested that the civil aviation industry was essential to meet possible wartime emergency conditions. Assistant Secretary of the Navy John Nicholas Brown went further, arguing that the nation needed a "manufacturing capacity that will meet our strategic requirements at all times. A well thought out, integrated aircraft production program is of the utmost importance to our national security."

If the military had to subsidize the commercial air industry, then the Department of Defense would become an indirect supporter of international trade and transportation. Alternatively, if the civilian transport system could support the military, then air commerce would be coordinate, if not subordinate, to the interests of military air power. The exact limit to which the defense establishment could subsidize the commercial fleet and industry depended on where one found the breaking point of a heavily burdened economy. As Dwight Eisenhower often suggested while Army Chief of Staff, defense was futile if the effort to achieve it exhausted the United States internally. But the whole industrial mobilization program, which itself created demands on the resources of the national economy in order to meet the requirements of industries such as aircraft, was an effort to strike an acceptable balance between adequate defense readiness and unacceptable spending.

Because of the pervasiveness of concern over levels of spending, it is important to understand precisely how large a program was regarded as safe for the national economy. In an interesting illustration, Secretary of the Army Kenneth Royall told the Air Policy Commission that it was essential to find a "criterion of what we can spend for military purposes." Disturbed, Arthur Whiteside argued that an actual shooting war would "cost us real money" and that a strong defense was therefore a good investment. Pressing Royall for an agreement that a strong military "would have some effect on averting war," Whiteside was reluctant to set a limit on defense spending since he feared that such a ceiling would diminish the psychological effectiveness of deterrence. In a revealing comment, which also offered a hint of a solution for inter-service squabbles over budgeting within the military establishment, Royall noted: "When I say we have reached a limit, I do not mean to indicate that I think a national expenditure of $10 billion, $15 billion or $20 billion would go beyond an absolute limit of what we could spend."

Government officials had consistently moved for the collaboration of private business, executive agencies, and the military departments ever since World War II. A special kind of mobilization—which would mean, for critical industries such as aircraft, not merely the adoption of an emergency plan but the acceptance and funding of a permanent working relationship—was a necessary element in achieving this collaboration. Even when this meant that the federal government through its armed services would subsidize civilian aviation development, this was a necessary price to be paid in the interest of defense. Administration officials with access to the President had hoped to use the civilian economy as an auxiliary to defense programs, largely to achieve a superior security position at a lower annual cost. Their vacillations were confined to questions of specific funding levels rather than to issues of basic principle. In all events, the military and civilian programs were to dovetail. The business leaders were more erratic; during and after World War II, they worked to reduce military influences in industry. Only when an adequate civilian market failed to develop did industry officials feel compelled to tie their future to government purchasing commitments. It took the fear of financial disaster to drive aviation businessmen to accept what the White House had urged for years. The enthusiasm of the armed services for the government program was also uneven, complicated by the divergence of their interests and by their involvement in restructuring the defense establishment itself. At the level of high policy, the most consistent, unswerving, and undaunted advocate of the "merger" of business and the military, as exemplified in the case of the aircraft industries, was the Truman administration itself.

SMALL BUSINESS AND LOCAL INTEREST GROUPS

Local interest groups and smaller businessmen, who were vastly less concerned with theories of national security and whose financial expectations were less sanguine than those of the major aircraft industrialists, contributed significantly to the achievement of Truman's defense objectives. Representatives of the large aircraft corporations believed that their best interests required independence of planning and action over the long run. Although they wanted favorable statements of profit and loss, they hoped that these could be secured without the risks of government control. Unlike the major corporate leaders whose concerns were national and international in scope, local industrialists, contractors, and merchants found the horizon of their futures at the borders of the town, the county, or the state.

Local interests affected the conduct of politicians, and local businessmen attempted to draft Congressmen into the service of regional prosperity. In this respect, the local interest groups conformed well to Truman's assessment of their motives. In the President's view, the profit motive strongly shaped business impressions about defense policy. While Truman was personally willing to use economic pressures or incentives to achieve his objectives in security policy, the local groups used the language of national security to justify their search for financial gain. They were alert and receptive to any apparent road to the main chance. Unaffected by the chimera of a flourishing national market in which to win profits, they did not share the reluctance of aircraft industrialists to establish lasting links with the government or with the military.

In their search for an easy and secure road to prosperity, local interest groups boosted the administration's industrial mobilization and dispersal programs. The construction of air bases and companion facilities represented a dollar pool that the White House could spend without reference to geography. The small-town and small-time groups pursued contracts and new commitments before, during, and after the war with little concern about sacrificing their power to control their own development.

Executive and legislative figures in Washington intended to channel defense spending to industrialize the West. Secretary of the Interior Harold Ickes had suggested to then Senator Truman in August 1941 that contracts be let for purposes of regional development rather than exclusively for defense production. Ickes warned that "the present defense emergency not only represents an opportunity of some importance for the industrialization of the area west of the Mississippi, but represents a danger that, if the opportunity is not utilized, the disparity between the industrialized East and the raw-material West will be increased rather than diminished." With the increasing range of effectiveness of aircraft, the margin of preference in strictly military terms for the location of air bases could shift in favor of the Midwest and the West. But the important fact was that the west and east coasts ought no longer to claim an overwhelming share of defense contracts.

East and west coast Congressmen were hard pressed to justify their claims for more spending in their areas. Thus they often coupled calls for reactivation of defense installations with both strategic and political arguments. An example was the effort of Congressman Louis B. Heller to capitalize on a succession of international problems to gain expanded use of the Brooklyn Navy Yard. On October 1, 1949, Heller wrote Truman that "the situation created by Russia's solution of the fission secret" made essential the revocation of Defense Department orders cutting the number of workers at the Brooklyn Yard. Heller argued that the new threat required a fuller, more total mobilization. The civilian work force was to be "as much a part of the defense establishment as the people in uniform." On July 11, 1950, Heller had new material to use in his fight to create employment in his district. "The ugly reality of the naked Korean aggression," he said, made it essential that the country "marshal all practicable strength both military and civilian to meet any eventuality." He suggested that attacks in Turkey, Iran, or the Balkans were possible. Once again, it was the Brooklyn Navy Yard that would supposedly produce the equipment for "our men on the firing line in Korea and wherever else International Communism shows its aggressive face."

A somewhat more revealing and characteristic case, as well as a more successful one, was that of then Congressman Mike Mansfield of Montana. In a memorandum and letter on June 26, 1952, Mansfield urged Truman to authorize funds for new construction at the Great Falls Air Base, a measure that he considered militarily useful and politically essential. To refuse funds on the grounds that they were needed for overseas bases would sit well neither with the people of Montana nor with the *Great Falls Tribune*, which Mansfield pointedly described as "the only Democratic and best newspaper in the State." The Congressman argued that the base was critical because of the new geopolitical facts of the air age. It was, he insisted, "the key air base in the entire United States because of its location on the route to Alaska, the North Pole and Siberia." But the Congressman again pointed out that his own support of the President "in the fight for foreign aid to our allies for international [cooperation] and for the strengthening of the United Nations," if not accompanied by funds for Montana, would place him "in a very delicate position and will rebound against me politically in the weeks and months ahead." The Great Falls Base was "the only defense project during World War II for Montana; consequently," Mansfield reminded Truman, "it has become an important factor in the economic life of Great Falls and Montana."

Although Mansfield offered geopolitical reasons for more funds for the Great Falls Base, political urgency prompted his letter and memorandum. It was that argument which he elaborated in greater detail for the President's consideration. In a brief note to the President less than a month after Mansfield wrote his letter to Truman, Secretary of the Air Force Finletter notified the President that he had directed an increase in construction at Great Falls totalling about $3,300,000. Truman commented briefly: "I think you did the right thing in this matter." What this incident revealed was the high degree of fluidity and interchangeability of military base spending and the developing connection between domestic political and military defense interests. As Mansfield himself noted, the air base was an "important factor" in his state's economic life. The increase Finletter ordered gave promise of making it a more important factor. Of additional interest is the symmetry between military planning in the new air age and visions of the political uses of defense contracts and construction. The air age might justify a massive infusion of money into the central states, the mountain states, and those along the Canadian border—an infusion that, while it seriously influenced economic life, would not necessarily influence the social affairs of the states in the direct way characteristic of welfare programs.

The correspondence concerning efforts to reactivate the old Army Air Force field near Harvard, Nebraska, is a miracle of candor in outlining the growing interest in the political applications of military contracts. C. G. Wallace, a businessman in the neighboring town of Hastings, asked his brother Lew in Portland, Oregon, to help channel his appeal for renewed use of the facility. The Nebraskan sent a copy of the letter to the President's aide William Hassett. Wallace admitted his reluctance to deal through his own Senators and Congressmen, generally Republicans, "since they want to take all the credit for anything that is done and then in turn blast the President for the things he tries to do." If only some project could be authorized for Nebraska, then it might be announced by the state Democratic leaders, who were out of office, and "we might be able to elect the next Governor, U.S. Senator, and some members of the house." Clearly revealing the order of his own interests, Wallace noted to his brother that "this would be an economical move and also a political one and not detrimental to the war effort." Although Wallace conceded to his brother that his major concerns were political and economic, he felt obliged to justify his requests, in a letter to the President's Secretary Matthew Connelly on August 13, 1951, with the President's defense measure of "giving 'blessing to industrial dispersal of industrial plants.' "

But soon Wallace returned to the political theme, telling Connelly that some "showing" of economic support would help put them in "a position to make an effort to send a delegation to Congress of Democrats that would support the administration in its policies." Wallace advised Connelly to "talk this over with the President and to do what you can in a practical way that will support the war effort." Nearly two months later, Robert L. Landry, the President's Air Attaché, sent Wallace a polite note to discourage his efforts. On October 5, Wallace again wrote to Connelly admitting defeat on the air base question. "We thought," he said, "its re-activation, if it did not interfere with national defense, would help us politically in Nebraska." Satisfied that this was now a dead issue, he noted that defense mobilizer Charles E. Wilson had stated that "he would like the aluminum fellows to move some of their plants into the mid-west for defence [*sic*] and security reasons." Not one to let his political interests die easily, Wallace inquired "if something can be done to make this location near our city."

The notion had become common that everyone was entitled to his own air-related facility. This was evident in the complaint of Arkansas Governor Sid McMath, who pointed out to Truman on June 29, 1951, that "at the present time Arkansas does not have an air operation of any type in the defense department, and is one of the few States in the Nation which does not." Therefore, he said, Arkansas "should have full consideration in any bases to be opened in the future." Echoing the line of argument that so many others were using at the same time, McMath explained that such an air base "would not only assist in the defense effort but forestall further economic distress."

The same attitude that had taken hold with respect to air bases and ground support facilities had also come to characterize thinking about development within the aviation industry as well. It was rare indeed for a region to resist the construction of a facility that would help support the local economy. Those who were uninterested in making sacrifices to move plants underground, in yielding bases, yards, or plants to other areas for the sake of a theoretically perfect dispersal, or in subordinating local interest to a comprehensive program of national mobilization still favored *ad hoc* defense expenditure that even a local or regional pressure group could hope to share. This pursuit of local special interests by businessmen and political leaders coincided with the long-standing objectives of the Truman administration. It created demand for government defense contracts, raised the call for military installations well integrated into the nation's economic life, and provided support for the principle of government intervention in and power over the discretely civilian sector of the economy for purposes of national defense.

CONCLUSION

At the high levels of policy-making, it was the Truman administration that consistently advocated the "militarization" of the economy, the placing of industry on a footing of permanent preparedness, and the integration of military and civilian sectors into a single system. As we have seen, important aircraft industry officials shifted their positions. At first many opposed an extensive pattern of interconnection, fearing the loss of their freedom of action and the compromising of their own control over their economic prospects. Although never clearly sympathetic to the defense vision that so affected Truman, these industry leaders reversed their position by 1947 and sought government contracts as insurance against their own economic failure. Meanwhile the armed services continued divided against one another and were even torn internally.

Smaller businessmen and regional and local political leaders were quicker to grasp the opportunities in the defense program. But the success of their efforts had waited on the period of semi-peace in the late 1940s. Although perhaps most of them were interested in defense only indirectly, industries and individuals finally reasoned that since spending was going to occur anyway, it might as well be ordered for their own greatest good. But for the government, there was implicit in the letting of contracts a degree of control over local and regional development and a measure of support for the defense effort.

All interested groups now used arguments based on the revised geopolitics of the air age—particularly the danger of air attack over Canada and the loss of "free security." Much of this use of geopolitical theory was undoubtedly a veil concealing self-interests and hopes for profits. But whether it was the comparatively sophisticated reference to polar air routes to the Soviet Union by a Montana Congressman or the rather crude use of the industrial dispersal concept by a politically active Nebraska businessman, strategic considerations had been hauled into ward-room politics and business calculations from the precincts to the White House. As a result, those who might have opposed the program of continuing defense mobilization which the administration hoped to serve up to the country swallowed it whole in their hunger for economic prosperity.

Notes

1.   Many writers have tended to understate or ignore the activity and creativity of civilians in government, acting independently of corporate links, in pressing for ties between military and industrial sectors. David Horowitz, in his introduction to Horowitz, ed., *Corporations and the Cold War* (New York, 1969) argued (p. 14) that the backgrounds of government officials demonstrate that: "In the postwar period, the strategic agencies of foreign policy—the State Department, the CIA, the Pentagon, and the Treasury, as well as the key Ambassadorial posts— have all been dominated by representatives and rulers of America's principal corpo-

rate financial empires." . . . To say that national ideology is corporate does not automatically mean that it was an invention of businessmen. . . . In a free-wheeling effort, Fred J. Cook asserted in *The Warfare State* (New York, 1962) that wartime Washington was divided between "the rapidly vanishing breed of New Dealers and even some of the dollar-a-year men who actually believed in democracy" and on the other side "the Military and the vast majority of Big Business." . . . For a recent work that accepts the thesis of control by a corporate elite but rejects the notion of military control over national policy, see Gabriel Kolko, *The Roots of American Foreign Policy* (Boston, 1969).

    2.   On the general framework of the thinking inside the Truman Administration concerning defense mobilization, see Donald J. Mrozek, "Peace Through Strength: Strategic Air Power and the Mobilization of the United States for the Pursuit of Foreign Policy, 1945-1955" (Ph.D. dissertation, Rutgers University, 1972).

    3.   The word "administration," as indicated above, here refers primarily to Truman and his close advisors such as Clark Clifford, George Elsey, and Samuel Rosenman. . . .

CONCLUSION

In the final essay, Louis Galambos and Alfred D. Chandler, Jr., employ an organizational framework to present a fresh view of the course of American economic history over the last century.

THE DEVELOPMENT OF
LARGE-SCALE ECONOMIC ORGANIZATIONS
IN MODERN AMERICA

By Alfred D. Chandler, Jr. and Louis Galambos

Scholars interested in modern industrial economies have for years devoted substantial attention to the growth and performance of large-scale organizations. Many of their studies have been the intellectual heirs of Max Weber's brilliant analysis of bureaucracy, for it is the bureaucratic structure of authority which most often characterizes such organization in the modern period. Economists, historians, and sociologists are all in debt to Weber for the basic ideas which have made the analysis of large-scale organizations so fruitful. . . .

In the American economy there were, we suggest, two distinct periods in the process of organizational growth. The first stage spanned the years from around 1870 to the early 1930's; the second from the 1930's through the 1950's. During the first of these periods, the major thrust of organization

Reprinted with permission from *Journal of Economic History* (March 1970). Copyright © 1970 by The Economic History Association.

building centered about the creation and refinement of primary organizations which had the following characteristics: (1) they tended to be national in organization and scope of operations; (2) they were largely in the private, not the public, sector of the economy; (3) they centralized authority along bureaucratic lines; and (4) they were constrained in their internal and external development by a particular set of boundaries which were traditionally or historically defined. The first three traits—nationalization; rapid growth in the public sector; and a high degree of centralization—are familiar. Numerous historians have discussed the creation of the national market and of the large firms, trade unions and professional associations which operated in it. Similarly, most students of bureaucracy have touched upon the centralization of authority in these private organizations.[1] The last aspect, however, probably needs to be illustrated.

By traditional boundaries we mean the kind of constraint exerted by the idea that a business firm in the iron and steel industry should continue to focus almost exclusively on the production of iron and steel goods. Was this necessary? Obviously not. But that was the way things had always been done—or seemed to have been done. Thus, the historically defined industry functioned as a constraint upon the expectational horizon of the firm's managers. The same thing could be said for the idea of a craft or skill and its impact upon trade union development. The concept of the profession—of engineering or social work—had similar effects upon professional organizations developing during these years. The boundaries of these bureaucracies were not determined solely by common interests or the existing ability to communicate information; historical categories of thought had important effects upon the way in which even group interests were perceived.

Within the primary organizations, this type of idea tended to constrain the process of internal differentiation. In the typical business firm, it was common to set up functional groups, such as those engaged in selling, in operating, or in financing the firm's activities. Again, these were traditional categories, although they were now restructured according to a new set of bureaucratic principles. In much the same way the trade unions organized shops in traditional crafts along regional lines. The shops in one city or district became the local and these united to form the national union. Yet a regional craft structure was soon outdated in many of the most rapidly growing, technologically advanced industries; production became concentrated in factories, so there were often the "shops" of several different craft unions in a single plant. These rarely joined forces to bargain for the workers in the plant. Like the business firms, the unions were constrained by traditional concepts.

During the years 1870-1930, organization building was concentrated in these primary bureaucracies—that is, large-scale, complex organizations which were essentially concerned with the job of organizing people in order to provide goods or services. The activities of the primary organizations created a new need, however, for a type of organization which could perform liaison and coordinating functions. Out of this need arose a second kind of large-scale organization which was largely concerned with coordinating the activities and with communicating between other organizations. These secondary organizations included trade associations, union federations, and some governmental agencies. Some secondary organizations were public, some private. Occasionally, large organizations (although not most) performed both primary and secondary functions. Some changed over time. Still, we think that most bureaucracies can be classified as either primary or secondary, and that this is an important distinction insofar as the history of organizational change in modern America is concerned.

One of the outstanding characteristics of the secondary organizations during this period (1870-1930) was their relative weakness. In terms of wealth, power, and prestige, they lagged far behind the primary organizations. In part, this reflected the widespread assumption that the relations between organizations would be determined, as they had been in the pre-bureaucratic age, by such natural forces as the gold standard or competition. This idea remained important even among leaders who were successfully achieving a substantial measure of rational control over the internal and external relations of their organizations. The need for inter-organization coordination and communication normally was acknowledged only after a significant crisis of some sort. Crises did occur, however, and after it was recognized that coordination was needed, this function was most often performed by weak federations in the private sector.

A glance at labor history illustrates our point. The major organizational developments in labor during these years centered about the rise of the national trade unions. Coordination of their activities was achieved through the AFL, a federation with very little power over its constituent unions. The AFL's officers attempted on many occasions to persuade the nationals to adopt certain policies. But aside from withholding support—itself a dangerous alternative—the Federation could do little to its constituent primary groups.

In the present day, we have become accustomed to thinking of the government as a coordinating mechanism. Furthermore, a number of scholars . . . have demonstrated that nineteenth-century America was not the laissez-faire haven it was once felt to have been. Nevertheless, before the 1930's there were few public bureaucracies which performed the special function of coordinating the actions of primary groups. True, there were populist and progressive reform movements which focused attention on business-government relations and the need for more regulation. One result was a set of new agencies, many of them independent regulatory commissions. But the major theme of their activities was the effort to discipline the behavior of individual primary organizations. The commissions tried to ensure that the new groups adopted the correct standard of organizational behavior in both their internal and external relations. Negative restraints were proclaimed, and occasionally invoked. Limits were established for organizational growth. But there was little consideration of, and even less action concerned with, the function of coordination. The first important exception to this rule came in the coordination and control of the nation's monetary supplies by the Federal Reserve System after 1913. To a lesser extent, the ICC, after the passage of the Transportation Act of 1920, came to have the same type of function among the nation's railroads.

The rule, however, remains: most regulatory activity was aimed at producing an economy in which each separate business or labor group behaved in the "proper" manner. If each of the organizations was "good," so to speak, it was assumed that the function of coordination would be performed by those natural forces which had seemed to work in the past. This represented a break with the classical position, which had been founded on the assumption that natural forces would ensure that individual behavior was proper, and out of the good behavior would flow the necessary coordination. Now it was widely felt that good behavior would ensure the necessary degree of coordination, but that the behavior might have to be achieved by exercising some control. These were the ideas that Theodore Roosevelt expressed with engaging simplicity when he made the distinction between good and bad trusts.

Roosevelt's effort to set rules of conduct for the nation's giant firms was one aspect of a general social crisis over the new organizations. During the first stage of their creation and internal organization building, 1870-1930, the primary bureaucracies generated numerous tensions. In part these conflicts were a product of new distributions of power and status. By their very nature bureaucracies are, as Weber so strongly emphasized, highly efficient instruments of human action. Developed to carry out economic functions, they soon came also to be used by their members to advance and protect their group interests. Most of the voluminous literature on the conflict between different social and economic groups has focused on elections and legislative action or on conflicting ideologies. We suggest that the development and outcome of these struggles for group power or protection should also be studied from the viewpoint of the inter- and intra-organizational activities involved.

Great size and bureaucratic controls created novel tensions, adding fuel to the existing socio-economic protest resulting from the redistribution of wealth and power. Local and regional systems were forced to give way before the nationally oriented bureaucracies; the new organizations usually severed relations with the kinship groups which had long played an important role in the economy. An interesting exception is provided by the Du Pont explosives combine. In this firm and in General Motors, Pierre S. du Pont was able to blend family control with bureaucratic management. But even in the Du Pont case, one can clearly see the conflict between the demands of the family and of the firm. In most large-scale businesses, the family gave way and professional managers soon occupied the leading positions of authority.

In part, too, the social crisis involved a fundamental conflict over values. Primary organizations, which stressed universalistic norms and group-oriented behavior, could hardly avoid trouble in a society geared to particularistic, individualistic values. National trade unions and large corporations subordinated the individual's special interests to those of the craft and the firm. The "soulless" corporation stood arrayed against the diffuse style of relationship which had always characterized the agrarian community. As these large organizations matured, they began to introduce norms which stressed neutral, not affective, responses—again this involved an important shift in values.

Another related cause of tension was the development within the organizations of new social roles. Roy Lubove has shown how this type of conflict arose between professional and voluntary social workers during the years 1900-1930: "The formal organization imposed rational system and order wherever possible and in the social agency the supervisor played a key role in reducing the influence of personal whim, emotion, and impulse. Undoubtedly the tendency of formal organizations to favor conditions which enhanced the possibilities of rational calculation hastened the substitution of paid, trained workers for volunteers."[2] Within business firms similar tensions developed when, for instance, heretofore independent salesmen were forced to conform to a new set of controls and role expectations. Understandably, this type of change generated a great deal of hostility toward the new bureaucracies.

By the early 1930's, however, many of these tensions had been relieved; the process of legitimation was well underway. This process cannot be understood solely in terms of power relations. In some cases, particular groups were able to achieve countervailing power and this eased their fear of the new organizations. Also, the performance of some of the primary organizations changed over the years. For the most part, however, the primary organizations retained and added to the wealth and power they had already acquired. Still, public hostility declined. The most important factor making for accommodation was undoubtedly the successful performance of the economy in the years 1900-1930. In a pragmatic, achievement-oriented society, such results were influential—whether they had anything to do with the new organizations or not. Then, too, the relative weakness in America of older, pre-industrial institution such as the extended kinship group made for a quick triumph on the part of the organizations. Many political measures also had a significant effect upon attitudes, even though we think that they were somewhat less important than progressive historians have suggested. The laws, the commissions, even the injunctions against unions, seldom worked in exactly the manner envisioned by their promoters, liberal or conservative; yet, as a symbolic response, political measures focused and handled discontent, easing relations between the public and the organizations. Those citizens troubled by the power and performance of the organizations could feel that the government was taking positive action to uphold the older values. As a result of these several factors, the process of accommodation was well along by the 1920's. Indeed, by that time bureaucratic values and perspectives on society were well entrenched in urban, industrial America.[3]

There were, however, problems inherent in this new structure of interrelated but loosely coordinated organizations, problems that were exposed by the Great Depression and by mobilization during the Second World War. One problem for the centralized business firm was the inherent limitation that centralization imposed upon growth. With highly concentrated control, top executives were so burdened with administrative data and decisions that they were unable to devote sufficient time to long-range, entrepreneurial decisions. Entrepreneurship suffered. Looking at this type of bureaucratized firm, Joseph Schumpeter clearly recognized that the administrative and the entrepreneurial functions were in conflict; in the long run, he felt, administration would win.[4] Furthermore, the single-industry and craft concepts tightly constrained organizational expansion. There was also a severe imbalance between the powerful primary organizations and the weak coordinating ones. In effect, the primary groups had partially freed themselves from traditional controls such as the market, without substituting organizational restraints of equal magnitude. The business bureaucracies had sacrificed the flow of information that the market had once given (automatically but not painlessly) to competing firms; the new means of acquiring such information were not equally efficient. Many of these weaknesses in the existing system were brought to light by the economic crisis of the 1930's.

A second major period of rapid organizational change began in the thirties. Now the central thrust of organizational development involved the coordinating units, particularly those in the public sector. Indeed, to many observers the Great Depression was a crisis of coordination. The secondary coordinating organizations in the private sector had failed; even when they were given a second chance and government support under the National Recovery Administration, they could not stimulate recovery. After 1935, attention increasingly turned to public, not private, organizations.

The new governmental policies which performed this function are familiar and do not call for any elaborate treatment here. Fiscal policy along Keynesian lines provided the major new tool. But in conservation, in agriculture, in money and banking, and in labor relations, new government agencies coordinated and guided economic activities in new ways.

Important changes also took place among the primary organizations. These organizations began to break out of the traditional, historically defined categories which had constrained their development in the years 1870-1930; administrators began to apply new and broader concepts of organizational potential. While of course the new categories also imposed constraints upon growth, the expectational boundaries were now far broader than they had been before the 1930's. This was certainly the case among labor organizations. The craft-oriented AFL unions were unable to prevent the rise of new industrial organizations. During these same years, many businesses began to diversify, to break away from the traditional concept of the single-industry firm. Du Pont and a few other companies had already adopted this policy, but during the 1930's and 1940's, the strategy of diversification spread throughout the industrial economy. With diversification came decentralization of authority within the firm. This structural innovation enabled managers to cope with the demands for both systematic management and vigorous entrepreneurship; decentralization was itself a basic innovation which Schumpeter could not foresee when he wrote *Capitalism, Socialism and Democracy*. By employing this new structure, firms were no longer limited by the growth rate of a single industry; geographical constraints on firm size also appear to have been pushed back dramatically. The large corporation could now handle far more complex and variegated problems.[5]

In this second phase—that is, from the 1930's through the 1950's—the external relations of the large-scale organizations also developed along new lines. The changes in the industrial firm were hardly noticed, let alone opposed; they were accepted as merely a slight variation on the earlier form of centralized company. During the 1930's, the regulation of big business became a political issue only briefly. Franklin D. Roosevelt revived the antitrust movement and received academic confirmation in the TNEC [Temporary National Economic Commission] reports. But this episode had little impact upon legislation and never became a major political issue.

Opposition in the late thirties and the forties to the growth of industrial unions and the expansion of the new federal "coordinating" agencies seems, however, to have been similar to the hostile reactions which the primary units had encountered at the turn of the century. At first glance, the protest of farmers, small businessmen, and professional people against big government and against big labor had much the same tone—and indeed some of the same rhetoric—as the earlier outcry against big business and the emerging craft unions. This response has been carried on into the sixties by the New Left, particularly its more youthful adherents, and also by the radical right as a protest against powerful bureaucracies and their behavior.

We suggest, however, that there were essential differences between the two stages in both the quality and quantity of the responses. . . . The negative reactions to large-scale organizations in the second period were weaker because of the previous accommodation with the primary units. Organizational values and roles were already firmly planted in America before the New Deal. This fact, as well as the atmosphere of crisis engendered by the Great Depression and the Second World War, made it relatively easy for Americans to accept the new primary and secondary organizations.

From the perspective of the 1930's, the innovations in government alone seemed revolutionary and the resistance fierce; from the vantage point of the late 1960's, however, both the revolutionary quality of the changes and the strength of the opposition seem diminished. This is particularly true when the public reactions to these measures are compared with the far stronger responses aroused during the 1890's by the early primary organizations. The most important dimension of organizational innovation in the 1930's was provided not by widespread ideological protests, but by the elaborate relationships among the organizations themselves. Every change in large-scale public and private institutions came under the scrutiny of existing, powerful organizations. The bureaucratic environment of the 1930's was far more complex than that of the 1890's. The primary and secondary organizations were well prepared to defend their special interests. It was the interaction of these various organizations which provided the most important aspect of the social response to organizational change during the thirties and forties. While these units vied for public support (in a characteristically systematic, rationalized way), the new type of inter-bureaucratic competition did not involve the same sort of fundamental social protest which had characterized the earlier response to the powerful primary organizations.

While this view of the development of large-scale economic organizations is highly simplified, we feel that it may be useful to historians working on the institutional aspects of change in the modern economy. To illustrate how it might be employed, we would first like to examine, very briefly, two episodes in American history from the vantage point provided by our framework. Our subjects are the mobilization of the economy during the first and second world wars.

Mobilization during World War I has customarily been described as a haphazard, chaotic process. Government officials had few if any clear precedents. The basic information necessary to decision-making was not available. Gradually, however, a few strong administrators—men such as Bernard Baruch in the War Industries Board—worked out more efficient administrative procedures; finally, they coordinated the flow of goods and services through the national economy. Baruch, according to Arthur Link, the foremost historian of the Wilson period, "established the WIB as the most powerful agency in the government, with himself as economic dictator of the United States and, to a large extent, of the Allied countries as well. And before many months had passed the Board had harnessed the gigantic

American industrial machine and brought such order into the mobilization effort that criticism almost vanished.''

Recently, this highly personalized interpretation has come under attack. Robert Cuff [in an essay included in this collection] concludes that Baruch consciously created this image of himself; in reality, Cuff says, Baruch's role in the WIB was not that of an economic dictator. Baruch mediated between powerful organizations. He depended upon a host of minor bureaucrats, most of them recruited from the private sector; he used the available organizations and appeared to be all-powerful only when he was able to achieve a compromise, a resolution of these existing forces. Cuff concludes that what really needs to be studied is the underlying organizational environment which dominated the activities of Baruch and his colleagues.

We agree with this re-interpretation and feel that our synthesis might be useful in analyzing the organizational environment that existed in 1917 and 1918. In the terms of our framework, the United States confronted the demands of wartime mobilization just as the new, centralized, national organizations were coming to power. The successful leaders of these organizations were attuned to the need for centralized authority and communications; centralization was the essential element in their organizational experience. Their concept of coordination involved an emphasis upon loose federations which arranged compromises (where possible) but did not really direct the activities of their constituent primary bureaucracies. When the wartime agencies were staffed with these men and began to deal with the primary organizations, the result was a de facto decentralization of power and responsibility. This did not result from a conscious commitment to decentralization, as such. The administrative tools for implementing an effective, decentralized program did not even exist at this time, nor were they developed during the war. Decentralization was the unplanned consequence of two factors: (1) a set of leaders who had a particular attitude toward organizational prerogatives; and (2) an environment in which the primary organizations were powerful and the secondary organizations weak and inexperienced. Given this organizational and intellectual setting, it is hardly surprising that such men as Baruch, as head of the WIB, Charles M. Schwab, as chairman of the Emergency Fleet Corporation, and even Newton D. Baker, the Secretary of War, became organizational mediators, not economic czars.

In World War II, the organizational setting and the patterns of mobilization were substantially changed. True, the mobilizers could now draw upon the experience gained in World War I. But equally influential were the new patterns of organizational development which had already begun to take shape before 1941. Wartime leaders from the government and from the private sector were attuned to the need for coordinated action—whether they had been implementing it or fighting it. In some cases, administrative experience with inventory control, forecasting methods, and formal decentralization in the private sector could be applied to the government's problems. The planners could draw upon that data generated by New Deal coordinating bureaucracies.

A significant example of the new situation is provided by the techniques developed to handle the most critical problem of mobilizing an economy for war—the allocation of basic, scarce materials. At first the war planners followed the pattern of World War I and made their allocation by setting priorities. As the priorities were soon being made on materials and components which were not yet produced, they became merely cards used by agencies and corporations in bargaining for goods. The solution came when the statistical and forecasting techniques developed by large industrial firms to coordinate the flow of goods through their organizations were modified to coordinate the flow through the economy itself. Before the adoption of the Controlled Materials Plan in 1942 and the Components Schedule Plan (which was approved a few months later), the War Production Board carried on much like its World War I counterpart, Baruch's WIB. Even in drawing up the new plans it acted as a mediator between powerful organizations. But once these plans were instituted, mobilization proceeded much more smoothly and effectively.

Under the schedule set up by these two programs, goods moved steadily and directly from the producers of materials and components to the processor or assembler on the basis of forecasted production. The producers of a few of the more critical and scarce items sent forecasts of their output for the next three months to the War Production Board, which then made allocations of expected output to the claimant agencies—that is, the Army, Navy, Shipping Board, Lend-Lease, synthetic rubber and high octane gasoline programs. These agencies (very large bureaucratic consumers) notified their prime contractors (large bureaucratic producers) of their quotas two months before the materials were scheduled to appear; then they allocated these materials to their sub-contractors one month prior to production.

The result was planned coordination and decentralization. As the New

York investment banker who proposed the plan explained: "The above system has the merit of confining decisions at the highest level to broad questions and decentralizing the detail. . . . The basic distribution of materials between the military, basic economic, Lend-Lease and other exports would be made by the War Productions Board . . . but the actual scheduling and directing of materials, particularly in the military field, would be taken over by those responsible for procurement and production, which cannot be carried out without control of the flow of materials in accordance with their schedules.'' Such carefully planned coordination made it easier to use effectively the other controls which were developed, such as those on prices. In general, these new modes of control allowed a much more massive mobilization of the economy in 1942 to proceed more smoothly than it had in 1917 and 1918.

As these developments illustrate, the patterns of mobilization in these two wars differed substantially, and one reason for the difference was the contrasting organizational environments of 1917 and 1941. Our analysis highlights these differences and thus, we think, helps the historian to develop a better understanding of these important episodes in American economic history.

We hope, too, that the framework will provide a tool for comparative analysis. It is clear that other countries followed different patterns of organizational development. In France, for instance, and in certain Latin American countries, the changes that we have described in our first stage appear to have been retarded. The centralized primary organizations did not sweep the field as they did in the United States. For one thing—as David Landes and John Sawyer[6] have pointed out—the kinship group provided a more substantial barrier to bureaucratization in the private sector in France than it ever did in the United States. The same was true, Professor Cochran has shown, in Latin America.[7]

On the other hand, coordinating organizations achieved greater power in France than in the United States. Usually this contrast has been associated with the overwhelming American opposition to government control in any form. Our framework suggests, however that this problem needs some reconsideration. It seems likely that the high degree of bureaucratization in the American private sector prior to the 1930's was actually more important in determining the outcome of policy than the oft-cited public resistance to governmental interference. Each new policy, each new measure of control had to be pushed through an incredibly dense organizational environment.

This environment, we think, had a decisive influence upon the degree of coordination achieved and upon the particular modes of implementing that policy.

Organizational analysis might also be used in growth studies. For one thing, such a framework should help us analyze and appreciate the social conflicts, inevitably generated by the process of organizational change. In America, these conflicts were particularly severe during the late nineteenth and early twentieth centuries, when the primary organizations were first acquiring great power and wealth. How much more serious would such tensions be in a society which is simultaneously introducing both primary and secondary organizations? This, it seems, is the policy adopted in many plans for modernization today, and we suggest that attempts might well be made to analyze more accurately the cost—both psychological and economic—of such a policy.

At any rate, we hope that these examples will serve to illustrate some of the ways historians might use middle-level generalizations about organizational development. Perhaps this synthesis can be used by future particularizers in case studies of economic organizations; such research, we trust, will eventually modify and improve our framework, and, incidentally, strengthen the historical dimension of the work done by the generalizers. If nothing else, we will be pleased if our own historical view encourages further research on the changing nature and external relations of economic institutions in modern America and abroad.

Notes

1.   Many of the organizations which we discuss do not meet all of Weber's criteria for a bureaucratic organization. But as Weber so strongly emphasized, his was an intellectual construct—an ideal type. All bureaucracies had some of the characteristics that he outlined, but none had all. In the U.S. the large corporations and government agencies come closest to the Weberian ideal type; the unions, trade organizations, and professional associations fall short of this type, in varying degree.

2.   Roy Lubove, *The Professional Altruist* (Cambridge: Harvard University Press, 1965), p. 170.

3.   Robert H. Weibe, *The Search for Order, 1877-1920* (New York: Hill and Wang, 1967), provides the best general study of this shift in values.

4.   Joseph A. Schumpeter, *Capitalism, Socialism and Democracy* (New York: Harper & Brothers, 1942), pp. 131-4, 139-42.

5.   Alfred D. Chandler, Jr., *Strategy and Structure* (Cambridge: The

M.I.T. Press, 1962). Robert Cuff has suggested that one of the important developments of the thirties was the tendency of some government agencies to perform both primary and secondary functions (TVA, for instance). This, in turn, may well have sharpened the hostile reactions of those who could approve of the government as a coordinating agent, but not as a primary organization.

6.   John E. Sawyer, "The Entrepreneur and the Social Order: France and the United States," in William Miller, ed., *Men in Business* (Cambridge: Harvard University Press, 1952), 7-23. David Landes, "French Business and the Businessman: A Social and Cultural Analysis," in E. M. Earle, ed., *Modern France* (New York: Russell & Russell, 1961), 334-353.

7.   Thomas C. Cochran, "Cultural Factors in Economic Growth," *Journal of Economic History,* XX (December 1960), 513-530.